Beyond the Courtroom

Beyond the Courtroom

Proven Strategies from the Legal Field for Leadership, Emotional Intelligence, and Well-Being in the Modern Workplace

Natalie Loeb

David B. Sarnoff

PLI Press • New York City • #447833

Legal Editor: Jacob Metric

LCCN: 2026930051

ISBN: 978-1-4024-4998-7

To my husband, Gordon, my partner in every way. I love you. Thank you for the ongoing support you have always provided. I will never forget it was YOU who told me to keep going when I was ready to give up and go back "in house." You saw in me what I couldn't see in myself. You are a natural coach and a true partner to me in every sense of the word!

To my children, Alec and Caroline, who tell everyone they grew up in a leadership workshop. They helped me to overcome the mommy guilt so I could pursue a career I love and build a business that aspires to make a positive difference in the work lives of others every day. To my daughter-in-law April, who joined our team, willing to accept and embrace our family workshop. Our gatherings together reinforce my daily "why." Together we are the "Loeb Team." I love you all more than you will ever know and am so proud of the people leaders you have become. Keep making the world a better place. Love you forevermore.

NATALIE LOEB
March 2026

To my wife, Paige, who I met by chance at the US Open Tennis Finals in 1996, your love, encouragement, and support over the decades have helped me through challenge and success. Thank you for being my partner and for all the adventures you have created.

To my son, Jordan, and my daughter, Bella—you bring out the best in me, inspire me daily, and fill my life with purpose and constant surprises. You keep life interesting in the best ways. I love you both.

To my parents, Lorraine and Jerry Sarnoff, your unconditional love, sacrifice, grit, and the values you instilled in me have shaped every step of my journey. I am forever grateful for the foundation you provided and the constant support.

DAVID SARNOFF
March 2026

About the Authors

Natalie Loeb is the founder and CEO of Loeb Leadership, a certified woman-owned, U.S.-based management and leadership development firm she has led for more than twenty-five years. A successful entrepreneur and working mother, Natalie blends business acumen with warmth and empathy, helping organizations build high-trust, high-performance cultures where people and results thrive.

Natalie's deep understanding and experience in professional development training and executive coaching in the legal space makes her a sought-after strategic partner and leadership development advisor to *Amlaw 100* firms, nonprofits, technology start-ups, and a range of other industries. Natalie and her team design and deliver flexible, research-backed leadership development programs that increase self-awareness, agility, and leadership capacity—unlocking the discretionary effort today's hybrid workforce demands. Personally, Natalie is known for helping leaders connect and engage with authenticity, emotional intelligence, and clarity.

Natalie is a trained executive coach through the Zicklin School of Business in New York City and holds a Master of Science degree in Industrial/Organizational Psychology from Baruch College. She is certified in more than fifteen leadership assessment tools and has authored numerous articles on law firm leadership. A sought-after speaker at legal conferences and a faculty member for the Practising Law Institute (PLI), her briefings include: "IQ vs. EQ: What Lawyers Need to Know About Emotional Intelligence"; "Active Listening for Lawyers"; "Law Firm Workplace Culture—Be Smart, Build a Healthy Culture"; and "Generational Challenges Between Law Firm Partners and Associates."

Clients consistently praise Natalie's intelligence, creativity, and genuine commitment to people. As a working mother, she brings empathy and practicality to the real-world challenges leaders face, making her a trusted partner in developing strong, inclusive, and resilient workplaces.

David B. Sarnoff is a highly sought-after ICF-Certified Executive Coach, leadership trainer, workshop facilitator, and conference speaker with an extensive track record of helping professionals elevate their leadership effectiveness. He is the founder of Sarnoff Group LLC, an executive coaching and leadership development firm, and also serves as a consultant to Loeb Leadership. With decades of multidisciplinary experience spanning the legal profession, executive search, business ownership, and board governance, David brings a uniquely integrated perspective to the challenges facing corporate executives, attorneys, managers, and high-potential professionals. He has coached scores of leaders, including managing partners, practice group leaders, general counsels, directors, SVPs, and C-suite executives.

As an executive coach, David helps clients strengthen emotional intelligence, enhance professional performance, expand leadership capacity, and build high-trust, collaborative teams. A dynamic and relatable speaker, he presents regularly at national conferences, law firms, corporations, and professional associations. His work includes numerous Practising Law Institute CLE webinars and Studio Briefings on emotional intelligence, leadership skills, active listening, bridging generations, workplace conflict, delegation, time management, culture, mission alignment, and inclusion.

David previously served six years on the Fort Lee Board of Education, including three consecutive years as Board President, and was appointed to the New Jersey School Boards Association statewide mental health task force on social and emotional learning. Passionate about allyship and inclusion, he also served as Co-Chair of the New York City Bar Association's Diversity, Equity & Inclusion Committee.

He is certified in the EQ-i 2.0 Emotional Intelligence Assessment and Everything DiSC®, integrating evidence-based tools and frameworks to help leaders and organizations achieve sustainable growth, stronger collaboration, and meaningful impact.

David is a graduate of Hofstra University and Rutgers Law School. He trained as an executive coach at iCoach New York, now iCoach Global, a program affiliated with the Zicklin School of Business at Baruch College, and he now serves as a member of the faculty of that program.

About the Contributors

Fritz Galette is a licensed psychologist in New York State and holds a doctorate in clinical psychology from Fordham University. He serves as an adjunct professor in the graduate Department of Applied Psychology at New York University.

Dr. Galette is a consultant and executive coach to leaders in the corporate and nonprofit sectors, specializing in leadership development, group dynamics, and workplace psychology. His recent work includes supporting multigenerational family businesses, strengthening nonprofit boards, and leading resilience and emotional-intelligence trainings for professionals across high-demand fields. He is also a frequent speaker and workshop facilitator and has collaborated on numerous CLE panels addressing mental health, stress, and professional well-being.

In his private counseling and coaching practice, Dr. Galette works with a diverse range of clients, helping them navigate stress, anxiety, relational challenges, and performance concerns through evidence-based and culturally responsive approaches.

Beyond his professional work, Dr. Galette is a seventh-degree black belt in Tae Kwon Do, has completed twenty-three New York City Marathons, and is an active musician.

Born in Brooklyn to Haitian immigrant parents, he lives in the New York City area with his wife, Helen Galette, Esq. Their two sons are now adults, and the family remains closely connected throughout the region.

Anjli Garg is an ICF-certified executive coach, leadership trainer, and former C-suite lawyer who helps high-achieving professionals lead with confidence, clarity, and sustainable success—without sacrificing their well-being. Her work bridges the *outer game* of strategy, productivity, and leadership execution with the *inner work* of self-trust, emotional intelligence, and burnout prevention.

Before becoming a coach, Anjli spent twenty-four years practicing corporate law at Sullivan & Cromwell, American Express, Citibank (as Assistant General Counsel), and State Street (as Managing Director). She led a global team of over thirty professionals and worked at the intersection of law, risk, strategy, and leadership inside complex, high-pressure institutions. Having navigated her own evolution from individual contributor to enterprise leader, she now partners with others during moments of professional and personal pivot.

Anjli works with partners, associates, heads of legal, in-house counsel, and senior and mid-level executives at critical inflection points—such as stepping into expanded leadership, navigating uncertainty, rebuilding after burnout, reshaping professional identity, or seeking to lead with greater authenticity and impact. Her clients often describe her as the rare coach who brings both strategic rigor and emotional depth, helping them gain clarity, dissolve self-doubt, and make aligned, high-stakes decisions with confidence and ease.

Her approach is informed not only by her legal and executive background, but also by her lived experience as a first-generation professional, mother, artist, kriya yogi, and certified energy practitioner. Her clients credit this integrative approach with tangible outcomes, including promotions, new leadership roles, stronger business development, increased confidence and visibility, renewed focus, and newfound fulfillment and ease.

Anjli facilitates workshops and delivers keynotes on leadership, navigating uncertainty, executive presence, visibility, well-being, and inclusion for global corporations, *Am Law 100* firms, professional associations, and nonprofits.

She is a Professional Certified Coach (PCC) through the International Coaching Federation, a Certified Professional Coach through iPEC, and is certified to administer the EQ-i 2.0® and EQ 360 emotional intelligence assessments. She holds a J.D. from New York University School of Law and a B.A., summa cum laude, from the University of Connecticut.

Table of Chapters

Part I
Leadership

Chapter 1 Why Lawyers Need Executive Coaches

Chapter 2 Taking Advantage of Executive Coaching

Chapter 3 It's Not Lawyering, It's Leading

Chapter 4 Partners, How Patient Are You?

Chapter 5 When Met with Opposition, Model the Way

Chapter 6 Great Leaders Are Made, Not Born from Promotion

Chapter 7 Looming Economic Downturn? How Do I Balance My Firm's Needs and the Impact on Our Associates?

Chapter 8 Does Your Executive Committee Understand the Merits of a Firm Retreat?

Chapter 9 What's Next for Law? EQ, Wellness, and Technological Change

Chapter 10 Be the Keel—How Can Law Firm Leaders Provide Stability During Uncertain Times?

Chapter 11 From Fear to Trust: How Law Firms Can Break the Cycle of Toxic Leadership

Chapter 12 Stepping Up Without Overstepping—Navigating Leadership Gaps with Care

Part II
Management

Chapter 13 How Can I Better Manage People and Administrative Tasks?

Chapter 14 Holding Your Colleagues Accountable for Destructive Behavior

Chapter 15 Preparing to Welcome Your New Associates? What You Should Know

Chapter 16 Is There Only One Lane on the Road to Partnership?

Chapter 17 Stretched Thin As Summer Associate Season Begins?

Chapter 18 Get SMART with Achieving Career Goals

Chapter 19 Feedback Matters: Creating a Two-Way Street

Chapter 20 A Path to Partnership Success—Why 360 Feedback and Coaching Matter

Chapter 21 Navigating the Noise—Dealing with a Difficult Boss

Chapter 22 When the Mentor Needs a Manual: Thriving During Summer Associate Season (Part I)

Chapter 23 When the Mentor Needs a Manual: Thriving During Summer Associate Season (Part II)

Chapter 24 When the Mentor Needs a Manual: Thriving During Summer Associate Season (Part III)

Chapter 25 Performance Reviews Should Be a Tool, Not a Chore

Chapter 26 Taking Leave Without Losing Ground

Part III
Emotional Intelligence and Communication

Chapter 27 Using Communication to Defeat Frustration

Chapter 28 If You're Happy and You Know It, Let Them Know

Chapter 29 Is Praise As Important As a Paycheck?

Chapter 30 Don't Let Senior Associates Slip Through the Cracks

Chapter 31 De-escalating Tensions in the Office One Kind Gesture at a Time

Chapter 32 Distinguishing Bickering from Bullying

Chapter 33 Navigating Political and Social Tensions in the Legal Profession

Part IV
Well-Being and Inclusion

Chapter 34 Is a Lack of Equitable Feedback Hindering Your Path to an Inclusive Workplace?

Chapter 35 Advocating for Your Attorneys' Mental Health

Chapter 36 Prioritize Belonging and Accessibility in Your Next Position

Chapter 37 Why Partners Shouldn't Ignore Associates' Mounting Stress

Chapter 38 Am I a Change Embracer or Change Resister?

Chapter 39 How to Prepare for Your Law School Journey

Chapter 40 Do Female Lawyers Have to Play by Different Rules?

Chapter 41 **"Why Do I Have To? Nobody Did It for Me"—Addressing Generational Diversity in Law Firms**

Chapter 42 **From Bates Stamp to Blockchain: How Immigrant and First-Gen Attorneys Bridge the Generational Divide in the Legal Profession**

Chapter 43 **Is There Life After Law? Career Transitions for Attorneys**

Table of Contents

About the Authors vii
About the Contributors ix
Table of Chapters xi
Preface xxi
Acknowledgments xxxi

Part I
Leadership

Chapter 1 **Why Lawyers Need Executive Coaches** 1
Natalie Loeb & David B. Sarnoff

Chapter 2 **Taking Advantage of Executive Coaching** 9
Natalie Loeb & David B. Sarnoff

Chapter 3 **It's Not Lawyering, It's Leading** 17
Natalie Loeb & David B. Sarnoff

Chapter 4 **Partners, How Patient Are You?** 25
Natalie Loeb & David B. Sarnoff

Chapter 5 **When Met with Opposition, Model the Way** 33
Natalie Loeb & David B. Sarnoff

Chapter 6 **Great Leaders Are Made, Not Born from Promotion** 41
Natalie Loeb & David B. Sarnoff

Chapter 7 **Looming Economic Downturn? How Do I Balance My Firm's Needs and the Impact on Our Associates?** 51
Natalie Loeb & David B. Sarnoff

Chapter 8 **Does Your Executive Committee Understand the Merits of a Firm Retreat?** 61
Natalie Loeb & David B. Sarnoff

Chapter 9 **What's Next for Law? EQ, Wellness, and Technological Change** 69
Natalie Loeb & David B. Sarnoff

Chapter 10 **Be the Keel—How Can Law Firm Leaders Provide Stability During Uncertain Times?** 79
Natalie Loeb & David B. Sarnoff

Chapter 11 **From Fear to Trust: How Law Firms Can Break the Cycle of Toxic Leadership** 87
Anjli Garg & David B. Sarnoff

Chapter 12 **Stepping Up Without Overstepping—Navigating Leadership Gaps with Care** 97
Natalie Loeb & David B. Sarnoff

Case Study **Steering Through the Storm—A Law Firm Leadership Moment** 105

Facilitator's Guide **Steering Through the Storm—A Law Firm Leadership Moment** 109

Part II
Management

Chapter 13 **How Can I Better Manage People and Administrative Tasks?** 113
Natalie Loeb & David B. Sarnoff

Chapter 14 **Holding Your Colleagues Accountable for Destructive Behavior** 121
Natalie Loeb & David B. Sarnoff

Chapter 15 **Preparing to Welcome Your New Associates? What You Should Know** 129
Natalie Loeb & David B. Sarnoff

Chapter 16 **Is There Only One Lane on the Road to Partnership?** 137
Natalie Loeb & David B. Sarnoff

Chapter 17 **Stretched Thin As Summer Associate Season Begins?** 145
Natalie Loeb & David B. Sarnoff

Chapter 18 **Get SMART with Achieving Career Goals** 153
Natalie Loeb & David B. Sarnoff

Chapter 19 **Feedback Matters: Creating a Two-Way Street** 163
Natalie Loeb & David B. Sarnoff

Chapter 20 **A Path to Partnership Success—Why 360 Feedback and Coaching Matter** 171
Natalie Loeb & David B. Sarnoff

Chapter 21 **Navigating the Noise—Dealing with a Difficult Boss** 181
Natalie Loeb & David B. Sarnoff

Chapter 22 **When the Mentor Needs a Manual: Thriving During Summer Associate Season (Part I)** 189
Natalie Loeb & David B. Sarnoff

Chapter 23 **When the Mentor Needs a Manual: Thriving During Summer Associate Season (Part II)** 195
Natalie Loeb & David B. Sarnoff

Chapter 24 **When the Mentor Needs a Manual: Thriving During Summer Associate Season (Part III)** 203
Natalie Loeb & David B. Sarnoff

Chapter 25 **Performance Reviews Should Be a Tool, Not a Chore** 213
Natalie Loeb & David B. Sarnoff

Chapter 26 **Taking Leave Without Losing Ground** 221
Natalie Loeb & David B. Sarnoff

Case Study **Managing the Mix at Harper & Stone LLP** 229

Facilitator's Guide **Managing the Mix at Harper & Stone LLP** 233

Part III
Emotional Intelligence and Communication

Chapter 27 **Using Communication to Defeat Frustration** 237
Natalie Loeb & David B. Sarnoff

Chapter 28 **If You're Happy and You Know It, Let Them Know** 243
Natalie Loeb & David B. Sarnoff

Chapter 29 **Is Praise As Important As a Paycheck?** 251
Natalie Loeb & David B. Sarnoff

Chapter 30 **Don't Let Senior Associates Slip Through the Cracks** 259
Natalie Loeb & David B. Sarnoff

Chapter 31 **De-escalating Tensions in the Office One Kind Gesture at a Time** 267
Natalie Loeb & David B. Sarnoff

Chapter 32 **Distinguishing Bickering from Bullying** 275
Natalie Loeb, David B. Sarnoff & Fritz Galette

Chapter 33 **Navigating Political and Social Tensions in the Legal Profession** 283
Natalie Loeb & David B. Sarnoff

Case Study **Reading the Room—Even on Zoom: Managing Emotions and Communication in High-Pressure Deals** 293

Facilitator's Guide **Reading the Room—Even on Zoom: Managing Emotions and Communication in High-Pressure Deals** 297

Part IV
Well-Being and Inclusion

Chapter 34 **Is a Lack of Equitable Feedback Hindering Your Path to an Inclusive Workplace?** 301
Natalie Loeb & David B. Sarnoff

Chapter 35 **Advocating for Your Attorneys' Mental Health** 311
Natalie Loeb & David B. Sarnoff

Chapter 36 **Prioritize Belonging and Accessibility in Your Next Position** 319
Natalie Loeb & David B. Sarnoff

Chapter 37 **Why Partners Shouldn't Ignore Associates' Mounting Stress** 327
Natalie Loeb & David B. Sarnoff

Chapter 38 **Am I a Change Embracer or Change Resister?** 335
Natalie Loeb & David B. Sarnoff

Chapter 39 **How to Prepare for Your Law School Journey** 343
Natalie Loeb & David B. Sarnoff

Chapter 40 **Do Female Lawyers Have to Play by Different Rules?** 353
Natalie Loeb & David B. Sarnoff

Chapter 41 **"Why Do I Have To? Nobody Did It for Me"—Addressing Generational Diversity in Law Firms** 361

Natalie Loeb & David B. Sarnoff

Chapter 42 **From Bates Stamp to Blockchain: How Immigrant and First-Gen Attorneys Bridge the Generational Divide in the Legal Profession** 369

Anjli Garg & David B. Sarnoff

Chapter 43 **Is There Life After Law? Career Transitions for Attorneys** 379

Natalie Loeb & David B. Sarnoff

Case Study **Balancing the Scales in Labor & Employment** 387

Facilitator's Guide **Balancing the Scales in Labor & Employment** 391

Preface

Natalie's Story

If you asked my parents what I was like as a child, they would tell you that I had a lot of friends, that I enjoyed being around both the adults and children, and that I always seemed to know when somebody wasn't feeling well or needed some support. My parents installed a phone in my bedroom when I was ten years old when I was sharing a room with my sister because the phone kept ringing downstairs in the kitchen and it was always for me. My sister was really envious that I needed my own phone. To this day she reminds me of that.

When I went to college, I knew I wanted to study psychology. I wanted to learn all about people and what makes them tick. I was fascinated by people. In my last semester, senior year, a course was added to the Psychology curriculum called Industrial/Organizational Psychology. I had always been interested in business too, however, I was not successful in the one accounting class I tried. Numbers didn't inspire me, but I was intrigued by how businesses put people with different needs, expectations, and life experiences together in high-performing organizations and expect everything to go seamlessly, because it doesn't. I struggled in the accounting class yet excelled in the Industrial/Organizational Psychology classes. I was fascinated by the research and theories around how to create workplace cultures where people could perform at their best. This area of study energized me: how to help others at work be productive, healthy, and happy. I was hooked.

Upon graduation, I returned to Staten Island, New York and began to explore graduate programs in New York City. At the time, there were three graduate programs available; one at Columbia University, one at New York University, and one at the City University of New York/ Baruch College. Baruch College allowed me to go part-time at night and was also easier on my bank account. The program was excellent. While in the program, I needed to work to support myself and I also knew I wanted to find a job in Human Resources (HR), the "people part" of organizations. I saw an advertisement for a job in HR for a large law firm and answered it. It just so happened that the Director of Human Resources at this firm (Skadden, Arps, Slate, Meagher & Flom LLP) at the time had completed the same graduate program I did and she thought it was important to have someone on the HR team with my training and background. I was interviewed, asked to do a formal training presentation, and was hired. This job became my connection to the legal field. Again, I was hooked. I loved the high energy and intensity in the office, the intelligent people, and the meaningful work to be done. I was also exposed to the best manager who I ever had. She set clear expectations, provided timely feedback, and held me accountable. I was given the support to offer a variety of professional development programs to all levels of staff members at the firm. My focus was on management development, however, I would continuously conduct needs analyses and offer programming that met individual department needs. This role gave me experience in program design, development, and delivery. And again, I loved it.

After spending ten years at the firm, my husband and I had our second child. The commute was about four hours round trip and, like many working mothers, I had to figure out how to continue with the career that gave me so much satisfaction while being the type of mother I wanted to be to my children. I quit my job and found a job closer to home. A few weeks later I received a call from the Director of Human Resources, asking if I would like to stay on in a "consulting" capacity; giving me the flexibility to work from home (design and development) and come to the office to deliver the programming a few days a month (delivery). I said "yes"; and this was the beginning of my consulting career. Skadden was always known for being progressive and innovative. This arrangement proved that once again.

In 1997, I was an individual training & development consultant. Twenty-seven years later, along with my husband and an excellent leadership team, we are a full-service management consulting firm called Loeb Leadership with over sixty consultants delivering our services to our clients. Simply put, our team is dedicated to unlocking the potential of organizations and their people. We care about developing extraordinary leaders, inclusive cultures, and engaged employees.

At the time of writing this book, over half of our clients are law firms. When I returned to Skadden as a consultant, I found that after spending ten years in-house in big law, other leaders in legal firms would seek out my services, giving me and others on our team the opportunity to work with a variety of law firms from big to small.

Working beside both lawyers and administrative staff for almost three decades has certainly taught me a lot. I have noticed patterns in human behavior in general and particular patterns in the behaviors of legal professionals. While attending and presenting at many legal conferences over the years, I have collected many stories and additional learnings.

In 2021, my colleague David Sarnoff and I were offered the opportunity to write a column about leadership for lawyers in the Practising Law Institute's online periodical, the *PLI Chronicle*. We were thrilled to answer questions about leadership from lawyers and legal professionals. The launch of our column was in July 2021. The title of the article was "Why Lawyers Need Executive Coaches" (now chapter 1 of this book). When writing the article, David and I were very aware that many lawyers were not familiar with or were perhaps intimidated by the idea of a leadership coach. In fact, when I would introduce coaching to lawyers, they immediately thought it was some type of therapy and followed that up with "I don't need therapy." Others thought I was some sort of sports coach. It became apparent that the field of industrial/organizational psychology where leadership coaching and training is a key component was not on the radar for most lawyers. At the same time, most of the lawyers I spoke to became curious and after allowing themselves to process the benefits of leadership coaching, began to ask more questions and show more interest. I will never forget one lawyer who was having difficulty giving feedback to associates who gave him subpar work. His aggressive, abrupt style left associates demotivated and unclear on what he wanted. When I suggested:

1. Do not throw the work at them (at the time, this lawyer was using hard copies), and
2. Instead of saying, "this sucks," to try "this is not what I expected," using a monotone, perhaps even supportive tone.

The lawyer told me, "it's not actually the crummy work that gets in the way, it's the way I 'feel' when I receive it. I don't know how to manage that emotion." That comment made me smile and it was then that

I asked the lawyer to sit down. And I introduced him to the world of emotional intelligence and how normal it is to be triggered by "crappy work," particularly when under pressure. This lawyer told me he didn't want to react this way, but didn't know what else to do. As I explained emotional intelligence to him, he listened, understood that his intelligence was in no way under attack, and if he did indeed want to respond in a different way to this crappy work, there was a path to getting there beginning with understanding how to respond to what triggers him. This lawyer made tremendous progress. We also uncovered his wonderful sense of humor during our conversations which he decided to allow to let into his performance management/coaching discussions with associates (appropriately). This warm sense of humor showed his "human side" and helped the associates to see him as the true developer of legal talent he aspired to be.

At our essence we are all human. It is people that fill our law departments and law firms. When these people are led by inspiring extraordinary leaders, healthy workplace cultures arise, performance is elevated, and the people offer their best efforts to help the firm thrive. In a healthy workplace culture, the people also learn how to manage their stress effectively so it does not distract from the work or impact their health negatively.

Leadership, however, is not easy. It requires self-reflection, intention, courage, and yes, some education around best practices. The good news is that over the years, we have found that the highly intelligent people we work with in law firms not only understand this, they embrace it once they commit the time to think and learn about leadership. Lawyers have told us over and over again, "I never learned about leadership in law school." Fortunately, there are many ways to learn. Robert F. Kennedy Jr. is known for saying "Leadership and learning are indispensable to each other." I have observed this over and over again in the over forty years of my career in a field dedicated to continuous learning. It is those leaders that adopt a learner's mindset and continuously learn that create workplaces where innovation and performance excels. It is for this reason that David and I are so honored to bring this book to those legal professionals who we admire so much. Legal work is tough, and meaningful and intense. Those practicing law can no longer do it alone. It is done with teams of folks. Leading high-performance teams is another key leadership skill; one that must be learned.

Preface

Our intention with this book is to provide smart people with a short guide for how to be better leaders. At the end of each column you will find three key takeaways and action items you can choose to experiment with and see if they make a positive difference for you. As they say, Rome wasn't built in a day. Identify a tip or two that seems achievable for you and try them out consistently for a period of time. Notice if you are getting closer to being an extraordinary leader, building an inclusive culture, and having engaged associates/employees. If it is working, keep going.

During times of growth and change, where leadership is most necessary, I have personally witnessed the growth and change of hundreds, perhaps thousands of lawyers and legal professionals.

This book does not need to be read in any particular order. Scan the chapter topics. See what resonates with you. What is happening today that catches your eye? Daily experiences and challenges will have you seeking some ideas on how to handle them. Within the chapters, scan the articles, what may be helpful today? What may you want to share with someone else that may be struggling or lack confidence in their leadership today. Use this book as a practical tool to help you solve today's leadership challenges.

If this book helps one more person to step back, reflect, and intentionally choose a new behavior for a better outcome for their firm, their colleagues, direct reports, and/or themselves, then my parents were right; I seemed to know when someone needed some type of support. Providing that support gives my work the meaning I believe is important: building extraordinary leaders, inclusive culture, and engaged employees.

Please feel free to email me with any thoughts, questions, or stories. I would love to hear them.

David's Story

How we are raised and educated and the experiences we accumulate throughout our lives shape our worldview, influence how we build trust, cultivate relationships, communicate with others, cope with failure, and develop the grit necessary to navigate adversity. These factors play a crucial role in determining the kind of leader we can become. This is especially true in the legal profession, where attorneys are often driven by intellect and technical expertise but may lack the self-awareness to fully understand how they show up, how they are perceived, and the impact of their words and actions on others, particularly when they are in high-stress and high-stakes situations. Leadership in the law requires more than knowledge; it demands an ability to inspire, cultivate high-trust relationships, manage teams effectively, and drive performance through others.

One of the biggest challenges in the legal profession is that most attorneys do not receive formal executive coaching or leadership training and if they do, it is typically later in their career. Instead, they learn leadership and management skills through observations and experiences, often following models that do not reflect best practices. Without intentional development and practice, attorneys may default to ineffective leadership styles that hinder their teams and organizations. In this book, Natalie and I aim to educate, raise self-awareness, and illuminate a path for leaders at all levels to enhance their leadership capabilities. By improving their skills, attorneys can create a ripple effect of positive impact throughout their groups, firms, and organizations, fostering stronger, more effective teams and a healthier workplace culture.

My story begins in New York City. I was born in the Bronx as one of four children, with my twin sister and I being the youngest by eight and eleven years, respectively, from our brother and sister. When I was a toddler, we moved to northern New Jersey. My family story played a large role in shaping the foundation of my values, building relationships, leadership philosophy, and understanding of resilience. My father was the son of immigrant parents who escaped persecution in Poland in the late 1920s. Raised by parents in the East New York section of Brooklyn who initially did not speak the language nor understood the culture, my father learned the meaning of hard work early on, shining shoes and selling newspapers at just nine years old to help support his family. My mother, the daughter of Latvian immigrants living in the Bronx, had to leave high school to help support her family after her father's untimely death at the age of forty-nine. When my parents married—my father at twenty-one and my mother at nineteen—they built a life centered around devotion, hard work, integrity, and perseverance. They remained together for sixty-four years until my father's passing in 2020.

My father was one of the last of the old-time seltzer-men in New York City, delivering siphon glass bottles of highly pressurized water, soda, beer, and syrups to apartments on the Upper West Side of Manhattan and throughout the Bronx. His day started at 4:30 am and he worked twelve-to-fourteen-hour days, enduring rain, snow, heat, and cold for thirty years. In 1973, my father was the victim of a hit and run driver, breaking both his legs. My dad was out of work for a year and my parents struggled to support the family. Striving through a grueling recovery, my dad was back on the seltzer truck a year later. When I was ten years old, in the late 1970s, I started to work on the truck on weekends and school holidays. It was back-breaking work but I learned more about life and people in that experience more than anything else I did. When we would go into an apartment building, my father would introduce me to the doormen, porters, and elevator operators and they would all tell me, "your dad is a great man." It was a source of pride that my father knew how to connect with people from a variety of backgrounds and cultures and he treated everyone with dignity and respect, whether you lived in the penthouse or the basement apartment. At ten years old and beyond, I was expected to knock on doors of strangers, take orders, and make deliveries. I learned how to engage people, make eye contact, and carry on a conversation; lessons that served me well throughout my career. On days working on Arthur Avenue in the Bronx, or on Central Park West in Manhattan, it was like being in a movie, delivering to social clubs, penthouse apartments, and people from a variety of cultures and socio-economic levels. There were interpersonal experiences, for instance, when I delivered to an elderly woman on Riverside Drive. She grabbed my arm and pulled me to the window to point out city landmarks and give me a history lesson. After a while, I had to pull my arm away to make other deliveries. I told my father what happened, and he said, "look, she is lonely and lives by herself. You gave her an opportunity to connect and have a conversation. It was a mitzvah." My dad was way ahead of his time in demonstrating empathy and compassion.

In the early 1990s, my father's body couldn't handle carrying cases of seltzer anymore and he transitioned to driving plumbing supplies to construction sites, working full-time until the age of eighty-three. My mother, known affectionately as "The Suit Lady," worked as a bank clerk and spent years selling men's suits at Lord & Taylor. People would wait in line for her to help them because they trusted her honesty. If a customer asked how a jacket looked, she would say, "Take that off and follow me." Despite her hours being reduced, she remained a top seller, earning the President's Recognition for excellence. Here directness and integrity was driven by compassion to do right by her customers and it was an invaluable lesson for me to learn.

While I grew up in northern New Jersey, I played team sports until I graduated high school. I played on highly successful teams in football and baseball and learned to hold myself accountable when others were counting on me to do my job as I was counting on them. This dynamic was also present throughout my legal career and beyond. When people didn't hold themselves accountable, it usually led to conflict. My twin sister and I were the first in our family to attend college, and I later became the first in my extended family to graduate from law school. While I was a senior in college, I took a job as a paralegal for a mid-size law firm in New York City called Gold & Wachtel LLP (N/K/A Wachtel Missry LLP). One of my earliest experiences as a paralegal involved working on the Commissioner of Major League Baseball's investigation into George Steinbrenner as one of our partners, William Dowling, was the former General Counsel of the Yankees. This was one of the first times I learned to function under highly stressful situations, working long hours, sometimes all-nighters, and expected to arrive back at work early the next morning. It was a foreshadowing of what was to come as a lawyer. I went to Rutgers Law School and clerked and worked summers at the firm throughout law school.

My parents took immense pride in telling people their son was a lawyer, though they did not fully understand the relentless grind of being a litigator in the 1990s on white collar defense and commercial litigation cases. My early legal career was filled with high-stakes cases, including second-chairing trials in state and federal court and participating in a multi-week arbitration in St. Louis before a panel of three judges. I also worked on money-laundering and insurance fraud cases where clients on occasion would cooperate and go undercover with the FBI. While I found the work exhilarating at times, the stress and relentless pace got the better of me. I ultimately transitioned out of the practice and into executive search, consulting with law firms and legal departments, and coaching attorneys at all levels.

After practicing law, I started my new career at an executive search firm and after five years, two colleagues and I left and started our own search firm called Morandi, Taub & Sarnoff LLC. I started MTS when my son was eighteen months old and my infant daughter was eight weeks old. Needless to say, that required managing quite a bit of stress, but my wife Paige and I managed to navigate those challenging times. This work opened my eyes to the nuances of leadership, communication, and career development in the legal profession. I observed examples of high-performing leaders, as well as poor leadership, which was more the norm than the exception. In 2015, I formed Sarnoff Group, LLC that evolved from a career-coaching focus to an executive coaching and leadership training mission. Eventually, I discovered my true passion—executive coaching and leadership training. Enrolling in the iCoach New York executive coaching program at the Zicklin School of Business at Baruch College was a transformative experience. I delved deeply into emotional intelligence, active listening, and leadership development, earning a certification from the International Coaching Federation (ICF) and multiple assessments, including the EQ-i 2.0 to measure emotional intelligence.

Concurrently, I served on the board of education in our town for six years, three of those years as board president. In that role, I learned how to listen, make people feel heard, and build consensus and address multiple constituencies. I also learned that if you give your word, you better back it up or you will cause irreparable damage to trust. I was appointed to the New Jersey School Boards Mental Health Task Force and contributed to its final report on social and emotional learning. I observed various dynamics of helicopter parents and snowplow parents who pave the way for their children not letting them fail or experience pain or discomfort. This impacts their ability to build coping mechanisms to manage stress, failure, and adversity. We see the impact of these behaviors in the workplace.

Since 2018, I have dedicated my career to executive coaching, facilitating training workshops and speaking engagements for associates, partners, practice group leaders, general counsels, and professionals on the business services side of law firms. I also coach leaders in other industries and professions and identify best practices applicable to all professions. The work is incredibly rewarding and aligns with the values instilled in me by my parents—hard work, honesty, high-trust relationships, empathy, inclusion, respect, and being direct. Meeting Natalie through a mutual friend further enriched this journey, leading to numerous collaborations, conference presentations, and the PLI column that serves as the foundation for this book. Since 2020, I have been a member of the Diversity, Equity and Inclusion Committee of the New York City Bar Association and served as co-chair of this committee for two years.

Leadership in the legal profession is not just about intelligence or technical expertise—it's about emotional intelligence, communication, feedback, inclusion, bridging generations, and conflict management. The lessons I absorbed from my upbringing, legal career, and transition into coaching have reinforced the idea that true leadership is about effective communication, resilience, adaptability, and the ability to foster trust. I hope this book offers insights that inspire legal professionals and professions in other industries to lead with purpose, empathy, and authenticity.

Acknowledgments

To my first boss, Sharon Armstrong, my first HR Director, Gayle George, and the labor and employment partner that modeled leadership for lawyers for me, Hank Baer.

To my extraordinary team that models the behaviors it takes every day to have a highly functioning collaborative team. We do not strive to be perfect, instead we strive to support each other every day in a way that is humanly possible; providing a healthy workplace culture and excellent services to our clients.

To Ted—you know why.

NATALIE LOEB
March 2026

I am grateful to the many people who shaped my understanding of leadership and management, beginning with my father, Jerry Sarnoff, who modeled what it means to lead with integrity. He showed me that being a strong leader means being caring and direct, courageous yet empathetic. His example continues to guide me every day.

My close college friend and mentor, Bruce J. Liebowitz, whose investment in my growth and development profoundly impacted my career and life. Bruce was a pioneer and thought leader in organizational development, an adventurous travel partner, and a trusted confidant. His loss was deeply felt but he left a legacy that impacted many and will live on into the future.

To my friend and law firm colleague, Evan Weintraub, thank you for your patience, your calm in the midst of chaos, and your invaluable mentorship, especially in refining my legal writing and navigating high-pressure situations with grace.

To Carl and Gloria LaGrassa, who began as clients and became dear friends. Your leadership, perseverance, resilience, and humility have been both a model and an inspiration. I'm grateful for the lessons you've taught me and the experiences you gave me.

And finally, to all the teachers, athletic coaches, colleagues, and mentors—both the great leaders and the not-so-great ones—thank you. Each of you, in your own way, helped shape my perspective on what it truly means to lead effectively.

DAVID SARNOFF
March 2026

To Our PLI Team—Together, We Are Stronger

It's been more than three decades since we each entered the legal field—through different doors, yet drawn by the same spark: the energy and intensity of working alongside brilliant minds doing meaningful work.

Over the years, we both chose to influence our workplaces in positive, human ways, leading with care, leveraging emotional intelligence, and striving to make a difference. At times, our efforts were met with resistance. But more often, they inspired curiosity: *How did you get others to follow?*

It's from these shared experiences that our columns for legal professionals were born. Writing was our first step in giving voice to what we've learned and experienced. Having others believe in that voice has been the next and most rewarding part of the journey.

That belief found a home at the Practising Law Institute (PLI). In a chance meeting with Kara O'Brien of PLI, David shared an idea that led to an introduction to Amy Taub, whose enthusiasm for our work on leadership, listening, and emotional intelligence sparked new opportunities and several PLI One-Hour Briefings. From there, we pitched the concept of a monthly column and were introduced to our incredible editor, Alyse Greer.

For nearly five years, Alyse has championed our vision, refining our ideas and ensuring every column met PLI's high standards. We are deeply grateful for her partnership. Alyse also connected us to our book editor, Jacob Metric, and the outstanding publishing team, a group as dedicated and passionate as they are talented.

We're equally thankful to Kenneth Min and Lisa Garcia, whose professionalism and guidance have made our PLI Studio briefings such an enjoyable experience.

As the saying goes, it takes a village. We are profoundly thankful to the entire PLI team for believing in us and, more importantly, for believing that leadership in the legal field truly matters.

Together, we are building better workplaces, stronger teams, and more connected communities.

Thank you for being part of this journey.

Natalie Loeb
David Sarnoff
March 2026

Part I

Leadership

Chapter 1

Why Lawyers Need Executive Coaches

Natalie Loeb & David B. Sarnoff

"I don't want to be a jerk, but when associates give me crappy work, what am I supposed to do?" The partner actually used a different word than "jerk." His tone was loud and direct. He was frustrated, maybe even angry. Time is valuable, and he was tired of having to edit or redo work. Quite simply, he wanted better results from his associates but didn't seem to know how to get it. Mental energy that was wasted on frustration and throwing work back and forth to his team of associates wasn't serving him or his clients well. He knew it, but what he didn't know was how to change it. Not until he had some time to work with his executive coach.

Traditionally, the law firm model has been a business structure that did not place great value on cultivating communication and leadership skills. Starting as first-year associates, attorneys are trained to focus most of their energies on practicing law in their area of expertise and billable hours. However, as associates become more senior, their responsibilities expand to overseeing matters and delegating work. Law school prepares one for lawyering; it does not prepare lawyers for managing teams. Many associates who are promoted to partner find themselves ill-equipped and lacking the skills necessary to delegate work to other people. Instead of coaching associates in the moment, senior lawyers often default to one of two counterproductive responses: (1) taking back the work and doing it themselves, or

(2) cutting the associate from the matter altogether. While these may seem like quick fixes, they create a long-term problem: underdeveloped associates, lower morale, and a weak talent pipeline for the firm.

However, the legal profession is embracing coaching, training, and development for attorneys focused on effective leadership, communication, emotional intelligence, collaboration, and other key skills.

From the early 20th century to the dotcom boom of the 90s, law firm management styles and practices rarely changed from decade to decade. There was little in the way of disruption in the practice of law for almost a century. However, that is changing at a rapid rate. Like many other industries, the practice of law is feeling the effects of disruption as well as pressure to modernize on many fronts. Global competition, economic pressures from clients, new expectations from associates, responding to a global pandemic, and the increasing integration of artificial intelligence and smart machines have fueled a transformation and substantive changes to the practice of law.

As a result, law firms and legal departments find themselves in a position where they have to maintain a high-caliber work product, increase efficiency and productivity, and retain talent. It is important to have both high-functioning administrative and management departments as well as legal practice groups. The primary way to achieve success is by nurturing and cultivating leaders at all levels of the organization. This requires a commitment from the firm to invest in professional development, leadership training, and targeted, individualized, and/or group coaching to raise the firm's collective emotional intelligence.

In a study commissioned by the American Management Association (AMA) and administered by the Institute for Corporate Productivity (ICP) entitled *Coaching: A Global Study of Successful Practices,*[1] researchers found that "[w]orking with an external coach is significantly related to a successful coaching experience, regardless of the coachee's level in the organization." The study indicated that the majority of leaders prefer external coaching (coaching provided by professional coaches outside of the firm) and that high-level employees

1. Am. Mgmt. Ass'n, *Coaching: A Global Study of Successful Practices, Current Trends and Future Possibilities 2008–2018* (2008) [hereinafter AMA/ICP Coaching Study], https://www.amanet.org/assets/1/6/i4cp-coaching.pdf.

"place a high value on confidentiality, [which] may only be possible with an external coach." Evidence suggests that external coaches may also "be more willing than peers or subordinates to deliver painfully honest feedback to a high-level employee and go on to develop a goal-directed plan of action."

External executive coaches have no agenda other than for the "coachee" to be successful and for the firm to leverage their talent. Executive coaches, training and development professionals, and organizational development professionals provide the tools and assessments that allow law firms to increase efficiency, productivity, and collaboration in a measurable way. Coaches and facilitators work in group and/or individual settings to align the firm so that all employees understand leadership skills and behaviors, which enables leaders to foster collaboration and ultimately make work life better and more satisfying. Law firms can also employ coaches to provide services to individuals and groups who can benefit from improved communication and presentation skills, conflict resolution, organization and time management, and management or leadership skills.

Over the past twenty years, executive coaching and management training have been widely embraced in corporate culture, and their benefits are broadly reported and documented. Law firms have been slower to accept training and development, but there are signs that this is changing as well. Many large law firms now have training for attorneys, management, paraprofessionals, and staff. This type of training enhances the culture of the organization and provides employees with the tools necessary to adapt to rapid change, lower anxiety, and alleviate disruption caused by changes within the firm.

While there are many companies and law firms that regularly engage in some form of coaching and training, there are also skeptics who believe that coaching is unnecessary or a luxury. However, the AMA/ICP Coaching Study dispels this myth. The findings revealed that "those who have received coaching were more likely than other respondents to say that their subordinates trust their leadership abilities and they're more likely to say that they set specific goals for performance at work."[2]

---

2. *Id.* at 10.

In 2017, there was a record number of law firm mergers and acquisitions in the United States.[3] A natural consequence of a law firm merger is the need to integrate different cultures, business practices, leadership styles, and firm citizenship. Executive coaches, trainers, and facilitators can play an integral role in smoothing the transition of two merged law firms. As a result of the rapid speed of change, technology, and economic pressures, law firms will be forced to address issues of leadership, management skills, succession, adaptability, conflict resolution, efficiency, and culture. External professionals can be a strong asset to law firms who recognize that coaching services can help them function on a higher level and increase their competitive edge.

Consider the well-intentioned managing partner who wants to create an inclusive work culture, attract and retain talent, meet client expectations, and enhance morale. Intentions are good, but behaviors and actions matter more. An executive coach will challenge that managing partner to reflect on his mindset and to commit to behaviors that move their initiatives forward.

How about the talented partner you brought into your Dubai office to share his expertise and offer his insights into how to grow the business in the region. What happens when you find out that the partner is struggling to build the necessary "sphere of influence" to be effective? Coaching will help this partner to increase self-awareness, adapt to the local office culture, and leverage his strengths to build high-trust relationships.

When set up correctly, executive coaching is a highly collaborative, individualized relationship between a leader and a coach. Both parties collaborate to reach an agreed-upon result with the objective of fostering sustained behavioral change and transforming the quality of the leader's effectiveness. Coaches work with leaders to enable their rapid development while navigating the ego of the leader. Unlike training, coaching focuses specifically on the issues that the firm and leader want to work through. Thus, it becomes a more practical and efficient way to improve skills and to achieve personal and professional objectives.

---

3. *See* Elizabeth Olson, *2017 Record Year for Law Firm Mergers*, Bloomberg L. (Jan. 3, 2018), https://news.bloomberglaw.com/business-and-practice/2017-record-year-for-law-firm-mergers/.

Coaching focuses on shifting a leader's mindset in a way that can translate into daily activities. The coach's role is to create a safe and confidential environment in which the coachee can reflect on their behavior, contemplate the steps that are necessary to achieve an objective, and practice new skills. In turn, the coachee's role is to identify an area they want to develop or explore during the engagement, to be willing and open to receiving feedback, and to hold themselves accountable for behavior change. The length of the coaching engagement varies and is usually determined by the area the coachee wants to develop or explore. In short-term engagements, the coachee may have a specific opportunity they want to tackle, and they simply need a trusted thought partner to help shape a path forward. Longer-term coaching engagements are needed when the coachee hasn't fully defined the opportunity or when the opportunity is complex.

At the end of an executive coaching engagement, the coachee has a heightened sense of self-awareness, greater confidence and resilience, better tools and strategies, and a more agile mindset that can effectively tolerate stress. The coachee also develops a growth mindset when it comes to giving and receiving feedback and viewing feedback as a gift that helps align one's intentions with one's actions. These are critical skills for partners and rising associates who lead and manage people and teams to create high-performing and high-trust teams.

Key Takeaways and Action Items

Key Takeaway One

Shift from Fixing to Developing Others

Rather than redoing or discarding associates' work, lawyers in leadership roles must develop the skills to coach in the moment—this builds capability, morale, and a stronger talent pipeline. Executive coaching helps leaders adopt this mindset and practice it effectively.

Action Items:

1. **Debrief Collaboratively:** Walk through the work with the associate, highlighting what was done well before addressing gaps or errors.
2. **Ask Reflective Questions:** Prompt them to share their thinking process ("What led you to approach it this way?") and explore alternatives together.
3. **Agree on Next Steps:** Co-create an improvement plan so the associate can revise and learn rather than just receive corrections.

Key Takeaway Two

Invest in Leadership Skills Beyond Legal Expertise

Lawyers are often promoted based on legal acumen, not leadership ability. Executive coaching fills that gap by helping leaders build emotional intelligence and improve delegation, time management, and communication—skills essential for leading high-performing, collaborative teams.

Action Items:

1. **Select a Focus Area:** Choose one leadership skill (e.g., feedback, delegation, time management) that will have the biggest impact.
2. **Practice with Intention:** Set a measurable goal (e.g., delegate one task each week) and track your progress over thirty days.

3. **Seek Accountability:** Partner with a coach, mentor, or peer to discuss wins, challenges, and ways to refine your approach.

Key Takeaway Three

Leverage Coaching As a Strategic Asset for Change

In a rapidly evolving legal landscape shaped by technology, mergers, and shifting cultural expectations, coaching provides a confidential space to reflect, receive honest feedback, and develop targeted behaviors. It supports both individual transformation and firm-wide growth and resilience.

Action Items:

1. **Engage in Reflection:** Explore how industry changes (tech, hybrid work, client demands) are affecting your leadership approach.
2. **Identify Blind Spots:** Ask your coach or peers for candid feedback on how your behavior impacts others.
3. **Align with Your Vision:** Work with your coach to set clear goals and create a plan to become the leader your team needs.

Chapter 2

Taking Advantage of Executive Coaching

Natalie Loeb & David B. Sarnoff

Dear Coaches:

> **I'm a senior associate at a large law firm and my Practice Group Leader (PGL) approached me and proposed an executive coaching engagement as a way to support my candidacy for partnership consideration. The PGL suggested I could strengthen my communication skills, giving and receiving feedback and cultivating relationships. I was the only one in my class that was approached for this. I don't understand why I was put in this position because I'm not interested in going into therapy. How should I respond to the PGL?**
>
> ***—Singled Out***

Natalie: Congratulations! Your PGL apparently is invested in your success. I'm not surprised you're a bit skeptical about being offered coaching. There is a history in law firms of associates being offered coaching when something is "wrong." The fact is that when a leader offers a coach to an associate to support their candidacy for partner in today's workplace, it means that something is "right" and the partner and firm would like to see the associate leverage their legal talent and build capacity for their ability to lead and influence others. David and

I often talk about emotional intelligence and how it is a way to predict and measure success for partners. The skills your PGL wants to support you in developing fall under that emotional intelligence umbrella and will help you not only to build business but to also build relationships, manage conflict, influence others, and lead teams. With a combination of strong legal talent and emotional intelligence skills, you will find success as a partner, and most likely less stress as you transition to the role. Thank your PGL for the opportunity for coaching.

You are probably wondering what today's coaching looks like for a talented lawyer (we call our coaching clients "highly talented, highly valued, high achievers"). Below are some of the questions you may be wondering about, along with the answers for you. After considering the information below, I suggest you bring a learner's mindset to your coaching engagement. I have no doubt you will enjoy the process and build additional foundational skills to help you become partner and remain successful and highly sought-after. Wishing you tremendous success!

Q: What is coaching exactly?

A: A supportive relationship with a trained coach to help the client build increased self-awareness and enhance the lawyer's ability to learn, try new behaviors and approaches for interacting with others, self-reflect, push themselves out of their "comfort zone" to make desired changes, solve problems, and achieve goals. Most coaches today work with their client virtually, typically in a series of regularly scheduled sessions. If the coach and coachee are located in the same area, they may meet face-to-face.

Q: How is coaching different from consulting, teaching, or therapy?

A: Coaching differs from consulting because the coach's primary role is not to give advice or design solutions. Coaches ask questions and suggest alternatives that guide clients to discover their own unique answers and choose their own path. A coach may provide ideas, expertise, and skill-building techniques, but doesn't solve clients' problems for them, nor tell them what to do. Coaching differs from teaching in that the coach doesn't determine what the coachee will learn, nor provide a curriculum to be followed. The coachee decides what he or she needs to know, and the coach facilitates learning by providing accountability, feedback, helpful resources, or useful models. Coaching differs from therapy because coaching sessions are primarily focused on learning and achievement, rather than healing or resolution. Coaches help coachees to make changes in their lives by observing present conditions, visualizing future goals, and determining action steps.

Q: What do people get out of working with a coach?

A: Coaching clients experience a sense of partnership and support in achieving their professional and personal goals that is often not available elsewhere in their lives. Regular coaching sessions provide clients with dedicated time to focus on what they truly want and what must happen to create it. Coaches help their clients design action steps to meet their goals, then hold them accountable to their own stated desires, providing perspective, feedback, and smart questions along the way. As a result, clients stay motivated, make significant changes, and achieve more than they may have thought possible.

Q: How does someone know if they are ready to work with a coach?

A: To get the most from a coaching relationship, clients need to be willing to learn new ways of doing things and make changes in their mindset and behavior. Anyone who is open to hearing new perspectives, willing to question how they are currently acting, and ready to take on new challenges in their career can benefit from working with a coach.

Q: How can I be a great coaching client?

A: It's simple, yet right from the start it requires action. Prioritize coaching. Prioritize coaching. Prioritize coaching.

Great coaching clients prioritize coaching by scheduling coaching sessions when they are at their best. Smartphones are off and attention is on the coaching session. Interruptions from your team or others are not allowed. For your coaching session to remain focused on you and your development, you need to keep yourself away from those disrupting interruptions. If your coaching session is virtual, do not spend your session talking with your coach while you are simultaneously checking your email.

Clear your mind for each coaching session. It helps to remember what you discussed in the previous session. You may want to take notes either during or after your session.

Plan for your coaching session in advance. Think about your short- and long-term goals. Be open to your coach's agenda as well. Tell your coach about wins you've experienced since you last talked. Talk about what you might be procrastinating on or any frustrations you are experiencing. Take risks in what you are talking about. Don't avoid important work topics. Every avoided work topic of importance is a potential leak in the coaching boat. If you avoid too many topics, you will spring too many leaks and your coaching boat won't make it to your desired destination.

Take risks in what you choose to talk about regarding work. Don't be afraid to talk about big dreams or challenges you experience. There are no dumb questions in this process. It's important to have definite goals but sometimes it's also important to wonder about things. Your coach is there to partner with you in both the goal-setting, goal-achievement process and the wondering. Both you and your coach are experts on you. Your coach's expertise will grow as you talk in more depth about your work experiences.

Your feedback to the coach about how on-target he is, or what has been helpful to you, will help the coach home in on being a better coach. You can also challenge your coach about what doesn't work for you. Also, tell your coach if you think something is missing from your coaching sessions. Honest feedback from both the coachee and the coach about what's going on in the coaching partnership is like the oil keeping the relationship running smoothly.

What You Can Expect

Coaching involves assignments and sometimes homework. Your coach expects you to complete any assessments which are part of this engagement. There also may be a series of articles which she wants you to read. Your coach may offer additional assignments, targeted to your development. Because this is a coaching partnership, you do not have to comply with every assignment your coach requests. You can say no. You can also counteroffer to do or read something else.

Confidentiality

Typically, what you say to your coach stays with your coach and is confidential. The boundaries of confidentiality are generally outlined during the contracting stage. Please be mindful that this is not a privileged conversation and under specific situations, disclosure may be required under law.

David: I echo Natalie's congratulations on being offered an executive coaching opportunity. It is an investment to prepare you for the challenges of the partnership track process and to be an effective leader and attorney. As Natalie also mentioned, coaching involves building emotional intelligence skills that help raise self-awareness to understand how you show up, how you are perceived by your colleagues, and what are the impacts of your words and actions on others. By having an external coach, you usually get more objective and direct feedback about areas that are ripe for growth and development that can be addressed in a confidential setting. Law firm associates often find themselves navigating a demanding and competitive professional landscape. Historically, the legal professional has always been known for its high-pressure environment, intense workload, and demanding clients. In such a challenging setting, it's easy for even the most talented associates to feel overwhelmed or uncertain about their career track. This is another value add where executive coaching can make a positive impact.

Firstly, executive coaching offers a unique opportunity for personal and professional development. While law school equips associates with the necessary legal knowledge and skills, it often falls short in preparing them for the complexities of law firm culture, leading and managing people and teams, managing clients, cultivating high-trust relationships, and career advancement. Executive coaching provides a customized approach to address these areas for growth.

Moreover, executive coaching can serve as a valuable sounding board for associates grappling with complex professional situations or challenges. Executive coaches provide a confidential and impartial space for associates to discuss challenges, brainstorm solutions, get direct feedback and observations, and gain fresh perspectives without fear of judgment or reprisal. As Natalie said, coaching is not therapy for the reasons she outlined. I would like to add that therapy typically looks into the past to understand how we got to where we are. Coaching typically establishes where we are and focuses on how we want to change going forward. It is forward-focusing in embracing change and developing necessary skills to be more effective in practicing law and leading others.

Executive coaches can provide insights into building effective working relationships with colleagues, managing conflicts diplomatically, and positioning oneself for career advancement within the firm. These behaviors require the skills found in highly emotionally intelligent leaders. As Daniel Goleman, a thought leader in emotional intelligence, says, "EQ is a differentiator among a group of highly intelligent people as to who is most able to lead."

Additionally, executive coaching can be instrumental in helping associates identify and leverage their unique strengths and talents. Executive coaching can help associates navigate transitions and challenges at various stages of their career. Whether it's transitioning to a new practice area, seeking partnership, or developing efficient strategies to manage time and prioritization in a more effective way. Executive coaches can provide guidance, support, resources and accountability every step of the way.

Lastly, investing in executive coaching demonstrates a commitment to continuous learning and growth, qualities that are highly valued in the legal profession. In a rapidly evolving industry, where new technologies, AI, and market dynamics constantly reshape the legal landscape, the ability to adapt and innovate is paramount. Executive coaching equips associates with the tools, insights, and growth mindset needed to thrive in an ever-changing legal environment.

In conclusion, while the journey of a law firm associate can be quite challenging, it is also filled with opportunities for learning, and professional development. By embracing executive coaching, associates can unlock their full potential, overcome obstacles, and achieve success on their own terms. Whether it's honing legal skills, navigating office politics, or charting a path to partnership, executive coaching can be a valuable resource in the toolbox of any dedicated law firm associate. I wish you the best in your coaching engagement.

Key Takeaways and Action Items

Key Takeaway One

Executive Coaching Is a Sign of Investment, Not Punishment

Although coaching has historically been offered reactively when issues arise, we reframe it as a proactive investment in high-potential talent. Being singled out for coaching ahead of partnership consideration is a strong signal that the firm sees leadership potential and wants to support growth in areas like communication, feedback, and relationship-building.

Action Items:

1. **Communicate the Intent:** Clearly articulate to lawyers receiving coaching that it is a proactive investment in their professional growth and leadership potential.
2. **Integrate into Talent Strategy:** Position coaching as part of the firm's leadership pipeline program, especially ahead of partnership consideration.
3. **Celebrate Coaching Publicly:** Have firm leaders share success stories of partners and senior associates who have benefited from coaching.

Key Takeaway Two

Coaching Builds Emotional Intelligence Skills Critical for Leadership

We emphasize that coaching focuses on enhancing self-awareness, relationship management, and influence—core elements of emotional intelligence. These skills complement legal acumen and are essential for thriving in leadership roles, managing clients, and leading teams effectively in the law firm environment.

Action Items:

1. **Assess Baseline EQ:** Use tools like EQ-i 2.0® or 360-feedback to identify strengths and areas for growth.

2. **Create Individual Development Plans (IDPs):** Set clear, measurable goals focused on self-awareness, empathy, communication, and influence.

3. **Practice Skills in Real Time:** Encourage those being coached to experiment with active listening, feedback delivery, and conflict management in ongoing matters.

Key Takeaway Three

Coaching Is Not Therapy, It's a Forward-Looking, Practical Development Tool

The column distinguishes coaching from therapy, consulting, or teaching. Coaching is described as a structured, confidential partnership that helps clients set goals, try new behaviors, receive feedback, and make lasting change. It's about unlocking potential and navigating challenges—not fixing problems from the past.

Action Items:

1. **Clarify Expectations:** At program launch, explain the difference between coaching and therapy so participants understand the purpose and boundaries.

2. **Set Developmental Goals:** Collaboratively establish clear objectives tied to current performance and future roles.

3. **Use Structured Check-Ins:** Schedule periodic reviews to celebrate wins, identify roadblocks, and recalibrate goals as needed.

Chapter 3

It's Not Lawyering, It's Leading

Natalie Loeb & David B. Sarnoff

Dear Coaches:

> **I was recently promoted to equity partner and invited to participate in the firm's management committee. I'm excited for the new opportunity and want to begin thinking about ways to contribute to the committee and how to lead my team for the best results. While I know I was promoted because I'm a good lawyer, I don't feel equipped to lead. Why do I lack confidence and feel like something is missing? Many of my colleagues aren't the best leaders, and I want to break the cycle of poor leadership, but I haven't personally had great leaders or mentors to draw from. What do I do?**
>
> ***—Learning to Lead with Intent***

Natalie: Let's begin with one of your strengths: you are demonstrating self-awareness. In the world of leadership development, heightened self-awareness is a strength, and you are self-aware about your confidence as a lawyer; however, since you have not yet had formal training on how to lead, you lack confidence in how to *effectively* lead. Our experience as leadership coaches for lawyers consistently shows us that lawyers often become uncomfortable when they lack confidence in their competence for a skill. Intuitively, you are right. Your self-awareness is signaling that you're missing a crucial stepping stone to becoming an effective member of your firm's management committee. In short, this is what you're "missing." The good news is, leadership is indeed a skill that can be developed, and with your continued curiosity and willingness to learn (both good leadership traits), you can effectively prepare yourself to be an extremely valuable contributor to your firm's management committee. I have seen many lawyers grow confidence in their leadership skills, and develop an ability to be very influential on committees.

When we are coaching lawyers, it is not uncommon for a lawyer to say something like, "I never thought of myself as a leader," or "I was never taught how to lead in law school." However, today it is extremely common for talented lawyers to be selected or offered leadership roles in their firms. Whatever that role may be, it will certainly require learning how to interact with a variety of personalities and issues. One of my favorite definitions of leadership is put forth by Jim Kouzes and Barry Posner, Ph.D., authors, researchers, and thought leaders on leadership: *Mobilizing others to want to struggle for shared aspirations.* Leading in a law firm means leading from whichever seat you are assigned. Sometimes this means leading with authority, and at other times it may mean leading with influence. Whichever is the case for you, it will be helpful for you to adopt the mindset of a leader. Although all leaders eventually develop their individual leadership philosophy, a common thread to leading effectively is to pay attention to both the results you want to achieve and the emotional needs of the people who will help you get there. Research tells us that lawyers often like to work autonomously, but leaders need to know how to work collaboratively. And for some lawyers, this is where it can get tricky.

Like any other skill we develop, leadership skills require a combination of learning and practice. Think back to when you learned a new skill/activity as a child, whether it be a sport, language, art class, computer language, or software. We all begin the same way. Prepare yourself. The language I'm about to use may make you bristle; however, it accurately depicts how human beings learn.

Here's the model:

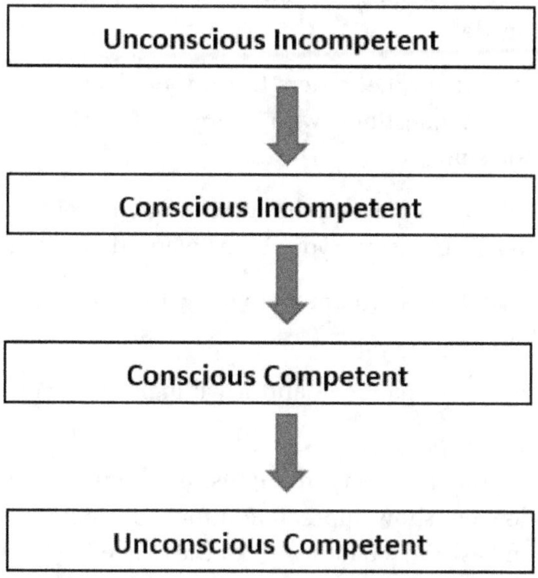

When I learned to drive a stick shift, I was excited but had no idea what I was getting into. I was unconsciously incompetent, meaning I didn't know what I didn't know. When I put the key in the car and tried to drive it around the block, I immediately moved to being "consciously incompetent." I very quickly became aware that I had no idea what I was doing and that this was going to be harder than I thought. I found a patient person to teach me and eventually learned how to use the stick shift and the gas pedals in sync to make the car move. I moved to a place of being "consciously competent" and found myself paying a lot of attention to what I was doing. As I practiced and got better, I eventually moved to the "unconscious competence" stage. Today, I can drive a stick shift without even thinking about how my hand and feet are interacting. It just comes naturally.

Learning to lead follows the same learning path. You are not "missing" anything. Since you have been placed on this committee and are expected to lead, you are finding yourself in the "conscious incompetent" stage. Congratulations! Now you can move to the "conscious competent" phase. And if you stick with it long enough, you may eventually grow to be a successful unconscious competent leader.

Leadership Tips for a Newly Conscious Competent Leader

There are many leadership behaviors to develop and practice. Here are five to consider.

1. Listen actively. Let others finish their sentences. Don't interrupt. Ask questions with a tone of curiosity rather than skepticism.
2. Seek the opinions and thoughts of others before providing an answer. Demonstrate you value diverse thoughts and opinions.
3. Smile and use eye contact to show interest in what others are saying.
4. Demonstrate patience and a willingness to consider others' ideas.
5. Share your reactions, thoughts, opinions confidently. When challenged, show appreciation for the willingness to contribute and ask the "challenger" for the reasoning behind the challenge. Listen actively.

If any of these behaviors are not yet natural for you, good for you. Your heightened self-awareness can lead you to committing to consciously practicing that behavior more frequently. And now you are on your way to becoming the kind of leader you aspire to be on your management committee.

David: Thank you for your question and congratulations on your promotion to the management committee. This promotion is significant and requires a mindset shift from being one of a group of partners to being a leader of partners. It is analogous to going from being an associate to being promoted to partner. There is a transition from being one of the team to leading the team, going from being a high performer, adept at a skill or practice, to now motivating and inspiring performance through others. Being a high-performing individual contributor and being a leader require significantly different skills. At its essence, in my opinion, it is IQ vs. EQ.

Attorneys tend to focus on IQ, which involves their competency in verbal, spatial, numerical, and logical intelligence. Essentially, they focus on how smart they are and how well they incorporate their intelligence into the practice of law. Emotional Intelligence (EI or EQ), however, involves the competency of self-perception, self-expression, interpersonal skills, decision making, and stress management. As Natalie referenced earlier, at its core, EQ is about raising self-awareness as to how one shows up and is perceived by others. It requires an understanding of the emotions we experience, identifying these emotions, being able to influence emotions, and understanding the impact of our words and actions on others. This requires leaders to cultivate and nurture relationships with members of their teams to build trust and be able to motivate and inspire others to perform at a level that meets or exceeds expectations.

What law firm partners are typically not taught before ascending to the ranks is the difference between management and leadership. Management is a fact. It is the "what" we do. Members of the management committee manage and oversee the law firm's operations and practice of law. It is "what" they do. However, leadership is a choice. It is "how" you do it. Management involves your IQ skills for developing budgets, finances, personnel decisions, technology choices, and so on. Leadership requires your EQ skills in creating a shared mission culture, understanding the goals and aspirations of your team members, and communicating how you will support them. As Natalie mentioned, communication is a critical EQ skill that involves demonstrating empathy, care, and inclusion. When a leader demonstrates empathy in an authentic way, the members of their team will typically respond in kind and want to contribute in a way that supports the team and its leader. Being an empathic leader also provides the environment to deliver direct feedback that is received in a productive way. It still may sting the person on the receiving end, but if they believe it is delivered with care, it will be better received than if it was delivered with a punitive intent. Members of your team will be motivated and inspired by your leadership skills, not your management skills. As I say over and over, "leaders model the behavior they expect of others." As a member of the management committee, you want to demonstrate consistency and compliance in your own behavior as well as the behavior of individual contributors. When there is contradiction between what a leader requires and how the leader behaves, there will be an erosion of trust and shared mission.

To echo Natalie's comment, you have demonstrated the self-awareness in understanding that leadership is important and that you may not currently have the most effective skills to be a highly impactful leader. The good news is that emotional intelligence and practicing leadership skills involves learned behaviors and can be developed with learning and practice. In order to start down your leadership journey, I recommend a few books to help teach you high-caliber leadership skills. They include the following:

- **Primal Leadership**, by Daniel Goleman, Richard Boyatzis and Annie McKee;
- **Leaders Eat Last**, by Simon Sinek; and
- **The Leadership Challenge**, by Barry Posner and James Kouzes.

Once you learn the foundations of leadership skills, it is important to practice those skills, seek feedback, and evaluate what strengths to continue leveraging and where there is opportunity for growth and development. Try to create a support structure of people you trust and confide in, in order to work through challenges and to collaborate on solutions. Keep in mind, leadership can be a lonely place and it is important to have trusted friends or colleagues to talk to.

Key Takeaways and Action Items

Key Takeaway One

Leadership Is a Learned Skill, Not an Innate Trait

Even highly successful lawyers feel uncertain when stepping into leadership because they have not been formally taught how to lead. Your self-awareness is not a weakness; it is evidence that you're ready for growth. Leadership requires learning, practice, and the willingness to move from "conscious incompetence" to competence.

Action Items:

1. **Adopt a Learning Mindset:** Read foundational leadership books (e.g., *Primal Leadership, Leaders Eat Last, The Leadership Challenge*) to build a conceptual framework for modern leadership.
2. **Seek Training and Coaching:** Enroll in leadership development programs or work with an executive coach to practice skills such as influence, communication, and conflict navigation.
3. **Choose One Skill to Practice Weekly:** Whether it's active listening or asking open-ended questions, deliberately practice one leadership behavior until it becomes more natural.

Key Takeaway Two

Leadership Requires High Emotional Intelligence (EQ), Not Just IQ

Lawyers often rely on intellectual intelligence, logic, analysis, and accuracy, but leading requires empathy, curiosity, communication, and relationship skills. Your impact will increasingly depend on how you make others feel, not just what you know.

Action Items:

1. **Practice Active Listening:** Let others finish their thoughts; avoid interrupting; ask clarifying questions with curiosity rather than skepticism.
2. **Build Trust Through Empathy:** Take time to understand your colleagues' motivations, stressors, and aspirations. Demonstrate care through tone, body language, and follow-through.
3. **Model Regulated, Inclusive Behavior:** Respond calmly when challenged, acknowledge others' contributions, and reinforce psychological safety in meetings and discussions.

Key Takeaway Three

Leadership Is About Influence, Not Authority

Being on the management committee is not just about making decisions, it's about mobilizing others toward shared goals. Leadership is the "how" behind the work: how you inspire, communicate, collaborate, and support the people who deliver the results.

Action Items:

1. **Engage Others Before Offering Your View:** Ask teammates for their ideas, concerns, and perspectives before sharing your own. This strengthens buy-in and shows respect.
2. **Demonstrate Behavioral Consistency:** Align your actions (timeliness, preparation, communication, follow-through) with your expectations of others. This builds trust instantly.
3. **Create a Leadership Support Network:** Identify two to three trusted colleagues or mentors with whom you can process challenges, gain perspective, and sharpen your judgment.

Chapter 4

Partners, How Patient Are You?

Natalie Loeb & David B. Sarnoff

Dear Coaches:

> **I'm a new associate and, like many others, have a hybrid working arrangement. The partner I report to has been very short with me recently and often declines requests for video calls to review assignments when I am working remotely. Instead, the partner tends to reassign work I have been working on to associates more senior to me who already know how to perform the work. I fear I'm missing out on learning and developmental opportunities as a result of this hybrid work. How do you suggest I approach the partner about my concerns?**
>
> ***—Passed Over in the Pandemic***

David: Thank you for this question—you are certainly not alone. In the early days of the pandemic and through the years that have followed, there has been a widening gap in training and mentoring for associates, particularly first- and second-year associates. In the Fall of 2021, I had a conversation with a senior HR professional at a well-known law firm. I asked her what impact she believes the pandemic has had on the development of junior associates. She said that it has had a "dramatic impact." She continued, "Remote work has impacted the learning and development of junior associates similar to how remote learning has impacted students in kindergarten." I thought that was a powerful statement. She also said, "If a junior associate does not have the courage to raise their hand and speak up and advocate for themselves, they get lost in the flow."

With respect to your specific question, one potential solution is to schedule a call with your partner and have a frank and honest discussion about the impact that the remote working environment is having on your skill development and seek solutions that can provide the oversight and mentoring that would address this challenge. In preparation for the call, I suggest you offer a plan to the partner such as having regularly scheduled check-ins to discuss challenges and progress on assignments. Conveying a significant interest in the practice area and willingness to invest the time and commitment to building the necessary skills may also influence the partner's behavior. If the partner is not willing to commit to this track, another possible solution is to seek peer feedback and input on your work product from more senior associates who have successfully worked with this partner.

I think it is worthwhile to discuss the broader issue of feedback in the legal profession. Just a few short years ago, most would have thought it unthinkable for the entire legal profession to function in a largely remote and hybrid format. In my opinion, the operations of the practice of law changed more during the pandemic and following two years than in the prior fifty years. While the ever-increasing use of technology has been eroding opportunities to interact in person, the pandemic caused a massive shift to remote and hybrid work and with it, the loss of spontaneous learning opportunities. The legal profession as a whole and law firm partners specifically have not been widely known for giving effective feedback to associates. This has only been exacerbated by remote and hybrid work environments. In fact, we have seen a sharp increase in the demand of law firms requesting training for giving and receiving effective feedback because of an awareness that ineffective feedback is impacting associate development and attrition. Prior to the pandemic, a partner would ask associates to attend a client conference call or a negotiation, where they could listen and observe without being noticed. Now, if a partner tries to do that on a Zoom call, the associates are typically visible, and the client may become concerned about being billed more. Law firm partners must be intentional in creating meaningful learning opportunities for associates, particularly when teams are dispersed across offices or working remotely.

Leaders in the profession are becoming increasingly aware that partners need to be more mindful about how they delegate work, provide effective feedback, and monitor progress on assignments. If associates do not receive oversight, effective feedback, and development opportunities, it will negatively impact their ability to learn and hone needed skills for a strong foundation to practice law. It is also a business imperative to make associates feel valued, invested in, and properly trained, otherwise they may consider seeking training at another law firm.

Natalie: Let me begin with saying, I echo everything David said. Seeking feedback when it is not offered or provided enough is necessary for career growth and is a skill utilized by effective leaders at all levels.

Here's more to think about: As coaches, one of our responsibilities is to challenge the thinking of our "coachees." Sometimes when a situation is "reframed," allowing for a shift in perception, we find another way of handling it. It seems pretty clear you are eager to grow and develop into a great lawyer, and you recognize that your partner has years of experience and a wealth of knowledge to tap into. You mention that the partner is very short with you and often declines your request for video calls. Consider the questions below.

Is this the partner's pattern of behavior both when you are remote and in the office or mostly when you are remote? If this is a fairly consistent pattern of behavior for this partner, David's advice about scheduling a call with your partner to discuss the impact of working remotely on your skill development and devise a plan that will provide you with the necessary oversight and mentoring is an excellent first option. "Run that play" and see what happens. It may very well open up the communication required between you and the partner to establish a pattern of work being assigned to you along with feedback via more frequent Zoom calls.

Ask yourself, "Does this behavior come to the surface more often as a result of remote work?" Might this partner be struggling with remote employees and having difficulty settling into Zoom calls and remote leadership? This partner wouldn't be alone if that was indeed the case. Some partners are better at managing stress than others. Some are more adaptable than others. And some have life priorities and home lives that are more challenging than others.

By asking yourself these questions, you are entering into what we call in the leadership world "managing up." High performers take the initiative to consider the context of their boss's world by asking, "What kinds of issues are they handling that may be impacting how they are communicating to me?" Sometimes a shift in perception can help you to see this behavior differently and ease into a different emotion and therefore a different action or behavior. One of my favorite stories, made famous by Dr. Stephen Covey, Ph.D.'s book, *The 7 Habits of Highly Effective People,* is a well-known story about an incident on a subway and a shift in perception:

> I was riding a subway on Sunday morning in New York. People were sitting quietly, reading papers, or resting with eyes closed. It was a peaceful scene. Then a man and his children entered the subway car. The man sat next to me and closed his eyes, apparently oblivious to his children, who were yelling, throwing things, even grabbing people's papers.
>
> I couldn't believe he could be so insensitive. Eventually, with what I felt was unusual patience, I turned and said, "Sir, your children are disturbing people. I wonder if you couldn't control them a little more?"
>
> The man lifted his gaze as if he saw the situation for the first time. "Oh, you're right," he said softly, "I guess I should do something about it. We just came from the hospital where their mother died about an hour ago. I don't know what to think, and I guess they don't know how to handle it either."
>
> Suddenly, I saw things differently. And because I *saw* differently, I *felt* differently. I *behaved* differently. My irritation vanished. I didn't have to worry about controlling my attitude or my behavior. My heart filled with compassion. "Your wife just died? Oh, I'm so sorry. Can you tell me about it? What can I do to help?" Everything changed in an instant.[1]

---

1. Stephen Covey, Ph.D., The 7 Habits of Highly Effective People, at 30 (Simon & Schuster Apr. 2020).

On March 11, 2020, everything seemed to change in an instant. The World Health Organization (WHO) declared the COVID-19 outbreak a pandemic. Just as the pandemic had a dramatic impact on junior associates, it has also had a dramatic impact on partners and law firm leaders. We must acknowledge that these times have affected people, including partners, in many different ways. Handling ourselves and each other during those unsettling times required some self-compassion and empathy for others. Empathy and compassion are valuable leadership skills and were widely used during the COVID-19 pandemic. Upon returning to work, partners and other leaders had to adjust to hybrid working arrangements. For some, this remains challenging. As today's law firms are a blend of in-office and remote work, each associate must abide by the firm's established policies. Perhaps this is a partner who is a better manager and mentor when you are in the office. If so, be sure to be visible when you are in the office. Seek the feedback David mentioned earlier and demonstrate your eagerness to learn. Practice the empathy and compassion we mention. All leaders, whether partners or operations professionals in law firms have much on their plates. The easier you can make it for the partner to use his time wisely and provide the guidance you need, the better. As you build a relationship with this partner in the office, it will undoubtedly make it easier for you to ask questions and seek feedback when you are remote. As your relationship strengthens and the partner begins to notice your desire to learn, there is a better chance that the partner will provide the direction you need and give you the opportunity you are looking for, rather than shifting the work to others. Just as leadership and partners acknowledge that they need to adapt their leadership styles to leading associates differently, associates may need to adapt and learn to be more assertive (e.g., initiate conversations with their partners and seek feedback from more senior associates). Hybrid work persists and learning to consider the context of others and how to take the initiative to make things better can be beneficial skills for associates' careers.

In conclusion, remember that career growth in the current landscape involves not just technical skills but also emotional intelligence, adaptability, and proactive communication. Embrace these qualities, and you will navigate your legal career successfully.

Key Takeaways and Action Items

Key Takeaway One

The COVID-19 Pandemic Deepened Gaps in Associate Development that Persist Today

Remote and hybrid work have disrupted traditional learning and mentoring opportunities. Many junior associates have struggled to gain visibility, feedback, and hands-on experience, especially if they don't proactively advocate for themselves.

Action Items:

1. **Initiate a Development Conversation:** Schedule time with your supervising partner to share how remote work has affected your learning and growth.
2. **Propose Specific Solutions:** Suggest practical steps like shadowing calls, weekly check-ins, or feedback sessions to accelerate your development.
3. **Show Initiative:** Express your eagerness to learn and contribute, signaling that you're taking ownership of your professional growth.

Key Takeaway Two

Partners May Be Struggling Too—Practice Empathy

Not all partners adapted easily to remote leadership. A partner's shortness or lack of availability may reflect stress, workload, or discomfort with managing remotely—not necessarily a lack of interest in your growth.

Action Items:

1. **Shift Your Perspective:** Pause and consider what pressures or stressors might be impacting the partner's behavior before taking it personally.

2. **Lead with Curiosity:** In your next interaction, open with a simple check-in ("How are things going for you?") to humanize the conversation.

3. **Strengthen the Relationship:** Use empathy to create a more collaborative dynamic, which can encourage more openness and support over time.

Key Takeaway Three

Managing Up Is a Key Leadership Skill—Even for Associates

Taking the initiative, understanding your supervisor's work style, and finding ways to make their job easier are all signs of leadership at any level. Managing up is about being proactive and aware of the bigger picture.

Action Items:

1. **Seek Insider Insights:** Talk to a senior associate who works well with the partner and gather tips about communication preferences and expectations.

2. **Adapt Your Approach:** Use what you learn to tailor how you share updates, ask questions, and deliver work product.

3. **Demonstrate Proactivity:** Anticipate the partner's needs—offer solutions, flag issues early, and show you're engaged in the bigger picture.

Chapter 5

When Met with Opposition, Model the Way

Natalie Loeb & David B. Sarnoff

Dear Coaches:

> **I'm responsible for building future generations of leaders at my law firm and retain outside consultants to administer leadership and mentorship training. One of the firm's highly qualified, talented, and successful partners refuses to engage in the process, which not only sets a bad example but also is a disservice to their direct reports. How should I—or the firm—handle this?**
>
> ***—Tenacious Trainer***

Natalie: Tough question. And you aren't alone. What I'm pleased to see in this question is that you are mindful of the fact that it sets a "bad example" and is a disservice to direct reports. My guess is the partner has not given much thought to how this behavior displays a lack of leadership.

In today's firms, there remain leaders who achieved success without the benefit of leadership and mentorship training. Often, these leaders see no value in spending time building these types of skills in future generations of lawyers. We have heard this described as "if it's not broken, why fix it?" Due to the present success of their firms, these leaders often see no reason to invest dollars and time in this type of programming. The thinking is "why waste valuable billable hours?" However, we all know that today's firms are filled with lawyers, the future leaders, who have a different mindset towards training and development. These future leaders are completely aware that their continued success in a volatile, uncertain, complex, and ambiguous (VUCA)[1] world depends on their ability to influence and lead others, keep junior associates motivated and inspired to do their best work, and earn the trust and confidence of their clients. Make no mistake, this next generation of lawyers are noticing the type of behaviors in the partner(s) you described, along with how it impacts them and their colleagues. As a result, firms that allow this type of behavior to continue unchecked risk losing associates, their future leaders, to another firm.

That said, how does someone in your role begin to influence this partner to take more of a leadership role in developing the future lawyers at your firm rather than undermining their development? Influencing is a leadership skill. So, in fact, what you are asking is how do I lead here to achieve the goal I am aspiring to?

1. Leadership is a relationship: Consider your relationship with this partner. What type of work have you done so far to earn this partner's respect and trust? How open do you think this partner will be to discussing your concern? If you do indeed have a relationship of trust with this partner, you have a much higher chance of successfully opening a productive and fruitful conversation about your concern.

2. Leadership and credibility go hand in hand, with credibility being the foundation of leadership. Be sure you are performing in a way that is seen as highly credible. If you are going to lead, you must demonstrate to others that you are someone they can believe in. Research tells us there are three behaviors that demonstrate credibility: trustworthiness, competence, and dynamism. When someone consistently demonstrates these behaviors, they are more likely to be seen as

---

1. *See* Nate Bennett & G. James Lemoine, *What VUCA Really Means for You*, Harv. Bus. Rev., Jan.-Feb. 2014), https://hbr.org/2014/01/what-vuca-really-means-for-you.

credible. Dr. Barry Posner, Department of Management and Entrepreneurship at Santa Clara University Leavy School of Business, and co-author of *The Leadership Challenge: How to Make Extraordinary Things Happen in Organizations,*[2] discusses the concept further in his video *Why Credibility Is the Foundation of Leadership.*[3]

3. Your previous success with building leadership skills in others at your firm lends credence to *your* leadership abilities and will help you gain support from others. You must consistently and unwaveringly believe in the benefits of what you are doing and be confident in sharing that message with others.

4. Seek "advice" from this partner. Partners are highly competent at giving advice. Perhaps if you ask for advice on this challenge; acknowledging that your first obstacle is this partner's lack of support, you may be surprised with the partner's answer. If the partner does not shut you down, share your desire to hire consultants to prime the firm's next generation of leaders. Be prepared to show your competence, research, and the pros and cons of moving this initiative forward. (Tip: any outside consultant you are talking to should be able to help you with this.)

5. Lastly, if the partner shuts you down, don't give up. Keep the idea on your radar. Sometimes leaders on the administrative side of a law firm have to bring ideas forward more than once. Leaders don't give up.

David: Thanks, Natalie. You make excellent points. I also commend the person who submitted the question because they and their firm see the value of professional development and training future leaders. After all, these are learned behaviors, and with enough dedication and effort, leaders can be developed from any seat in the organization. What it essentially comes down to for me is that *leaders model the behavior they expect of others*. Period! Hard stop! As we have described

---

2. Barry Posner & James M. Kouzes, The Leadership Challenge: How to Make Extraordinary Things Happen in Organizations (Wiley 2017).
3. *See* Barry Posner, *Why Credibility Is the Foundation of Leadership*, YouTube (Feb. 5, 2015), https://www.youtube.com/watch?v=QmMcSBQvQLQ.

in prior columns, just because an individual contributor is highly skilled at their profession does not mean that this person will be an effective leader or manager. In my experience in the legal profession, I have seen many attorneys elevated to partner based largely on revenue generation and less on their ability to manage individuals and teams. Effective leaders are able to motivate, inspire, and drive performance through others.

Natalie provides sound advice for how to engage this partner to raise their awareness about why leadership training, development, and mentorship provides significant value for the firm and its employees and why the partner needs to participate. I agree with Natalie's approach, and these strategies largely appeal to the emotional intelligence of this partner. Briefly defined, emotional intelligence (EI), also referred to as emotional quotient (EQ), involves the ability to recognize one's own emotions, identify them, and have the ability to influence them. At a higher level, EI involves recognizing emotions in others and understanding how to influence their behavior. Individuals who possess these skills generally make effective leaders. They have the self-awareness to understand how they show up and are perceived by others. However, attorneys on average have a lower average emotional intelligence score than the general population.[4] Even though attorneys in general are not known for high EI, emotional intelligence skills are learned behaviors and can improve over time with coaching, practice, and life experience.

In addition to addressing EI issues, I would also suggest simultaneously appealing to this partner's *IQ* to help them understand the far-reaching benefits of investing the time to cultivate high-trust relationships and develop future leaders. From my perspective, this is an absolute business imperative for the firm. You may want to share with this partner the hard costs of replacing high-performing associates in the lateral market. Some studies put the figure up to 150% of the annual salary when you factor in recruiter fees, multiple rounds of interviews, signing bonuses, onboarding, and lost revenue opportunities while the

---

4. *See* RONDA MUIR, BEYOND SMART: LAWYERING WITH EMOTIONAL INTELLIGENCE (ABA 2d ed. 2005); Natalie Loeb & David Sarnoff, *EQ Versus IQ: What Smart Lawyers and Law Firms Need to Know About Emotional Intelligence*, 4 PLI CURRENT: THE JOURNAL OF PLI PRESS (2020).

position remains vacant. When this partner sees how their behavior impacts the firm, revenue, and their individual income, it may cause a renewed understanding in making others feel valued and developed.

In January 2022, the *MIT Sloan Management Review* published an article entitled "Toxic Culture Is Driving the Great Resignation."[5] In this article, the authors surveyed thousands of workers who left their jobs in many different industries. What they found was that compensation was less of a predictor of attrition than corporate culture. Employees feeling valued, heard, developed, and recognized for work done well was toward the top of the list of what employees identified as priorities. There are also generational dynamics at play in many cases. Associates' expectations with respect to mentoring, receiving feedback, inclusion, and culture have changed significantly in the last twenty years. Lastly, in my opinion, the burden should not be placed on you alone to help this partner see the benefits and necessity of leadership development.

Firm leadership and executive committee members should also model the way by communicating clear and unambiguous expectations that this partner is required to participate in the above-described programming. By doing so, they can then measure, at a time certain, whether or not this partner met expectations, and if not, communicate the consequences. At the end of the day, it is all about holding people accountable, and this is where most law firms fall short. Accountability is the mechanism that holds people responsible for not engaging in the mutually agreed-upon behaviors. Accountability also demonstrates to others what will happen if they decide to act outside the agreed-upon boundaries. Good luck.

---

5. Donald Sull, Charles Sull & Ben Zweig, *Toxic Culture Is Driving the Great Resignation*, MIT Sloan Mgmt. Rev. (Jan. 11, 2022), https://sloanreview.mit.edu/article/toxic-culture-is-driving-the-great-resignation/.

Key Takeaways and Action Items

Key Takeaway One

Resistance from Senior Partners Can Undermine Firm Culture and Talent Development

When highly visible partners opt out of leadership and mentorship training, it sends the wrong message to others—especially junior attorneys—and damages the firm's long-term investment in its future leaders.

Action Items:

1. **Have a Candid Conversation:** Meet one-on-one with the partner to share your observations and the impact on junior attorneys and firm culture.
2. **Invite Their Perspective:** Ask for their advice on how to address the issue—this reframes the conversation as collaborative rather than confrontational.
3. **Highlight Long-Term Impact:** Emphasize how their engagement could strengthen the firm's talent pipeline and legacy, appealing to their influence and role-model status.

Key Takeaway Two

Emotional Intelligence Is a Learnable Skill—But Often Undervalued in Law Firms

Many lawyers are promoted based on technical or financial performance, not leadership ability. Yet managing people requires self-awareness, empathy, and influence—all key components of emotional intelligence (EI), which can be developed over time.

Action Items:

1. **Connect EI to Business Outcomes:** Share data or examples showing how higher EI improves client satisfaction, team productivity, and retention.

2. **Tell Success Stories:** Use real-world case studies or anecdotes where EI training led to measurable improvements in leadership or team dynamics.

3. **Position EI As Strategic:** Frame leadership development as an investment in firm growth and risk mitigation, not just a "soft skill."

Key Takeaway Three

Accountability and Top-Down Support Are Critical for Cultural Change

It shouldn't fall solely on talent or professional development staff to enforce participation. Firm leaders must model the behavior they expect and hold partners accountable for opting in—or opting out—of leadership development efforts.

Action Items:

1. **Collaborate on Expectations:** Work with leadership to establish clear participation requirements for training and mentorship programs.

2. **Communicate Firm-Wide:** Encourage leaders to articulate the importance of these initiatives in meetings, emails, or firm-wide updates.

3. **Follow Up and Measure:** Set a timeline for reviewing participation rates and outcomes and share results to reinforce accountability and progress.

Chapter 6

Great Leaders Are Made, Not Born from Promotion

Natalie Loeb & David B. Sarnoff

Dear Coaches:

> **My law firm recently promoted several senior associates to partner based on their strong performance. They have a strong work ethic, are excellent with clients, and meet or exceed billable hours requirements. But these newly minted partners are underequipped to manage and develop their direct reports and at a loss when it comes to delegating work, managing conflict, and how to communicate to their associates. What advice do you have for getting the new class of partners up to speed and better preparing future partners' managerial skills in advance of promotions?**
>
> ***—Steer Me to the Right Track***

David: Thank you for this question, which contains one of the most common observations we hear about attorneys in general and newly promoted partners in particular. In my opinion, the legal profession has not focused enough attention or resources on developing and training effective attorney managers and leaders. I believe this leadership deficit begins in law school.

I went to law school in the early 1990s and can't recall the school offering a class on how to manage and lead people and teams, nor how to effectively delegate and drive performance through others. What I did find in law school was an indoctrination of assigning blame, the proximate cause of damages, who is liable, who is responsible. There was no elective on smart collaboration, creating an inclusive culture, or how to give developmental feedback.

The good news is help is on the way. Barry Posner, co-creator of the Leadership Challenge®, a widely used leadership development program, and Dean Emeritus Donald Polden, at Santa Clara University School of Law, published a book entitled *Leading in Law: Leadership Development for Law Students.*[1] This book introduces law students and attorneys to the foundational principles of best practices pertaining to leadership and management. Firms should consider assigning this book—or one like it—to their associates as early as possible in their careers.

Attorneys typically get promoted because they have excellent practical legal skills that make them exceptional lawyers. There is a primary focus on the IQ of the attorney and how well they draft briefs, argue motions, negotiate deals, or finance transactions. However, just because an attorney is an excellent practitioner doesn't necessarily make them a skilled leader or manager. To motivate, inspire, and build trust, an attorney needs to focus on EQ, or emotional intelligence. In my opinion, high-performing leaders are able to lead with care and empathy and connect on a personal level with the members of their team. Leading with care and empathy, however, does not equate to being soft. On the contrary, leading with empathy allows a partner to deliver extremely direct feedback or delegate assignments because it is coming from a place of care and genuine interest in the growth and development of the associates on their team. This takes time, effort, and intentionality to nurture and cultivate high-trust relationships. When it is done well, associates will outperform colleagues who work for partners who lead with fear and intimidation. There is a quote attributed to Theodore "Teddy" Roosevelt that says, "People don't care how much you know, until they know how much you care." In fact, in

---

1. Barry Posner & Donald J. Polden, Leading in Law: Leadership Development for Law Students (Carolina Academic Press 2022).

a Bloomberg article, the private equity goliath KKR & Co. found that employees performed at a higher level when leaders demonstrated higher empathy towards employees. The article also highlights that empathy is a behavior that can be learned.[2]

I have facilitated group coaching cohorts of newly promoted partners, during which they share their challenges, obstacles, and successes. In many cases, they voice frustration with not knowing how to have a difficult conversation, deliver developmental feedback, or communicate to an associate that they are not meeting expectations on billing requirements. The root of the frustration is that they have never had to do these things or were never trained to during their years as an associate. They also experienced a wide variety of leadership styles from the partners they worked for, and there were no structured or defined expectations of leadership requirements. This lack of leadership skills has been exacerbated by managing teams in a remote and hybrid environment.

Additionally, partners tend to get frustrated with associates when they delegate work and it does not come back as expected. Partners need to own some of the responsibility for this result. Did the partner adequately assess the skillset of the associate, provide a reasonable time frame, and provide opportunities for follow-up and questions? Many partners delegate work and ask the associate, "do you understand what I am asking?" In most cases, the associate responds "yes," even if they don't know. A best practice is for the partner to lead with care as follows: "David, I want to position you for success on this assignment and to confirm that we are on the same page, please tell me in your own words what I am asking you to do." This provides the opportunity to course-correct at an early stage and not wait until the draft is submitted to see that it is not what the partner wanted. This is an example of incorporating emotional intelligence into supervising others. According to Daniel Goleman, emotional intelligence is more important than IQ for all stakeholders, and in my opinion, especially for leaders. Goleman says, "when I calculated the ratio of technical

---

2. Heather Landy, *Empaths at the Gate: KKR and a Stanford Psychologist Measure People Skills*, Bloomberg (Apr. 23, 2025), https://www.bloomberg.com/news/articles/2025-04-23/kkr-s-pete-stavros-spearheads-program-to-train-company-leaders-in-empathy?embedded-checkout=true.

skills, IQ, and emotional intelligence as ingredients of excellent performance, emotional intelligence proved to be twice as important as the others for jobs at all levels."[3]

Natalie: This is a great question; one that doesn't surprise me at all. As David says, lawyers learn to be great lawyers in law school, not necessarily great leaders. When coaching newly elevated lawyers moving into a role that requires leading a team, I often like to start with a classic *Harvard Business Review* article titled "What Makes a Leader?" by Daniel Goleman. In this article, Daniel Goleman reminds us that "IQ and technical skills are important, but emotional intelligence is the *sine qua non* of leadership."[4]

However, let's take one step back. The common reaction I get after sharing this article with a lawyer leader is something like, "I'm a lawyer, I've never seen myself as a leader." Bam. Drop the mic. That's a significant moment. If one does not see oneself as a leader, why would one be concerned with how one behaves as a leader? How would one understand the responsibilities and expectations that come along with being a leader? And why would one even concern oneself with developing the skills required to be an effective leader?

The first lesson for your senior associates who have been promoted is to be crystal clear that in addition to being great lawyers, they are now expected to be great leaders. These senior associates have become role models for the associates on their teams. They are now being constantly observed, their behaviors and reactions and emotions are being noticed, and most likely they are the topic of conversation at dinner tables. So, the first step in being promoted is accepting that others now *see you* as a leader.

Armed with this new mindset and an appetite for learning, your senior associates need to prepare themselves for something that is very uncomfortable for lawyers. And that is not being the smartest person in the room when it comes to leadership. These senior associates are clearly great lawyers; however, building leadership capacity requires learning a new set of skills. And like learning any other skill, we all start as beginners. When leaders are in training, they will make

---

3. Daniel Goleman, Working with Emotional Intelligence (Bantam 1998).
4. Daniel Goleman, *What Makes a Leader?*, Harv. Bus. Rev. (Jan. 2004), https://hbr.org/2004/01/what-makes-a-leader.

mistakes. Making mistakes is not comfortable when practicing law—and perhaps not even acceptable. However, when someone is learning to lead, some of the best education will come from trial and error: try something new, see the result, and decide if that result is the best outcome. If it is, keep doing it. If it isn't, one must self-reflect and decide on a new course of action . . . and try it! Since a leader's behavior is on display, others will notice, and the lawyer leader must be prepared to dig into their ability to be resilient and keep trying. To make this come alive, let's consider "Pat." Here's a short story.

> *Pat stared out the office window as the sun sank behind the horizon. Today was a particularly rough day. One of the firm's most demanding clients continued to insist on an unrealistic deadline, raising his voice and speaking over others during the weekly conference call with Pat and her team. The client's outburst was just one of many stressors affecting Pat throughout the day. Pat's go-to associate was in the emergency room after breaking his foot, and Pat's spouse had been texting her repeatedly to request information she needed about the details of their upcoming family vacation. And to top it off, the firm's Chief Talent Officer, Maria, left a second voicemail about introducing Pat to an executive leadership coach to begin the process of addressing feedback she had received from members of Pat's team.*
>
> *Pat was well aware of the critical feedback as she became a senior associate. Some associates described Pat as unapproachable and that, at times, her tone and directness were off-putting. Associates felt more comfortable seeking assistance from other senior associates, which was the impetus for Maria's calls. These senior associates were starting to complain. Pat sighed heavily as she listened to Maria's message. They don't get it, she thought. She dropped her head and was briefly consumed by thoughts of her recent accomplishments and what it took to achieve them.*
>
> *In only three years, she had helped to double the size of the practice group and positioned it as one of Chicago's top M&A teams. So, Pat couldn't help but feel resentful of the request to speak with a coach. Were things so bad and her behavior so outlandish that it required an intervention by an executive coach? She didn't think so, but she also didn't want to be disrespectful to Maria, so she picked up her phone and dialed Maria's extension.*

"Sorry for the delay in getting back to you," Pat said. "It's been quite a week to say the least." "I'm glad we are able to connect," replied Maria. "I'd like to get this coaching engagement initiated soon and want to be sure you feel comfortable and informed."

"Yeah, about that coaching," Pat added. "I do have questions, particularly as to why I'm being singled out. It seems unfair."

"I understand," replied Maria, "but I think we need to take a quick step back to ensure we are on the same page." Maria spent the next several minutes explaining to Pat that her offer to connect her with an executive coach was neither punitive nor a corrective intervention. "Coaching," she explained, "is a safe space that lets us explore ourselves and the impact our behavior has on others. It is particularly helpful for newly promoted senior associates. Listen, Pat, you are important to the firm, but so too are all of our associates," Maria continued. "When associates raise concerns about how your natural leadership style is impacting the team's morale, then I see that as a learning opportunity for you. And what better way to engage in that learning process than within a coaching engagement."

Pat wasn't buying it. "I don't need a coach," she replied. "I don't mean to be a jerk," Pat told Maria, "but what am I supposed to do when my associates give me crappy work? Or how about when they tell me that they have a bachelor party on an upcoming weekend and our deadline for one of our biggest clients is the following Monday? I am under a lot of pressure, and I need associates who feel a sense of ownership and consistently deliver high-quality work."

Maria sensed Pat was becoming irritated. "Perhaps," she added, "but there are other senior associates here who have similar responsibility and pressure, and they're handling it in a healthier manner. You don't see that?"

"No," Pat snapped.

"That's exactly my point," Maria quipped. "Perhaps there are things you can't see, and those are the things that are getting in the way. Coaching can uncover those."

"Well, that's something to consider I suppose," Pat sighed.

"Good!" Maria replied. "So, I can move forward with connecting you to the coach?" Pat reluctantly agreed.

Pat's learning opportunity consisted of three important takeaways, which will be important for any newly promoted senior associate. They will help in delegating work, managing conflict, and communicating effectively with their associates. Present the following exercise to your firm's newly minted partners to get started:

1. Adopt the Leader Mindset.

   How? Read a current book on leadership, listen to a podcast, or find a YouTube TEDx talk. Google "leadership" and choose what appeals to you. Tell your favorite AI program that you want to be an effective leader, share a bit about yourself and your situation, and see what it recommends.

2. Identify and hold yourself accountable for behaviors that will build trust, demonstrate respect, teach, and offer helpful feedback to associates on their work product.

   How? Think about your favorite boss/leader and model the behaviors they exhibited that inspired you.

3. Find strategies to strengthen resilience.

   How? From self-care to confidence building to learning how to cope with volatility, locate resilience strategies that will work for you. There are many "wellness" organizations and consultants that specialize in helping lawyers build resilience to manage stress. A quick search of the web will help you find many. Other lawyers can probably make good recommendations. Any organizations you belong to can probably guide you.

Key Takeaways and Action Items

Key Takeaway One

Legal Skills Alone Do Not Prepare Attorneys for Leadership—Management and Emotional Intelligence Must Be Developed Intentionally

Without structured development, even the most technically gifted attorneys may struggle to lead teams, influence others, or navigate conflict effectively.

Action Items:

1. **Launch Early Leadership Programs:** Introduce training for associates on leadership fundamentals—self-awareness, emotional intelligence, and collaboration.
2. **Integrate Practice Opportunities:** Use simulations, peer feedback, and mentoring to give associates a safe space to practice management skills.
3. **Create a Development Roadmap:** Provide a clear progression of skills and expectations so attorneys see leadership growth as part of their career path.

Key Takeaway Two

Newly Promoted Partners Must Embrace Their Identity As Leaders and Understand that Their Behavior Sets the Tone for the Team

New partners who see themselves as culture carriers build trust more quickly and create psychological safety that elevates team performance.

Action Items:

1. **Facilitate Reflection Exercises:** Encourage new partners to journal, discuss, or work with a coach to explore their leadership values and style.

2. **Curate Leadership Resources:** Recommend books, articles, or podcasts that emphasize the transition from individual contributor to leader.
3. **Host Peer Learning Sessions:** Create forums where partners share challenges and strategies for leading teams effectively and modeling firm values.

Key Takeaway Three

Delegation and Communication Require Clarity, Empathy, and Active Follow-Up to Ensure Team Success

When partners delegate thoughtfully and communicate expectations clearly, they empower associates while reducing preventable errors, rework, and frustration.

Action Items:

1. **Train for Clear Delegation:** Teach partners to clarify goals, deadlines, and quality standards, and to ask associates to repeat back assignments to confirm understanding.
2. **Promote Constructive Feedback:** Encourage regular check-ins and feedback loops so associates know where they stand and can adjust in real time.
3. **Build Open Communication Channels:** Foster a culture where team members feel safe to ask questions, raise concerns, and request support.

Chapter 7

Looming Economic Downturn? How Do I Balance My Firm's Needs and the Impact on Our Associates?

Natalie Loeb & David B. Sarnoff

Dear Coaches:

> **I've practiced law for over thirty years and worked through several economic downturns. Reports of a possible recession have people at my firm on edge, including associates who are concerned they may be cut. And they have reason to be nervous. My last firm cut associates and staff during the Great Recession—too many if you ask me. When the market recovered, those who remained barely kept up with client work, and the firm scrambled to rehire associates and staff. How can I, as a partner, help influence my firm's staffing decisions if we do enter another recession?**
>
> ***—Partner Preserving the Firm's Assets***

David: Throughout the last twenty-five years, multiple financial crises have significantly impacted the national and global economy.

Companies prepare and react to these crises in a variety of ways, from strategically planning for these downturns and reserving capital to cushion the blow on one end of the spectrum, to slashing headcounts and budgets with little strategic thinking on the other end. In my opinion, the legal profession in general has followed a repetitive game plan in economic downturns. I have seen this replicated in various forms by law firms over the past couple decades. Even though the consequences of implementing the game plan can have far-reaching consequences, few make the necessary adjustments, learn from mistakes, or adapt to changing generational perspectives and experiences.

For background, I started my career as a paralegal in 1989 and entered law school in 1991. There was an economic recession during this time that led to large-scale layoffs at large firms around the country. While I was a summer associate, a partner left an article on my office chair about how the editor of the law review at a law school in New York was having difficulty finding a job. I interpreted the partner's action as communicating to me that I should be grateful that I have a law firm job. As I was entering my fifth year as an associate, I decided to leave the practice, and in 1998 I transitioned into executive search and spent seventeen years consulting and coaching law firms, legal departments, and attorneys.

From the late 1990s to 2015, I witnessed multiple financial downturns and recoveries. The Groundhog Day cycle I observed was that in downturns, many law firms would cut associates, business services, and staff in large numbers to maintain the profits-per-partner metric as much as possible. Then during economic recoveries, law firms would spend significantly more on salaries and headhunter fees to recruit mid-level associates to handle the pent-up legal work clients needed serviced. Inevitably, highly trained mid-level associates were in extremely short supply because of the massive junior associate layoffs over the one to two years prior to the recovery. Many of these associates left the practice, accepted in-house opportunities, and moved to smaller firms. Some even started their own firms.

In my opinion, the consequences law firms suffer from this continued practice is that, in many cases, they spend millions on recruiting fees, taking people offline to interview and for onboarding, and experience lost business opportunity while associate and partner positions remain unfilled. The associates who were hired during a recovering economy lacked necessary skills and experienced low professional satisfaction, and partners were frustrated by the quality of work product they would receive. This cycle repeated itself multiple times over the past couple of decades, but the one constant was that associate salaries increased, sometimes significantly, but improved workplace culture, training, and mentoring did not. Some think that salaries alone address the challenge. However, even with the significant pay raises, associates still leave.

I pose a question: What if law firms set aside rainy-day funds during the prosperous years and perhaps partners take a modest pay reduction during downturns to invest in relationship building and training their high-performing and competent associates in order to capitalize on economic recoveries? I see the downturns as an opportunity to train and develop associates to write briefs, draft deal documents, and build a high-trust culture and shared mission. However, I witnessed few firms adopt this practice while they continued to deal with employment and quality shortages during recoveries.

Additionally, the way firms conducted layoffs and downsizing impacted them for years, eroding reputation, trust, and firm culture. Business thought leader Simon Sinek wrote the book *Leaders Eat Last*[1] in which he discusses the concept of servant leadership, where leaders focus on the needs of their teams and model the behavior they expect of others. I believe it would positively impact the legal profession if this philosophy were followed; I know some leaders who already practice servant leadership, and their teams are incredibly dedicated and loyal.

During economic downturns, we inevitably see a regular flow of articles announcing large-scale layoffs at law firms. I'm aware that during economic declines layoffs are necessary, but I caution law firm leaders to be mindful of how their layoff strategy may impact firm reputation and culture. Leaders should also calculate the recovery costs of recruiting and lost business opportunities compared to taking a temporary pay cut to retain and train talent. Maintaining and training talent during recessions may actually position a firm to outperform during economic recoveries and create a dedicated, high trust, and motivated workforce of associates.

---

1. SIMON SINEK, LEADERS EAT LAST (Penguin Publ'g Grp. 2014).

Ernst & Young published the "2022 EY US Generation Survey: Addressing generational preferences in the workplace," based on a survey of "3,000 full-time, white-collar workers in the U.S. at organizations with 5,000 employees or more."[2] One of EY's key findings is that firm culture matters: "92% of workers surveyed said company culture has an impact on their intent to stay with their current employer. . . . Those who said company culture had a 'great deal of impact' on their intent to stay [included] 39% of millennials, 39% of LGBTQ+, 39% of Gen Z and 38% of workers with children living in their homes."[3] Again, in my opinion, law firm leaders should take heed that money alone will not solve retention challenges and employee job satisfaction.

However, if layoffs are inevitable, try and conduct them demonstrating care and empathy; offer generous severance, outplacement services, and practical skills training. These practices will be noticed by law students and will impact the firm's perception during interview season and when recruiting laterals.

Natalie: Like David, I have been employed during economic downturns. I remember the feelings of uncertainty and anxiety. I remember being distracted until I knew "next steps." In one case, I remember being responsible for helping those who survived the "rightsizing" adapt their mindsets to the future. It was tough work. In another case, I was told I was being "let go" as part of the organization's rightsizing strategy. That was tough too. In addition, I have led a business through the global COVID-19 pandemic, which initially began with a significant downturn in business. This was probably the toughest experience of all. Because of these experiences, I look at this question through a personal lens. I have learned that handling this tough situation can look different depending on where you place your focus. I've also learned that balancing the needs of the business with the needs of your employees does not need to be a zero-sum game.

With introspection and clarity on your intentions, you can navigate this tricky situation with intention to minimize the negative impact

---

2. Ernst & Young, 2022 US Generation Survey (2022), at 1, https://www.ey.com/content/dam/ey-unified-site/ey-com/en-us/campaigns/diversity-equity-inclusiveness/documents/ey-generational-exec-summary.pdf.
3. *Id.* at 2.

on your associates and reputation of your firm, while aspiring for a healthy bottom line.

Here are a few considerations to reflect on now:

What is my firm's long-term strategy during tougher economic times? As David mentions above,

- Might your firm turn to a "rainy day" fund and weather the storm as opposed to reducing staff?
- Might your firm's strategy be to take a focused look at performance and make decisions on who is and who is not meeting the firm's performance expectations and perhaps manage "underperformers" out?
- Might your firm focus on cutting "non-essential" expenses for a defined period of time in lieu of staff reductions?
- Might the firm stay the course and weather the storm as "business as usual"?
- Might the firm choose a combination of one or more of the above (or other strategies)?

Whichever strategy chosen, firm leadership will likely prioritize the firm's financial health and overlook the "emotional" side of the strategy. In addition to the financial health of the firm, don't forget to pay attention to the emotional reactions from your firm's members. Remember, your firm is made up of people. Smart people. They are very aware of the economic consequences of a recession; but how leadership chooses to communicate its strategy and the resulting consequences will have a lasting and memorable impact on everyone at the firm along with the firm's culture. As Maya Angelou reminds us, "I've learned that people will forget what you said, people will forget what you did, but people will never forget how you made them feel." Even high-achieving lawyers and business professionals will have feelings triggered. Being sensitive to this can encourage you to give some thought to how you empathize with the mixed feelings colleagues often have as your firm responds to a looming economic downturn.

Although you ultimately have no control over someone else's feelings or behaviors, as a leader in your firm, you set the stage with your behaviors and words that others will notice and most likely emulate.

Your behavior during turbulent times is especially important. Followers look to leaders for direction and certainty. Whether your messaging is about upcoming staff reductions, embracing the status quo, or investing in training during economic downturns, create a communication plan and follow it diligently. People need to have as much information as they can to make wise decisions for themselves and their families.

It is impossible to "overcommunicate" during times of uncertainty and change. Keep the communication flowing and strive for as much transparency as possible. Without a communication plan, the smart people in your firm will seek to understand or guess what the firm's strategy is by putting together whatever pieces of information they hear or behaviors they observe from those in leadership roles. Often the conclusions rendered are incorrect and lead to an increase in rumors and anxiety. All of this can distract focus and have a negative impact on client service and deliverables.

Ask yourself the following questions as you think through your communication plan:

- How clear and easy to understand is your recession strategy?
- How can you communicate your strategy in a way that acknowledges an emotional impact on those in the firm?
- What options are in place to support those that are experiencing the strongest negative impact?

If your strategy does indeed include a reduction in staff, utilize every resource your firm has available to minimize the "human" impact. As David mentions above, demonstrate care and empathy while delivering tough messages, offer generous severance, outplacement services, and practical skills training. There is no doubt that demonstrating these practices will be noticed by both law students and other talented lawyers following the trends in the industry.

Michael Mankins wrote in an August 24, 2022, *Harvard Business Review* article, "In Uncertain Times, the Best Strategy Is Adaptability," "Stephen Hawking is famously credited with saying: 'Intelligence is the ability to adapt to change.' If it is impossible to predict what is around the corner, then the secret to success is adapting quickly to what appears."[4] Do not wait until a recession hits to adapt to the change. Think ahead about your strategy and how to manage both the financial impact and the human impact.

The economy will recover. It always does. A leader's responsibility is to adapt to the economy they are facing. Take a holistic approach to adapting. Consider both the financial health and the emotional health of the members in your firm.

---

4. Michael Mankins, *In Uncertain Times, the Best Strategy Is Adaptability*, HARV. BUS. REV. (Aug. 24, 2022), https://hbr.org/2022/08/in-uncertain-times-the-best-strategy-is-adaptability.

Key Takeaways and Action Items

Key Takeaway One

Cutting Staff During Downturns Often Harms Long-Term Firm Performance, Culture, and Reputation

Short-term cost savings rarely outweigh the long-term loss of trust, talent, and institutional knowledge that accompanies layoffs.

Action Items:

1. **Develop a Financial Cushion:** Work with leadership to create a "rainy day fund" to help stabilize operations and minimize layoffs during downturns.
2. **Explore Alternatives to Layoffs:** Recommend short-term partner pay adjustments, reduced discretionary spending, or temporary sabbaticals before cutting staff.
3. **Present the Business Case:** Share data, research, and case studies that illustrate the long-term financial and cultural costs of mass layoffs.

Key Takeaway Two

How Layoffs and Tough Decisions Are Communicated Has a Lasting Emotional and Cultural Impact

Even necessary decisions can damage morale if delivered poorly, while clear and empathetic communication preserves trust during uncertainty.

Action Items:

1. **Craft Transparent Messaging:** Ensure communications clearly explain the rationale for decisions, the criteria used, and the support available for those affected.
2. **Lead with Empathy:** Train leaders to deliver difficult news compassionately, acknowledging the emotional impact and validating employees' experiences.

3. **Keep Everyone Informed:** Provide regular updates to prevent misinformation, maintain trust, and reassure staff about the firm's direction.

Key Takeaway Three

Downturns Can Be Used As Opportunities to Invest in People and Strengthen Firm Loyalty and Capabilities

Firms that invest in development during slow periods emerge stronger, more unified, and better prepared to capture future opportunities.

Action Items:

1. **Offer Skill-Building Programs:** Launch initiatives that allow associates to deepen technical skills (e.g., drafting, client development, research) during slow periods.
2. **Reinforce Firm Culture:** Use downtime for team-building activities that foster connection and shared purpose across practice groups.
3. **Signal Long-Term Commitment:** Communicate that these investments are part of the firm's strategy to grow talent and prepare for future client needs.

Chapter 8

Does Your Executive Committee Understand the Merits of a Firm Retreat?

Natalie Loeb & David B. Sarnoff

Dear Coaches:

> **I'm a partner at a firm that has decided to maintain a hybrid work arrangement. With appearances in the office staggered, the sense of camaraderie and belonging feels diluted, and colleagues appear to be disengaged (despite the firm arranging a holiday party and a few happy hours over the past several months). A friend of mine who works in another firm told me about a retreat her firm organized, and I believe my firm could gain from the same type of team-building activity. How do I approach my executive committee with the idea and what benefits should I emphasize?**

—Challenging Assumptions

Natalie:

Tell me and I forget, teach me and
I remember, involve me and I learn.
-Benjamin Franklin

Our hybrid workplaces provide new challenges for leaders. Leading a mixed team of in-person and remote workers requires extra intention and attention. The COVID-19 pandemic of 2020–2022 instantly triggered "work from home." Everyone had an opinion about the effects of working remotely, and leaders in all industries had to make decisions on what they thought was best for their organizations.

The week we originally answered this question, the CEO of Citigroup, Jane Fraser, who had made an unusual decision for an elite Wall Street firm to adopt a flexible hybrid work culture, announced that those performers who are not meeting expectations would be required to come back to the office. Another example of adapting to hybrid work policies: We saw our law firm clients adopting a wide variety of flexible working options, with a goal of retaining talent while meeting both employee and client expectations. No matter which policies were adopted, consistent requirements for all workplaces included quality communication, heightened emotional intelligence (EQ), and diligent meeting cadences. To create a positive hybrid work experience, leaders must be intentional about all of this.

Along with adapting to hybrid workplaces, new opportunities emerged. An abundance of research continues to support the relationship between effective communication, high emotional intelligence, and overall productivity. With a continued focus on high expectations for team results and exceptional client service delivery, today's leaders must be intentional about strengthening their communication and emotional intelligence skills for both themselves and their team members. Think about this: As applications such as ChatGPT have ingrained themselves into our professional and personal lives, finding answers to almost anything (albeit whether they are accurate or not is yet to be seen) is accessible to all of us online. But how we use the information we gather as human beings—such as challenging assumptions, internalizing the impact, drawing on our creativity and empathy—dictates our willingness to work together for overall results versus promoting our personal agendas. Competitive edges within our firms will evolve requiring highly intellectually and emotionally intelligent lawyers who can use the artificial intelligence to solve complex problems in an ever-changing workplace. Our lawyers and business professionals will need to challenge assumptions appropriately, confidently envision the future, and comfortably tap into creativity while sustaining the energy and enthusiasm to partner with their clients to solve today's problems and anticipate the needs for tomorrow's success. Experts overseeing artificial intelligence in our organizations will teach us and guide us.

How do we build judgment, confidence, comfort, and sustainability in our partners, associates, and business professionals? First, as leaders we need to develop these qualities in ourselves, and then as leaders we need to commit to developing the next generation of lawyers. And how does one launch a big initiative like this as a firm? Not with an email, not with a staff meeting, not with an "All Hands" or "Town Hall." One launches a commitment to developing and preparing others for the future with an activities-based retreat—a combination of traditional and non-traditional experiential learning methods.

Ben Franklin was on to something: *involve me and I will learn.* Adult learning theory reminds us that adults learn best when placed in a situation where they have an experience. Our parents were wise: *experience is the best teacher.* This is why mentoring is in such high demand and associates compete to accompany partners to client meetings to learn. Nothing replaces the experience.

When structured correctly, firm retreats can provide memorable experiences that can transform behavior. And here's an idea: remove or limit the alcohol from the experience. Instead, try adding wellness activities to activate one's mental and physical abilities. Skilled facilitators will help the participants to notice how they respond to challenges, what they are feeling when pushing themselves from their comfort zones, or how to experience the rewards of allowing oneself to innovate and expand or set boundaries. These learnings can be brought into the day-to-day activities of practicing law.

In short, your challenge is to leverage the data available today, proving there are still many unknowns ahead of us in how we work. Perhaps ask ChatGPT to help you?

Whether we are hybrid, in the office, or completely remote, our leaders, associates, and professional staff members always need to know how to push themselves and others out of their comfort zones in a way that will exceed our clients' expectations. Lawyers need to optimize both their intellectual capabilities as well as their emotional and mental capabilities. A well-structured retreat outside of the office (the change of scenery immediately transforms the atmosphere of the gathering) can include an array of activities and meetings that can prepare you for the future. Challenge the status quo. And good luck.

David: Thank you for the question. I suggest you include the feedback from your friend and other attorneys who have had positive retreat experiences and share the data you collect with your executive committee. I would ask attorneys at other firms: What made your retreat valuable? What were the key takeaways and learnings from your experience? Attorneys typically like evidence and data, and this feedback could support your mission. While law firm retreats, and partner retreats in particular, have been around for a long time, they seem to have taken on new importance as the profession emerges out of remote work and firms start navigating the hybrid work environment. In fact, we experienced a significant increase in presenting and facilitating workshops and dialogue sessions at law firm retreats in 2022. In my opinion, retreats can be a highly effective tool to cultivate and nurture relationships, create an inviting learning environment, contribute to team-building, and improve organizational culture. However, there is a big "if," and that is, if the retreat is thoughtfully planned and competently executed.

Quite often, leaders in law firms delay retreat planning, put it on the back burner, question the ROI, and do not consider it a priority. When any of these factors are at play, it can negatively impact the experience and effectiveness of the retreat. In the past, retreats were used to review economic factors, revenue, and budgeting, and *maybe* a firm would invite a guest speaker and have a big retreat dinner. Now, more often retreats are viewed as opportunities to focus on professional, team, and individual development. They also provide an opportunity for colleagues to reconnect and, in many cases, introduce themselves for the first time in person to colleagues who joined the firm during the remote work period. I want to emphasize that successful retreats require advanced planning, goal setting, and a substantive and organized agenda so that the retreat is structured and professional. All too often, leadership doesn't afford retreats the level of seriousness they deserve, leading to the retreat lacking purpose and intent, which tends to leave participants with the feeling the retreat was a waste of time.

In too many cases, firm administrators tasked to organize and execute events for the retreat are given little notice and budget to do it effectively. In my opinion, this is a mistake that not only impacts the experience at the retreat but also leaves the firm's partners and stakeholders feeling less valued, included, and connected. In my experience, most people attending a retreat want to be challenged, learn new skills and practices, and contribute feedback and ideas to improve the firm's processes, procedures, culture, and climate.

Moreover, when retreats are viewed by law firm leaders as an important and meaningful exercise that serves multiple purposes, they can be highly impactful. Attendees leave the retreat feeling energized with renewed purpose, with key takeaways for practices and skills they can implement post-retreat, and wanting to re-engage and collaborate with colleagues.

After many firms began working remotely in March 2020, there was a mass implementation of hybrid work policies in 2021. The hybrid model in most cases required a minimum number of days for in-office attendance, but there was little enforcement or coordination of teams being in the office together. This diminished morale and organizational culture. We would consistently hear that coming into a sparsely populated law firm reduced the sense of shared mission culture, frayed relationships, and lessened communication. Also, the lack of spontaneous interaction and communication typically experienced in the office diminished problem-solving capabilities. Law firm retreats can be customized for partners, associates, business services professionals, and support staff, all of whom would benefit from the outing. They can range in duration from two hours to half-day or multi-day retreats. They can be at an off-site location such as a hospitality center or hotel meeting room or on-site in a conference room or meeting space (though, as Natalie mentioned, a change of scenery may help attendees shift their mindset).

In my experience, when participants were asked what they liked most about the retreat, most of the responses included interacting with colleagues in a non-work setting. Participants appreciated the opportunity to listen to others' opinions, receive advice from colleagues, and collaborate on projects. This experience is enhanced when colleagues from multiple offices are brought together in the same space. Some of the other common responses included enjoying the opportunity to discuss challenges and engaging in strategic planning and team building. Participants also appreciated focusing on improving management and leadership skills. These skills included giving and receiving feedback, managing difficult conversations, the difference between management and leadership, EQ v. IQ, respect in the workplace, and generational challenges, among many other topics. Retreat presentations can also include self-care, wellness, motivation, and at-risk behaviors.

In-person retreats also allow for participants to break out into small groups, which encourages higher-level collaboration, builds trust, and inspires active listening. When retreat workshops or dialogue groups are facilitated by a third party, attendees are challenged to be direct, address conflict, discuss challenges, engage in role playing, and improve direct communication.

In my opinion, law firm retreats, when well planned and executed, provide an excellent opportunity to learn to improve practical and EQ skills, continue to build relationships, and engage in dialogue to resolve firm challenges. Leadership should set ground rules prior to the retreat, such as not using computers, cell phones, or other devices during sessions. Participants should be respectful to others when speaking, encourage debate and allow for activities that are fun and involve team building.

While cost is typically a high-level concern to leadership when proposing a retreat, that should be balanced with the impact on culture, skill development, and improving communication and morale.

Key Takeaways and Action Items

Key Takeaway One

Hybrid Work Has Weakened Firm Culture and Relationships—In-Person Retreats Offer a Meaningful Way to Rebuild Connection and Engagement

When people reconnect face-to-face, it restores trust, strengthens collaboration, and re-energizes a shared sense of purpose that is difficult to replicate virtually.

Action Items:

1. **Build a Compelling Proposal:** Gather examples and data from other firms that have hosted successful retreats and highlight improvements in morale, engagement, and retention.
2. **Emphasize Relationship-Building:** Present the retreat as an opportunity to rebuild trust, cross-practice collaboration, and firm-wide connection.
3. **Secure Leadership Buy-In:** Present your findings to the executive committee and frame the retreat as an investment in culture and long-term performance.

Key Takeaway Two

Retreats Are Most Effective When They Are Intentionally Planned with Clear Goals and Are Professionally Facilitated, Not Treated As Casual Social Gatherings

A retreat with purpose creates alignment, deepens insight, and strengthens leadership capabilities far more effectively than unstructured social time.

Action Items:

1. **Form a Planning Team:** Recommend a diverse planning committee or hire an experienced facilitator to ensure all perspectives are represented.

2. **Design a Structured Agenda:** Include sessions on feedback, conflict navigation, generational communication, and other relevant leadership topics.

3. **Align with Firm Goals:** Ensure retreat objectives connect to business priorities (e.g., client service, collaboration, talent retention) to maximize ROI.

Key Takeaway Three

Experiential Learning During Retreats Fosters Deeper Leadership, Communication, and Problem-Solving Skills that Benefit the Entire Firm Post-Retreat

When participants actively practice skills rather than just hear concepts, the learning sticks—and translates directly into better team performance after the retreat.

Action Items:

1. **Highlight ROI Beyond Morale:** Present retreats as leadership and professional development opportunities, not just social events.

2. **Incorporate Interactive Activities:** Suggest breakout sessions, simulations, and wellness exercises to encourage engagement and reflection.

3. **Plan for Post-Retreat Impact:** Propose follow-up sessions or action plans so participants carry their learning back into daily work and team dynamics.

Chapter 9

What's Next for Law? EQ, Wellness, and Technological Change

Natalie Loeb & David B. Sarnoff

As we entered 2025, the legal profession found itself adapting to a rapidly changing landscape. Change was the headline. Our work with law firm members, from associates to partners and administrative professionals to C-suite leaders, over the past three decades has given us some insight into their response to change. Change has always been and will be a constant. The speed of change has accelerated as a result of AI and supercomputing. Today's pace of change demands we pay attention to what is going on around us. We can no longer choose to push anything "under the rug." Staying relevant, competitive, and sought after requires effectively responding to challenges and opportunities in the moment, anticipating what is next, and building a collaborative workplace culture where your people can bring their best legal skill and other talents to your firm and clients on a regular basis.

However, change can be overwhelming in and of itself. For some it is exhilarating. For others it is exhausting and produces anxiety. And for many others, it is somewhere in between. What we know for sure is that tumultuous change requires leadership. Change brings questions, uncertainty, unknowns, stress, excitement, and optimism. Leaders need to harness that excitement while addressing many of the very human components of uncertainty and stress. How a leader does this requires some self-reflection. A commitment to learning about one's own visceral response to change and using that data to set an intentional roadmap on how to "show up" and lead their firms and legal departments in 2026 and beyond. Which description below most accurately reflects your reaction to change? Are you where you want to be? Are your reactions helping you, your team, and the firm to lead change effectively?

LOEB LEADERSHIP — **Reactions to Change**			
Change Embracer	**Change Rejector**	**Change Skeptic**	**Change Driver**
I love new things. Bring it on!	*I prefer stability and consistency, so I avoid change at all costs.*	*I'm open to it but need to understand how it benefits me.*	*I only embrace change when it's my idea.*

What Is Change Management?

Change management draws on theories from several disciplines, including psychology, behavioral science, engineering, and systems thinking. And there are many different models to choose from. For example, Lewin's Change Management Model[1] splits the change process into three key stages known as "unfreeze-change-refreeze," while Kotter's 8-Step Change Model[2] provides a more comprehensive guide through change.

A central idea of **all** change management theories is that no change ever happens in isolation. In one way or another, change impacts the whole organization and all of the people in it. But with good change management, you can encourage everyone to adapt to and embrace new ways of working, including yourself! Sometimes, leading change may need to begin with changing ourselves.

1. Melanie Bell & Cat MacLeod, *Lewin's Change Management Model: Understanding the Three Stages of Change*, MINDTOOLS, *available with subscription at* https://www.mindtools.com/ajm9l1e/lewins-change-management-model.
2. Simon Bell & Cat MacLeod, *Kotter's 8-Step Change Model: Implementing Change Powerfully and Successfully*, MINDTOOLS, *available with subscription at* https://www.mindtools.com/a8nu5v5/kotters-8-step-change-model.

No matter where you fall on your personal response to change, we can offer you three specific areas to learn more about to help you internalize being a change agent and lead your law firm successfully into the future.

Emotional Intelligence Unites Legal Teams

Emotional intelligence (EQ) has become an essential skill for law firm leaders. Historically largely undervalued, overlooked, and misunderstood in the legal profession, EQ at its core is the ability to recognize, understand, and manage one's emotions while empathizing with others—EQ is emerging as a vital skill set for attorneys. The integration of EQ across culture, technology, and leadership in the legal profession signals a quintessential moment, underscoring the industry's progress (some faster than others) and potential for continued growth.

From what we hear from our clients, the EQ deficit is becoming more pronounced across generations. The legal profession today is more diverse in age than ever before, with Traditionalists, Baby Boomers, Generation X, Millennials, and Generation Z working side by side. These generational differences bring a diversity of experiences, perspectives, work styles, and expectations, creating both challenges and opportunities. Emotional intelligence fosters understanding and collaboration among these groups by encouraging effective communication, feedback, empathy, and active listening. This EQ deficit can become even more of a hindrance as AI takes on a larger role in the practice of law. The work left over that AI cannot do is high-level, challenging, and difficult work. To solve these problems, law firm leaders have to cultivate trust and relationships in order to effectively motivate, inspire, and drive performance to meet the needs of their clients.

As an example of generational differences in the workplace, Traditionalists and Baby Boomers generally value hierarchical structures and in-person interactions, while younger Millennials and Gen Z attorneys may prioritize flexibility and digital communication from devices. EQ enables partners and leaders to bridge these gaps by acknowledging the unique strengths that each generation brings and collaborating to find the most efficient and mutually beneficial way to work together. By creating inclusive environments where mentorship and reverse mentorship thrive, law firms can ensure knowledge transfer and skill development while fostering innovation.

Cultivating a Healthy Legal Culture

In addition to the challenges of intergenerational communication and work preferences, another area that is growing in prominence is well-being. The prioritization of well-being represents a cultural shift in the legal profession. Historically, long hours, high stress, and burnout were seen as an initiation to practicing as an attorney. However, firms are increasingly recognizing the importance of mental and physical well-being for sustaining performance and retaining talent.

That said, there remains a noticeable resistance to wellness practices because they are viewed by some as being soft, lazy, and not serving the needs of clients and the demands of the profession. While some firms wholeheartedly embrace well-being, modeling, and making a variety of services available to their members (both administrative staff and lawyers), others balk at offering resources to avoid acknowledging that well-being is necessary at their firms. The thinking is, "Why offer well-being practices when all of our team members are already mentally and physically healthy?"

Today's work environment and extensive research in the well-being space provides data proving the impact and benefits of well-being on workplaces, client service, and delivery. Pushing well-being under the rug has consequences. Acknowledging it, talking about it, and most importantly modeling it at the senior levels contributes to a work culture that today's employees respond favorably to. Like anything else, each individual's well-being is unique to them. Promoting a high-performance work culture with room for well-being allows your highly talented team to sustain the high performance that is expected.

Evaluate whether your culture and mindset are navigating towards well-being. Is it impacted by your generation? Life experiences? Note it and make an intentional decision on how to be clear about strong performance expectations while leaving room for your team members to embrace wellness practices that make sense for them.

The Institute for Well-Being in Law (IWIL), a nonprofit organization dedicated to transforming the legal profession's approach to well-being, provides resources to help those in the legal profession explore wellness.[3] Through advocacy, research, education, technical and resource support, and stakeholder partnerships, IWIL strives to lead a culture shift in law to establish well-being as a core centerpiece of professional success.

The Human Side of Legal Tech

Other hot button issues in the legal profession are technology and generative and agentic artificial intelligence (AI). Agentic AI (AI 3.0) refers to AI software that can work autonomously, without much human supervision. It understands natural language, sets goals for itself, plans workflows, makes decisions, adapts to changing circumstances, and, finally, learns and improves from interactions. The legal profession has traditionally been slow to embrace technological change, but recent advancements have transformed the way attorneys practice law and how firms operate. From AI tools for legal research and drafting to e-discovery platforms, technology is streamlining processes and enhancing efficiency. Rolling out and learning new technology always contains a "change management" component. Intellectually, most people can accept that new technology is required and makes sense. Emotionally, many people remain attached to older ways of accomplishing tasks. Maybe you have heard, "If it ain't broke, don't fix it," or, "We've always done it this way."

We can always learn from the past but MUST adopt a growth mindset for leaning into the future. For many, technological change is uncomfortable, while for others, it is exciting. Be curious and bring a learner's mindset to the technology being introduced at your firm. To quote John F. Kennedy, "The best leaders are the best learners." As leaders, we are responsible for learning, continuing to grow, and leading our organizations safely and confidently into the future.

Technology advancements raise challenges that require the emotional intelligence mentioned at the beginning of this chapter. Leaders lean on their emotional intelligence to motivate and inspire attorneys to solve higher-level problems. This requires the ability to give and receive direct feedback, manage conflict, and empower others to make

---

3. *See* https://lawyerwellbeing.net/.

decisions. For instance, the automation of routine tasks may lead to anxiety among junior attorneys about job security. Leaders with EQ skills can address these concerns by fostering open communication and emphasizing the value of human skills that technology cannot replicate, such as cultivating interpersonal relationships with clients and colleagues and working in a team setting that leverages everyone's strength and skills. By integrating technology with thoughtfulness and empathy, firms can harness its benefits while mitigating its potential downsides. Being human remains a strength!

Returning to Our Roots to Chart the Path Forward

In many ways, the legal profession is coming full circle as it re-embraces the human elements of practice. Historically, the law was seen as a respected profession of service and advocacy. Over time, the pressures of billable hours and profitability shifted the focus toward revenue generation. Today, amid rapid changes, the legal industry is rediscovering the value of emotional intelligence to enhance professional relationships and outcomes, fostering a collaborative culture that boosts retention, profitability, and revenue.

For example, client expectations are evolving. Clients increasingly seek attorneys who not only provide legal expertise but also demonstrate understanding of the client's specific industry, organizational culture, and circumstances. Emotional intelligence enables lawyers to build stronger client relationships by addressing both the legal and emotional dimensions of their clients' challenges.

The legal profession has been making strides to address these issues. However, there is still room for significant growth. One area ripe for improvement is collaboration. While some firms have made progress, many firms continue to struggle with creating truly collaborative environments where all individuals can thrive. Emotional intelligence can play a key role in advancing collaboration by fostering two-way feedback, empathy, conflict resolution, and mutual respect.

As we step into the future, the legal profession must embrace change, with emotional intelligence serving as both a guiding principle and a goal. Across culture, technology, and leadership, EQ will enable the industry to navigate challenges, embrace opportunities, and build a more resilient future. Leverage your emotional intelligence to foster intergenerational collaboration, prioritize wellness, deploy technology with empathy, and adopt collaborative leadership practices. In this way, you are supporting the legal profession as it charts a path toward continued improvement. In doing so, you are reaffirming your commitment to change as you work toward meeting the needs of your attorneys, professional staff, and clients.

Key Takeaways and Action Items

Key Takeaway One

Emotional Intelligence Is Essential for Leading Change in the Legal Profession

As law firms face accelerated change driven by technology, generational diversity, and shifting client expectations, emotional intelligence (EQ) has emerged as a critical leadership competency. EQ enables legal professionals to manage stress, communicate across generational lines, cultivate inclusive cultures, and motivate teams through uncertainty. It is no longer optional—it is a competitive differentiator.

Action Items:

1. **Train on Core Competencies:** Facilitate workshops on self-awareness, empathy, adaptability, and managing stress—tailored to the legal environment.
2. **Coach Through Change:** Provide executive coaching for leaders navigating transformation, helping them model calmness and clear communication.
3. **Foster Generational Dialogue:** Create structured opportunities for cross-generational conversations, mentoring, and reverse mentoring.

Key Takeaway Two

Sustainable Legal Culture Requires Prioritizing Well-Being

The legal industry is beginning to challenge the long-held belief that stress and burnout are badges of honor. Embracing well-being is not about being "soft"—it's a strategic move to enhance performance, talent retention, and workplace sustainability. Firms that model and normalize wellness at the leadership level are better equipped to foster high-performing, resilient teams.

Action Items:

1. **Model from the Top:** Encourage firm leaders to visibly prioritize well-being (taking vacation, setting healthy boundaries, using firm wellness programs).
2. **Normalize Conversations About Mental Health:** Host panels, fireside chats, or small group discussions that reduce stigma and open dialogue.
3. **Provide Resources and Training:** Offer resilience-building programs, mindfulness sessions, and time management training.

Key Takeaway Three

Legal Tech Adoption Must Be Paired with Human-Centered Leadership

AI and automation are reshaping legal workflows, but technology alone isn't the solution. Effective leadership in 2026 requires integrating tech with empathy and communication. Leaders must address fears, inspire curiosity, and emphasize human skills—like relationship-building and team collaboration—that machines can't replicate. The best legal leaders are also the best learners.

Action Items:

1. **Communicate the "Why":** Before rolling out new tech, explain the business case and benefits clearly to reduce resistance.
2. **Offer Training and Support:** Provide hands-on, user-friendly training and designate "tech champions" to support adoption.
3. **Address Fear and Resistance:** Hold listening sessions to surface concerns and provide reassurance that technology is a tool, not a replacement.

Chapter 10

Be the Keel—How Can Law Firm Leaders Provide Stability During Uncertain Times?

Natalie Loeb & David B. Sarnoff

Dear Coaches:

> **My colleagues, attorneys, and staff in my firm seem anxious and unfocused, and I want to ensure we maintain our performance and morale. In turbulent times how can I, as part of my law firm's leadership, give my colleagues/firm stability and structure?**
>
> ***—Steadying the Course***

Natalie: Thank you for your question. Today's legal firms are still made up of people, and together we are experiencing accelerated change. As described above in chapter 9, What's Next for Law? EQ, Wellness, and Technological Change, people have different reactions to change. Reactions to change can vary from being a change resister to a change embracer. While we can certainly observe others and make good guesses about what they are experiencing, observation alone is not 100% accurate.

Your question reminds me of an event where I misread someone's reactions to turbulence. In fact, this event taught me that the simple act of "checking in" can give me greater confidence in those around me. It also taught me what great leadership looks like through a threatening squall. Literally.

About eight years ago, my brother, who is a licensed United States Coast Guard sailing captain, asked me and my husband to join him on a thirty-foot sailboat while he tested it for future boating adventures. We met him in downtown New York City on the Hudson River where the boat was located. It was a small vessel; however, it was large enough for us to go below deck if necessary. It was a beautiful sunny afternoon, and my husband and I were looking forward to this experience. We set sail and admired the scenery in New York's harbor—certainly a sight to be seen.

About thirty minutes into our trip, the sky darkened, the wind picked up, and the captain instructed us to go below deck. We were hit by a squall. A squall is a sudden violent gust of wind or a localized storm, one bringing rain, snow, or sleet. It seemed to come out of nowhere. The boat was rocking hard and my amygdala got hijacked. I was triggered by immense fear. Below deck, I frantically searched for the life preservers so I could be sure we all had one if we were to capsize.

The captain stayed at the wheel. He remained focused and steady. He led us through the squall safely. When it was over, I went above deck, and the captain had red patches all over his face. I thanked him, smiled, and commented on his "hives" that must have come from being so anxious. He told me the red patches were not hives; instead, they were welts from where the hail had hit him. He also told me that he was not worried. He was trained to handle these types of incidents. He began to educate me about his training, his crew, and the boat's keel—the structural beam that runs from the bow to the stern (front to back) of the boat, providing stability and balance. His training and expertise had certainly prepared him to weather this squall.

This story came to mind as I read your question. First, are your colleagues indeed anxious and unfocused, or have they adopted behaviors that look that way to successfully weather the uncertainties surrounding them? If performance and morale are not suffering, then perhaps you are observing coping mechanisms to navigate the seas of change. If you are noticing performance slip and morale suffer, then there is reason for concern. Either way, there are some things you can consider that I learned from the captain of the ship during that intense squall.

The captain was well trained and prepared to handle the storm. As a leader, you need to prepare yourself to handle turbulent times. Leadership is easy when it is smooth sailing. Leadership is hard when there are winds of change, especially daily.

How to prepare:

(1) Become familiar with how you react to challenges and change. Are you exhibiting the kind of behaviors that will create more confusion and chaos, or behaviors that will elicit confidence in you from others?

(2) Model the behaviors you expect from others during times of change. Others will be watching you and noticing how you handle what is in front of you. Are those behaviors creating more anxiety or calming others? Although I was below deck during our squall, I would peek up to see how the captain was doing. He was always calm, forcefully directing others, making quick and confident decisions, and remaining focused on keeping us out of danger.

(3) Trust the resources available to you. If you have trust and confidence in the people, protocols, and services you have, you can keep focused and trust that you are moving in the right direction. If necessary, remind those around you that you and the firm are prepared. You have weathered storms before, and you will weather them once again.

After the storm, I became particularly interested in the keel of a ship. Its purpose is:

- **Stability:** The keel helps the ship resist tipping over, especially in rough waters or when it's windy.
- **Control:** The keel helps the ship maintain a straight course and resist sideways motion.
- **Efficiency:** The keel helps the ship cut through the water more efficiently.
- **Counterbalance:** The keel helps right the ship if it capsizes.

With excellent training and resources, and confidence in a successful outcome, a leader can be the "keel" that moves the team forward by optimally influencing others and creating a sense of stability. Give this some thought and revisit your question. I am confident you will determine specific actions for yourself that will help you navigate the stormy seas.

David: Natalie, thank you for sharing this powerful sailing story—it offers a compelling metaphor for leadership in uncertain times. Just as a captain must navigate the unpredictable conditions of the sea, leaders in law firms must steer their teams through uncertainty and rapid change, and typically in high-stakes situations and under heightened stress.

As Natalie noted, one of the most critical responsibilities of a leader is to model the behavior they expect from others, particularly under stress and in times of rapid change. Leadership is not just about setting strategy or making key decisions; it is about demonstrating resilience, clarity, self-regulation, and emotional intelligence when faced with adversity. People take their cues from leadership, and how a leader reacts under pressure significantly impacts the confidence, focus, and morale of those around them. I continually quote Martin Luther King Jr. to my clients, "Be a thermostat, not a thermometer." Set the climate and tone in a situation; do not just react to what you are presented with. Emotions are contagious and impact the people you are communicating with. If a leader appears calm, focused, and clear, that will impact the people around them. Likewise, if the leader is stressed, anxious, or angry, then those emotions will set the tone when communicating with others.

In your story, Natalie, I see your three important key leadership qualities in moments of high stress: managing one's own emotions, influencing the emotional state of others, and delivering clear, direct communication. These are vital skills in any high-stakes profession, but they are especially crucial in the legal profession, where ambiguity and rapid change are part of the landscape and how they are managed can impact whether you have a successful outcome. Other factors that leaders need to be mindful of are the emotions and reactions members of their team are communicating. It is important to ask ourselves whether we are aware and mindful of the facial expressions, body language, and tone that is being communicated back to us.

Just as the keel of a boat provides stability in rough waters, leaders serve as the stabilizing force in their organizations. However, maintaining that stability requires self-awareness and emotional regulation. Leaders must first recognize their own emotional triggers and stress responses. Natalie, just as your amygdala hijacked your thinking during the squall, leaders under stress can default to reactive behaviors when, for example, a witness changes a story in the middle of testimony, or they discover an email that impacts their client's case in a negative way and must address it immediately. Sometimes, leaders may respond by becoming overly controlling, withdrawing, or expressing frustration. Self-awareness allows leaders to pause, regulate their emotions, and choose a response that fosters confidence rather than chaos.

Being able to respond to those highly stressful and challenging moments, especially when you may not get it right in your initial response, requires resilience to overcome the situation. Resilience is not about suppressing emotions; it is about channeling them productively. Your brother, as the captain, undoubtedly felt the force of the storm, yet he remained focused and steady. Similarly, effective leaders acknowledge challenges without letting fear or uncertainty dictate their actions. Sometimes, acknowledging those fears and moving forward can cause a team to rally to your cause.

If a leader demonstrates panic or doubt, the team will mirror that anxiety. If the leader remains composed, confident, and solution-focused, the team is more likely to adopt the mindset of calm and focus. I repeat, "be a thermostat, not a thermometer."

Amid rapid change, ambiguity can breed fear, resistance, and confusion. One of the most effective tools a leader has is clear, direct communication. Where I often see leaders stumble is in letting the stress of a given situation overwhelm their ability to communicate clearly. They may lash out in frustration, or they may go quiet with little direction to their teams. Unclear or inconsistent messaging can create unnecessary stress and confusion for members of the team. Leaders should ensure that their communication is straightforward and actionable, reinforcing a sense of direction even when they are not sure how to solve a particular problem and are taking steps to work through it. Transparency, and communicating a spirit of care that we are all in this together, will foster trust. Even when the path forward is unclear, acknowledging uncertainty, while providing a plan for navigating it, reassures the team and increases trust.

In today's rapidly evolving legal landscape, leaders cannot prevent storms, but they can prepare for them, respond with composure, and guide their teams to calmer waters. By managing their own stress, influencing the emotional climate, and providing clear communication, they embody the resilience and stability that teams need to thrive. All the behaviors we have described in this chapter are learned behaviors. They need to be practiced and modeled on a regular basis. It is incredibly difficult to be confronted with a challenge under high stress and to navigate through it without any practice. I highly encourage our readers to practice emotional self-awareness, practice stress management, and practice communicating with clarity and care.

So, as you reflect on the behaviors of your colleagues, ask yourself: Are they reacting with distress, or are they demonstrating their own strategies for navigating uncertainty? More importantly, ask how you, as a leader, can model the calm, focused leadership that will inspire confidence and success. The answer to the second question is practice, practice, practice.

Key Takeaways and Action Items

Key Takeaway One

Great Leaders Are the Keel During the Storm

Just as a keel stabilizes a boat through rough waters, effective leaders serve as a grounding force during times of uncertainty and rapid change. Their ability to remain composed, focused, and confident directly impacts team morale, clarity, and performance. Leadership isn't just about steering—it's about steadying.

Action Items:

1. **Model Calm Under Pressure:** Practice pausing before responding to challenges to set a composed tone for the team.
2. **Focus on Priorities:** Identify and communicate the top three priorities during periods of disruption to help the team stay aligned.
3. **Recognize and Celebrate Wins:** Highlight progress, even small things, to reinforce confidence and motivation during turbulent times.

Key Takeaway Two

Emotional Self-Regulation and Awareness Are Essential Leadership Skills

Leaders must understand and manage their own emotional responses in high-stakes situations to avoid reactive behavior. Emotional intelligence—including self-awareness, emotional regulation, and empathy—enables leaders to model calm and resilience, which helps teams navigate anxiety and ambiguity with greater confidence.

Action Items:

1. **Practice Reflection:** After key decisions or difficult conversations, take time to assess your emotional triggers and responses.

2. **Pause and Reframe:** In tense moments, count to ten, breathe, or step away briefly to respond thoughtfully rather than reactively.

3. **Model Vulnerability:** Share (appropriately) how you manage stress and setbacks, normalizing emotional intelligence as a leadership strength.

Key Takeaway Three

Clear, Consistent Communication Builds Trust in Uncertain Times

Ambiguity can trigger fear and resistance, but leaders who communicate transparently—even when the path forward is unclear—foster trust and alignment. The most impactful leaders acknowledge challenges, clarify next steps, and convey a shared sense of direction, reinforcing psychological safety across their teams.

Action Items:

1. **Establish Regular Communication Cadence:** Use weekly updates, team huddles, or firm-wide messages to share updates and reduce uncertainty.

2. **Clarify Next Steps:** Even if all answers aren't known, explain what decisions are being made and what is still in progress.

3. **Invite Questions and Feedback:** Create opportunities for two-way communication (Q&A sessions, anonymous surveys) to address concerns.

Chapter 11

From Fear to Trust: How Law Firms Can Break the Cycle of Toxic Leadership

Anjli Garg & David B. Sarnoff

In the high-pressure environment of law firms, many of us have either witnessed or heard stories of partners losing their temper—berating junior lawyers in front of peers, slamming doors, or even throwing objects in frustration. These incidents often leave associates feeling shocked, demoralized, and helpless. The prevailing sentiment becomes, "What can you do?" Addressing such behavior directly seems risky, especially when the partner in question is a significant rainmaker. Consequently, the cycle continues, and the firm's culture suffers. In many of these situations, partners may have their behavior acknowledged or addressed informally by the executive committee or HR, but they are rarely held accountable. Often, they receive little to no direct feedback that their conduct is inappropriate, which contributes to the behavior continuing unchecked.

But what if there is a solution? What if, instead of accepting this as the norm, firms could address the root causes of such behavior and foster a more supportive and productive environment?

What Is Fear-Based Leadership?

Fear-based leadership is characterized by dominance, control, and the threat of consequences. Common behaviors include:

- **Public Shaming or Belittling:** Undermining individuals in front of peers and others.
- **Withholding Information:** Maintaining control by limiting access to knowledge.
- **Micromanaging or Punitive Oversight:** Undermining autonomy through excessive control and imposing disproportionate consequences for mistakes.
- **Mood-Driven Decision-Making:** Allowing personal emotions to dictate professional decisions.

These types of behaviors can meet the criteria for workplace bullying. According to the Workplace Bullying Institute (WBI), more than 30% of American adults report experiencing bullying on the job.[1]

How Does Fear-Based Leadership Impact the Workplace?

These behaviors create an environment where employees are constantly on edge—focus frays, confidence erodes, and well-being suffers.

More specifically, the personal toll on individuals, who are on the receiving end of fear-based leadership, often manifests as follows:

- **Chronic Stress and Burnout:** Fear triggers constant fight-or-flight responses, sapping energy and well-being.
- **Loss of Psychological Safety:** Employees suppress ideas, questions, and feedback, which stifles growth and innovation.
- **Imposter Syndrome and Low Self-Worth:** Constant criticism without developmental support damages confidence, which can result in talented people exiting the organization and/or the profession altogether.

---

1. Workplace Bullying Inst., 2021 WBI U.S. Workplace Bullying Survey (2021), https://workplacebullying.org/wp-content/uploads/2024/01/2021-Full-Report.pdf.

- **Physical Health Implications:** Elevated blood pressure, insomnia, fatigue, and other stress-related health issues, which undermines the physical health and well-being of the individual.

In addition, the organizational impact of fear-based leadership should not be underestimated. This type of leadership often results in:

- **Culture of Silence:** Employees avoid raising concerns or surfacing problems, fearing retaliation.
- **High Turnover and Low Engagement:** Fear leads to disengagement and prompts valuable talent to leave.
- **Stagnant Innovation:** A fearful environment inhibits risk-taking and creativity.
- **Diminished Trust in Leadership:** Mistrust spreads beyond the individual leader, weakening the entire leadership pipeline.
- **Reputation Risk:** Word spreads, affecting recruitment and client trust.

All of this means that not only do organizations and individuals not thrive under fear-based leadership, over time, neither the organization nor the individual can sustain the unchecked consequences of this leadership style.

Understanding the Fear Behind the Behavior

Interestingly, some fear-based leaders are unaware that they lead through fear. In their minds, they are holding people accountable or maintaining high standards and either aren't aware of the negative impact on others or feel that the character it builds outweighs any negative impact. But often, these behaviors stem from the leader's unexamined fear—of failure, criticism, loss of control, or appearing vulnerable.

Drawing on over fifteen years of research, Tepper, Simon, and Park identified key drivers of toxic leadership behaviors in their 2017 article titled "Abusive Supervision"[2]:

- **Identity Threat:** Leaders' own insecurities and fear of criticism can lead to defensive behaviors.
- **Self-Regulation Impairment:** Inability to manage emotions and self-regulate can result in lashing out, especially under stress.
- **Social Learning:** Exposure to fear-based leadership in past roles or organizational cultures can normalize abusive behaviors, as leaders model what they have observed or experienced.

These factors suggest that some leaders may not be aware of the fear they instill, as their actions are rooted in their own fears and learned behaviors.

The Cost of Silence

When other leadership stands silent and appears powerless or unwilling to address this behavior, they become silent enablers. The only choice those with less power have is to leave and disengage. In the meantime, they suffer, and their work suffers, creating a contagion effect all around them.

Research indicates that leaders with low self-awareness often exhibit toxic behaviors, such as micromanagement and dishonesty, leading to negative outcomes like employee disengagement and decreased performance.

According to a National Institutes of Health study[3] on workplace bullying in healthcare, incivility and bullying not only harm employees' health but may also carry significant economic costs for employers. While identifying the problem is relatively straightforward, designing and implementing effective interventions is far more complex.

---

2. Bennett J. Tepper, Lauren Simon & Hee Man Park, *Abusive Supervision*, 4 ANN. REV. OF ORG. PSYCH. AND ORG. BEHAV. 123–52 (Jan. 2017).
3. Erika L. Sabbath, et al., *Mental Health Expenditures: Association with Workplace Incivility and Bullying Among Hospital Patient Care Workers*, J. OCCUP. ENV'T MED. 737–42 (Aug. 2018).

However, such efforts—though challenging—have the potential to deliver meaningful benefits for both employees and organizations alike.

Stuck Between a Bully and the Bottom Line? Avoid the Zero-Sum Game by Cultivating Emotional Intelligence

Traditional interventions typically don't work—few, if any, want to challenge the rainmaker. Policies exist, but they often come off as hollow or ineffective. Fear-based leaders rarely face external correction because their authority often shields them from honest feedback. As a result, meaningful change can't be imposed—it must be driven by the leader's own willingness to reflect, grow, and shift their mindset.

Leaders who cultivate emotional intelligence—particularly empathy, self-awareness, and transparency—build trust, resilience, and innovation within their teams. They create environments where feedback is welcomed, mistakes are learning opportunities, and people feel seen rather than surveilled.

This is where executive coaching can be a powerful tool and process. A meta-analysis found that executive coaching significantly impacts behavioral outcomes, particularly in enhancing self-awareness and emotional intelligence. Coaching provides a safe space for leaders to explore and address their underlying fears, leading to sustainable behavioral changes.

David once worked with a senior leader who was a highly respected subject matter expert but was perceived by their team as intimidating and fear-inducing. When David asked how the leader believed they were viewed by their team, the leader confidently responded, "They think very highly of me."

To build self-awareness, David introduced a simple but revealing exercise. He asked the leader to write down three words or phrases they would use to describe themselves. Then he encouraged the leader to ask multiple team members to do the same—write down three words or short phrases that described the leader and leave them anonymously on the leader's chair.

When the responses came in, they painted a very different picture. Words like *vindictive, micromanager, mean,* and *untrustworthy* surfaced repeatedly. The leader was stunned. After sitting with the feedback for a few moments, they turned to David and said, *"I don't want to be that person."*

That moment marked the beginning of a transformative journey. Over the following year, the leader committed to developing greater emotional intelligence, empathy, and self-awareness. In time, their team experienced a fundamentally different leader—one who listened, empowered, and inspired.

The key takeaway? Emotional intelligence is neither innate nor set in stone. With intention, feedback, and dedicated effort, anyone can build these skills. It does, however, require self-awareness and a willingness to act on that awareness.

A 2025 Bloomberg article[4] highlighted how private equity giant Kohlberg Kravis Roberts (KKR)—not known for fostering a culture of psychological safety—uncovered a surprising truth: Companies led by high-empathy leaders significantly outperformed those led by low-empathy ones. Yet even KKR executive Pete Stavros had to have a wake-up call about empathy—one that's now reshaping how the firm develops its leaders.

Why? Because empathy isn't about being "nice." It's about driving performance, accountability, and loyalty—especially in uncertain, high-stakes environments.

As Stanford psychologist Jamil Zaki explains, empathy enables leaders to:

- Deliver honest, effective feedback while preserving dignity;
- Pinpoint the real barriers to performance;
- Build trust that fuels collaboration and innovation; and
- Foster connection, increasing retention and discretionary effort.[5]

Empathy isn't merely a soft skill—it's a strategic advantage.

---

4. Heather Landy, *Empaths at the Gate: KKR and a Stanford Psychologist Measure People Skills*, BLOOMBERG (Apr. 23, 2025).
5. *See id.*

And when the waters get rough, empathy isn't something to set aside. It's what helps you rally your team, build resilience, and row through the storm—together.

Conclusion

Fear-based leadership is unsustainable. While it may yield short-term compliance, it erodes trust, stifles innovation, and damages organizational culture over time. Recognizing that such leadership often stems from the leader's own fears and lack of self-awareness opens the door to transformation. Executive coaching emerges as a vital tool in this process, offering leaders a mirror to reflect on their behaviors and the impact they have on others.

In many law firms, confronting fear-based behavior directly—especially when exhibited by high-performing partners or rainmakers—is fraught with risk. The potential fallout from challenging these influential figures often leads to a culture of silence, where issues remain unaddressed, and the well-being of associates is compromised. It's a difficult calculus: the firm may feel it's more palatable to lose valuable associates than to confront an influential partner.

However, there's another way. If the partner is coachable and willing to engage in the process, executive coaching can serve as a powerful intervention. Coaching provides a confidential, judgment-free, and supportive environment where leaders can explore their behaviors, understand the underlying fears driving them, and develop healthier, more effective leadership styles. This inside-out approach fosters genuine change, benefiting not only the individual leader but also the broader organizational culture.

To foster a sustainable firm with a strong associate bench, firms must prioritize creating environments that encourage self-awareness, emotional intelligence, and open communication—qualities that are increasingly becoming non-negotiables for junior lawyers. By investing in leadership development and fostering a culture of trust and psychological safety, firms can move away from fear-based practices and towards a more empowering and effective leadership model.

When leaders confront their fears, they don't just change how they lead—they change the culture around them, creating space for others to thrive.

Key Takeaways and Action Items

Key Takeaway One

Fear-Based Leadership Erodes Culture and Performance

Fear-driven behaviors—public shaming, micromanagement, and mood-driven decision-making—create stress, disengagement, and high turnover. Left unchecked, they harm both individuals and the firm's reputation.

Action Items:

1. **Identify Fear-Based Behaviors:** Conduct anonymous surveys or focus groups to surface where fear-driven leadership shows up in your firm.
2. **Track the Impact:** Monitor turnover data, engagement scores, and exit interview feedback to connect toxic behaviors with tangible costs.
3. **Build Awareness Among Leaders:** Share research on the organizational and financial consequences of fear-based management to create urgency for change.

Key Takeaway Two

Emotional Intelligence Is the Antidote to Fear-Based Leadership

Self-awareness, empathy, and emotional regulation are essential to replacing fear with trust, psychological safety, and high performance.

Action Items:

1. **Develop Self-Awareness Practices:** Encourage leaders to solicit honest feedback (e.g., 360 reviews or anonymous word exercises) to see how they are truly perceived.
2. **Train for Empathy and Communication:** Offer workshops or coaching on delivering feedback constructively, listening actively, and regulating emotions under stress.

3. **Model EI at the Top:** Have senior leaders share their own growth stories and demonstrate vulnerability, signaling that empathy and reflection are valued.

Key Takeaway Three

Coaching and Culture Change Create Sustainable Transformation

Fear-based behaviors rarely shift through policy alone—leaders must do inner work to uncover fears, adopt healthier mindsets, and build new habits.

Action Items:

1. **Offer Executive Coaching:** Provide confidential coaching for high-impact leaders to explore underlying fears, improve emotional regulation, and adopt empowering behaviors.
2. **Foster Psychological Safety:** Create formal mechanisms for associates and staff to raise concerns without retaliation, reinforcing that their voices matter.
3. **Invest in Leadership Development:** Embed EQ, trust-building, and feedback skills into partner retreats and leadership training to shift the culture over time.

Chapter 12

Stepping Up Without Overstepping—Navigating Leadership Gaps with Care

Natalie Loeb & David B. Sarnoff

Dear Coaches:

> **Your last column about handling a horrible boss[1] resonated with me. My boss was the same when I worked in a firm. Now, I'm in-house as Assistant General Counsel. My current boss isn't terrible, but they aren't the best either.**
>
> **I'm looking for ways to improve my work experience and interactions with colleagues without stepping on my boss's toes. Should I approach my boss about this, or do you think it would be acceptable for me to take the initiative here?**
>
> ***—Initiate or Wait?***

David: Thank you for sharing this question. It is unfortunate that you have had a couple of bosses that do not appear to have been modeling high-level leadership skills and may be low on emotional intelligence. Having a boss who is "not terrible" still seems a long way from

1. *See* chapter 21.

having a "good boss." Many professionals find themselves in a middle ground of not being in a toxic workplace and living in a constant state of heightened stress, but still wanting a better boss who mentors, develops, builds skills, and creates a more positive working experience. However, being in-house might give you space to build strong relationships and shape your work environment—sideways with peers and even upward with leadership—especially if you're intentional about it.

One of the key questions you may need to think about is, "Can I develop a relationship with my boss that improves our communication, interactions, and collaboration?" You may consider taking the initiative; however, I encourage you to do it in a thoughtful way, being strategic and respectful. This can avoid the perception that you are stepping on toes or creating unintended tension with your boss.

In preparation for this conversation, you may want to take some time and reflect on what a successful outcome looks like. What behaviors would you like to see more of and which ones less of? Do you want a stronger collaborative relationship, clearer communication, a sense of camaraderie, or more opportunities to lead projects? Once you have determined the answers to these questions, think about what aspects of these behaviors are in your control and which ones are out of your control. You may want to propose to your boss creating time for informal check-ins or mentorship sessions or suggest ideas to create more efficiency in the group. If you do not feel ready for this step or are not comfortable, consider engaging peers and people who report to you to create opportunities to interact in knowledge sharing, collaborate on matters, or engage in team building. By engaging with colleagues, you create an opportunity to "model the way" and enhance the workplace experience for you and others.

If you decide to engage peers and direct reports to facilitate a more interactive environment, you may want to keep your boss in the loop, or even include them in the exercise, to avoid appearing like you're doing an end run around them. You may want to frame it as an opportunity for you to contribute to the betterment of the team. You may say something in the spirit of, "I have noticed that some of the junior attorneys could benefit from a practical skills session, and I am interested in leading a breakfast-and-learn. Would you be open to me working on this activity?" Ideally, you will communicate in a collaborative tone. As you communicate with your boss, be sure to actively listen to their response and take note of their body language and facial expressions as these will be the data points indicating whether or not your boss is aligned.

Your desire to make things better without causing friction is exactly what emotionally intelligent leadership looks like. By focusing on what you can influence, communicating clearly, and staying aligned with your team's broader goals, you can make a meaningful impact, without needing your boss to change first.

Natalie: It's great to hear you've transitioned into an in-house role as Assistant General Counsel. That move often brings new opportunities to make an impact—and sometimes new challenges in leadership dynamics. While it's a relief that your current boss isn't actively difficult, I understand the desire to improve your work experience and relationships without disrupting the chain of command.

In a legal department—especially in a corporate or regulated environment—hierarchy, precision, and discretion are key. But that doesn't mean you have to wait for top-down permission to make your experience more positive or productive. In fact, this is where your personal values can serve as a strong guide.

In my opinion, every leader should prioritize personal value clarity. Research on credibility by Jim Kouzes and Barry Posner indicates that clarifying our personal values helps us to align our behaviors with and to make intentional decisions true to our values.[2] When our values and behaviors are aligned, we increase our credibility. With heightened credibility, we have a higher chance of influencing others. Influence can be used to manage conflicts, lead teams, and to establish a leadership presence.

Values clarity also helps us to make decisions. Those decisions can be small daily decisions or larger team decisions. Let me give you an example. Family has always been a leading value for me. When my son was young, the Yankees won the World Series. My husband wanted to take him to the ticker-tape parade in New York City. I also value education. Attending the parade meant missing a day of school. When faced with this decision, my family value came out ahead, and my husband

---

2. James M. Kouzes & Barry Posner, Credibility: How Leaders Gain and Lose It, Why People Demand It (Wiley 2011).

and I decided that he and my son should surely have that experience, a decision I was very comfortable with.

Here is an example from my professional life. In my organization, my team values feedback. Due to this, we put a process in place to collect bi-annual feedback for everyone. We all participate, and we all receive feedback. Creating the process took time, energy, and intention. Remaining committed to the process has also required energy. However, we value feedback, so we make this initiative a priority.

Think about your top five core values. What may they be? And what would it look like as you demonstrate intention around them. May that help you make decisions on how to handle this situation.

For example, if you value integrity, collegiality, or proactive problem-solving (which are often core to legal professionals), then embodying those values in your daily work—in how you approach matters, support colleagues, or collaborate across teams—is entirely appropriate and often welcomed. These values can subtly but powerfully shape the tone of your interactions and help create a more respectful, solution-oriented culture around you.

Of course, when your efforts begin to touch on broader team dynamics—such as proposing changes to legal review processes, onboarding procedures, or interdepartmental workflows—it's wise to involve your boss early. This isn't just about hierarchy; it's also about strategic alignment. Framing your ideas as supportive of departmental goals or efficiency improvements can help your boss view your initiative as collaborative rather than disruptive.

Think of it as operating within your "lane," but with thoughtful leadership. Start small: mentor a junior team member, initiate more structured communication with business partners, or volunteer for cross-functional projects where your legal perspective adds value. These actions reflect your values and often lead to organic improvements in culture and performance.

Then, when something larger is on your mind—a new idea, a suggestion, or even just feedback on how the team functions—approach your boss not with a complaint but with curiosity and respect. Ask for their thoughts and position your ideas as opportunities, not judgments. That gives you room to lead by example while still honoring the structure you work within.

Early in my career, as I was growing as a professional development trainer, one of the learnings that stuck with me is that every employee is responsible for "taking initiative to make things better." I have found this is always welcomed in the workplace. In your case, as you think about your approach, make sure your solution includes being respectful and keeping your boss in the loop.

Key Takeaways and Action Items

Key Takeaway One

Thoughtful Initiative Can Improve Your Work Experience

Taking the initiative doesn't mean overstepping—it means finding ways to enhance collaboration and culture while keeping your boss informed and aligned.

Action Items:

1. **Clarify Your Desired Outcome:** Reflect on what would make your work experience better—clearer communication, more collaboration, more opportunities to lead—and write it down.

2. **Start Small:** Identify one or two low-stakes opportunities to contribute positively (e.g., mentoring a junior colleague, organizing a short "lunch-and-learn," or proposing a small process improvement).

3. **Keep Your Boss in the Loop:** Frame your ideas as supportive of team goals, and present them as a question: "Would you be open to me taking the lead on this?"

Key Takeaway Two

Align Actions with Your Core Values to Build Credibility

When you act in accordance with your values, you build trust, influence, and a stronger professional presence—without waiting for top-down change.

Action Items:

1. **Clarify Your Top Five Values:** Write down the principles that guide your professional decisions (e.g., integrity, collaboration, problem-solving) and use them as a filter for your choices.

2. **Demonstrate Your Values Daily:** Look for small, visible ways to live your values—respond promptly to colleagues, share knowledge generously, and approach conflicts with respect.

3. **Communicate with Intention:** When you propose an idea or initiative, explain how it supports the team's mission or shared values. This helps colleagues see your actions as aligned with group priorities.

Key Takeaway Three

Collaboration with Your Boss Builds Trust and Influence

Maintaining open communication ensures your efforts are seen as collaborative, not competitive, and creates space for your boss to support your initiatives.

Action Items:

1. **Schedule Informal Check-Ins:** Ask for periodic time to discuss priorities, share updates, and get feedback on how you're supporting the team.
2. **Listen Actively:** Pay attention not just to what your boss says, but to tone, body language, and reactions—these can signal support or hesitation.
3. **Frame Initiatives As Partnership:** Use language like, "I'd like to contribute to team success by . . ." and invite your boss to participate or provide input so they feel included.

Case Study

Steering Through the Storm—A Law Firm Leadership Moment

Background

Wallace & Pierce LLP is a law firm with about 200 attorneys across four offices. The firm recently merged with a smaller boutique firm, increasing headcount, workload, and internal cultural tension. Simultaneously, Wallace & Pierce is navigating client budget pressure, rising associate attrition, and a competitive lateral market.

Key Participants

- **Teresa Lin (Managing Partner):** Known for her integrity, strategic thinking, and people-centered leadership.
- **Jordan Sloane (Recently promoted partner):** High performer with client praise but little experience managing people.
- **Maya Patel (Fifth-year associate in Jordan's practice group):** Respected by peers but recently disengaged.
- **Derrick Wells (Senior litigator and member of the Executive Committee):** Skeptical of wellness and coaching efforts.
- **Maria Chen (Director of Professional Development):** A quiet advocate for leadership development.

Scenario

In January 2025, Teresa receives two concerning but unrelated messages within a week:

1. A senior client of Jordan's emails Teresa with praise for Jordan's legal analysis—but adds that "the team seems to be rotating a lot lately" and suggests "more continuity would be beneficial."

2. Maria privately shares results from an anonymous associate pulse survey. In Jordan's group, morale is down. Comments include:

   "We're doing good work, but there's zero feedback."

   "It feels like Jordan sees us as tools, not teammates."

   "We're afraid to ask questions, it's always urgent and reactive."

Teresa arranges a check-in with Jordan. He arrives late, clearly distracted, and says, "I know morale's low. Honestly, I'm doing everything myself because I can't rely on the team. And this AI rollout is making everything messier, not easier. I don't have time to coddle people."

Later that day, Maya walks past Teresa in the hallway. Teresa stops her to ask how things are going. Maya hesitates, then says, "I don't want to step out of line, but there's a lot of stress in our group. We want to do good work, but it's hard to ask for help or raise concerns without feeling like we're being disloyal."

At the next Executive Committee meeting, Teresa raises the topic of team performance and professional development. Derrick interjects:

"We've got bigger fish to fry, clients are shrinking budgets, and you want to spend more on coaches and wellness retreats? People need to toughen up and do the work."

Maria counters:

"Actually, the firms that invest in resilience and EQ are seeing better retention and client trust. We can't afford to burn people out."

The group agrees, reluctantly, to fund coaching for one partner as a pilot. Teresa selects Jordan. She frames it carefully with him:

"You're a valued leader. I'd like to support your continued growth, particularly around communication and team dynamics. Coaching isn't remediation, it's an investment."

Jordan responds, "Fine. I'll do it. But I'm skeptical this will change anything."

Meanwhile, the firm is rolling out a new AI research platform. Maria holds optional trainings. Younger associates attend; older partners skip them. One junior associate jokes in Slack, "Wonder how long until HAL replaces us all?" The message gets forwarded to Jordan, who snaps in a group meeting, "If you don't want to be here, leave."

Later, Maya quietly tells Teresa:

"We're not scared of AI, we just don't know where we stand. Some of us are wondering if we'll still be needed."

Six Weeks Later:

- Jordan has met a few times with his coach and admits in a small leadership huddle, "I didn't realize how much I was shutting people down. Coaching's uncomfortable, but helpful."
- Maria proposes a mini-retreat focused on intergenerational communication, EQ, and the future of law. Teresa brings it to the EC. The vote is close—but passes.
- Maya receives positive feedback on a recent brief. She tells her coach (part of a small peer group pilot), "It's the first time I felt seen in months."
- Jordan schedules a team lunch to thank the group for their work and opens the meeting with: "I've realized I haven't been giving enough support. That's on me. I want to do better."

Instructions for Reader:

As you read the case study, consider:

1. Which actions or behaviors reflect effective leadership and emotional intelligence on the part of each participant in the case study?
2. Where were there missteps, blind spots, or missed opportunities by any of the key participants?
3. Overall, what additional steps could improve communication, inclusion, trust, and performance?

List:

- Two examples of positive leadership behaviors demonstrated by any of the key participants.
- Two examples of behaviors that need improvement from any of the key participants.
- One recommendation you would make to either Teresa, Jordan, or the Executive Committee.

Facilitator's Guide

Steering Through the Storm—A Law Firm Leadership Moment

Analysis & Conclusions

Behaviors Done Well

1. **Teresa's Framing of Coaching As Growth-Oriented Leadership Development**

Rather than treating coaching as a fix, Teresa wisely presents it as an investment in Jordan's continued growth. This aligns with the messaging in chapter 1, Why Lawyers Need Executive Coaches, and chapter 2, Taking Advantage of Executive Coaching. It also models the idea that high performers need new tools when stepping into leadership roles—not just more responsibility.

2. **Maria's Quiet but Strategic Influence on Culture and Learning**

Maria leverages data from the associate survey, makes the business case for resilience and retention, and proposes a relevant retreat. She's a behind-the-scenes culture carrier whose actions reflect the lessons of chapter 6, Great Leaders Are Made, Not Born from Promotion, and chapter 8, Does Your Executive Committee Understand the Merits of a Firm Retreat?

3. **Teresa's Emotional Intelligence and Timely Interventions**

Teresa reads between the lines during hallway interactions (with Maya), handles resistance diplomatically (EC meeting), and creates what is widely known as psychological safety by sharing a past leadership struggle. These are examples of "being the keel" as described in chapter 10, Be the Keel—How Can Law Firm Leaders Provide Stability During Uncertain Times?

4. **Jordan's Coaching Breakthrough and Public Accountability**

Despite resistance, Jordan shows growth by naming his blind spots in a team meeting and shifting from defensive to developmental leadership. This reflects learning from chapter 4, Partners, How Patient Are You?, and chapter 10, Be the Keel—How Can Law Firm Leaders Provide Stability During Uncertain Times?

Behaviors That Need Improvement

1. **Jordan's Early Dismissiveness and Micromanagement**

Jordan's initial reaction—"I can't coddle people"—reflects a mindset focused on control and output over development and trust. His failure to delegate or offer feedback created avoidable morale issues. He needed coaching sooner, ideally before promotion, as emphasized in chapter 6, Great Leaders Are Made, Not Born from Promotion.

2. **Executive Committee's Resistance to Soft-Skills Investment**

Derrick's comment dismissing coaching and wellness as luxuries shows a narrow, short-term mindset. His reaction undermines firmwide psychological safety and fails to recognize that today's legal leadership demands empathy, agility, and team resilience as explained in chapter 7, Looming Economic Downturn? How Do I Balance My Firm's Needs and the Impact on Our Associates?, and chapter 9, What's Next for Law? EQ, Wellness, and Technological Change.

3. **Poor Change Management in AI Rollout**

The tech rollout lacked sufficient emotional framing and change navigation. Jokes in Slack and fear-based silence are signs that the rollout stirred anxiety that was not addressed. This missed opportunity connects directly to the discussion in chapter 9, What's Next for Law? EQ, Wellness, and Technological Change, and chapter 5, When Met with Opposition, Model the Way.

4. Missed Use of Feedback Channels

There was no mention of formal upward feedback or 360 reviews prior to Jordan's promotion, which could have surfaced readiness gaps earlier. This highlights the need for integrating EQ and communication assessments into promotion processes as shown in chapter 6, Great Leaders Are Made, Not Born from Promotion.

Recommendations for Strengthening Leadership and Culture

1. Embed Coaching into the Leadership Pipeline

Make coaching a standard part of partner development—before and after promotion. Normalize it as a high-performance tool rather than a reactive fix.

2. Equip the Executive Committee with EQ and Change Management Training

Educate leadership on how investing in people directly impacts profitability, client satisfaction, and innovation. Use firm and industry data to drive buy-in.

3. Humanize Technology Adoption

Pair every major tech implementation with empathy-based change management. Offer spaces to address fear, encourage learning, and show how human judgment and creativity still matter.

4. Develop Feedback Infrastructure

Implement upward feedback mechanisms and peer evaluations to catch leadership challenges early and reinforce a culture of learning and accountability.

5. Continue Modeling and Storytelling

Leaders should continue sharing their own learning journeys to de-stigmatize uncertainty and demonstrate vulnerability as a strength.

Part II

Management

Chapter 13

How Can I Better Manage People and Administrative Tasks?

Natalie Loeb & David B. Sarnoff

Dear Coaches:

> **As a partner, how do I manage all the administrative and management stuff I have to deal with? Other people's problems, practice groups, evaluations, bills, hours, etc. I know it needs to be done, but it's not why I went to law school. I am sure I could be better and more efficient at it.**
>
> ***—I Just Want to Practice Law***

David: Natalie and I appreciate the submission of this question, and it is one we commonly see in various forms. Quite often, when an attorney is promoted to partner, they are ill-equipped to effectively manage people and teams. Furthermore, law schools, by and large, spend relatively little time addressing leadership, collaboration, cultivating relationships, time management, effective delegation, and communication. I recall during my first day of law school in 1991, a member of the faculty said that "when you graduate, you will never think the same way again." He continued, "You will think in terms of consequences and not possibilities. You will walk past a playground of children playing and not see the joy of play, but rather the many ways a child may get injured on the playground." Those words stuck with me, and I believe that it was an accurate summary of my law school experience. Law school curriculum spends a significant amount of time perfecting the assignment of blame, proximate cause, liability, and damages. It spends much less time on possibilities, innovation, and optimism. To paraphrase positive psychologist and thought leader Martin Seligman, if you didn't have pessimism going in, law school will teach it to you. I believe it is this mindset that also explains why it can be difficult for law firm partners and managing attorneys to be effective leaders.

Natalie: This question is a reasonable one. It's also an inquiry commonly asked by all high achievers, no matter the industry. When I hear this question, I ask one in return: *What is in your control and what is NOT in your control?* One of my favorite lines to share with clients is "If you don't control the events in your life, the events in your life will control you." If we can control something, we can step up and take responsibility. If we can't control something, we must learn to be flexible and adapt and/or perhaps "let go."

Let's take "other people's problems." Can we control how others react to events in their lives? Of course not, but we can control how we notice those problems and to what extent we want to address them. When in a leadership role, it is often necessary to address others' "problems"; particularly if the problems are affecting work performance.

We live in a world today where we can assume everyone has a lot on their plates. If we are starting to notice someone's "problems" impacting their performance, we have two choices:

1. Ignore it; or
2. Address it.

You have a choice. This *is* where you have control. Remember, all choices have consequences. So think about your end goal.

> Choice 1: Ignore it:
>
> Some people believe "if I ignore it, it will go away." I have found this to be just the opposite. If you ignore it, the problem will usually show up some other way and often gets worse. It's your choice to ignore other people's problems. Just be realistic about the impact of this decision.

> Choice 2: Address it:
>
> In my opinion, the best choice is to address other people's problems. This is where you have control. When you choose to "address it," you are placing this task as a priority in a busy day. More often than not, the fifteen to twenty minutes set aside to address the person's problem will save huge amounts of time down the road. Addressing others' problems effectively requires skills additional to lawyering. It requires a solid understanding and demonstration of what is known as "emotional intelligence."

David: When attorneys begin their careers, they tend to focus on demonstrating their IQ (Intelligence Quotient), lawyering skills, meeting billable hour targets, and receiving professional development for practical skills such as drafting briefs, agreements, and other documents. While it is growing in popularity in recent years, attorneys, by and large, did not receive professional development in management and leadership skills, team building, and effective communication. Going from being an individual contributor or member of a team to then leading that team or department is a difficult transition for many. It requires a mindset shift and intentionality about what kind of leader the attorney wants to be.

In my opinion, effective leaders possess what is known as emotional intelligence. Emotional intelligence is a complex discipline; however, for purposes of this chapter, emotional intelligence, commonly referred to as "emotional quotient" or "EQ," refers to a leader's self-awareness about how they show up and are perceived by their team. It is understanding how you are known in the firm and being aware of non-verbal communication and body language. Emotional intelligence also involves a recognition of one's own emotions as they are happening, the ability to identify those emotions, and having the skills to influence those emotions. At a high level, leaders with emotional intelligence also have the ability to recognize emotions in others and use that information to effectively influence behavior.

In order to be an effective leader in a law firm or legal department where stress and pressure can be pervasive, it is important to be an active listener for members of your team. Active listening requires you to be present, focused on the speaker, and not distracted by calls, texts, or emails. Leadership also requires clear and unambiguous communication of expectations between team members and the leader. It is critical to give direct feedback about areas on which individuals need to improve or when they did something well and can leverage their strengths. Lastly, a critical leadership skill is to seek feedback from individuals and the team as to what you can do better and how you as a leader can improve. This builds trust, enhances direct communication, and creates a shared mission team culture.

With respect to evaluations, I cannot emphasize enough that it is vital to provide substantive feedback and direction for career and professional development. We hear feedback from individuals that reviews and evaluations were often meaningless and diminished their trust in a manager or leader because it was interpreted as a lack of caring. The last thing someone wants to see on an evaluation is "meets expectations," "needs improvement," or "keep doing what you're doing." Be thoughtful and give specific feedback and guidance. It will be greatly appreciated. When these behaviors are prioritized and become habits, you will reap the benefits of fewer "people problems."

As for managing client bills and tracking billable hours, this has been a continuous challenge in the legal profession. I recall as an associate that the office manager would get frustrated with certain partners who were consistently late entering their time, and the partners would get upset when they were constantly asked for their time sheets. Fast-forward almost thirty years, and I still hear about these same challenges. Even with the advent of sophisticated billing software, getting partners to enter time is still a chore.

Practicing law requires focus on the work product, especially when an attorney is working on multiple client matters at the same time. All things considered, it is difficult to recap in time sheets what an attorney worked on throughout the day. There are various practices and strategies for entering time, and it may take a sampling of different practices before you find the one that works for you. Some attorneys are diligent and organized and enter meticulous time on matters as they are working on them. For some attorneys, juggling multiple matters is difficult to do. Another practice to consider, if your billing software doesn't send alerts, is to set reminders on your computer or phone to prompt you at regular intervals (e.g., every two hours) to stop what you are doing and accurately enter your time on matters you are working on.

Natalie: We either get up every day with the intention to prioritize where we spend our time (control), or we get up every day and let others prioritize our day from their demands (lack of control). Realistically, we probably have a bit of both in our days. However, if one values all of the above responsibilities, then one must "take control" and place a priority on scheduling the time to get them done. It may not be realistic to take on all of this work yourself, so it's worthwhile to spend five minutes each day evaluating and prioritizing all of the items that need to be completed to determine what you need to do versus what you can delegate to someone else. And often, that is all it takes. This is a habit that can be built, but it takes intention. Try it!

Key Takeaways and Action Items

Key Takeaway One

Leadership in Law Requires a Shift in Mindset

Law school teaches attorneys to focus on risk, blame, and precision—but not necessarily on people leadership, communication, or emotional intelligence. The transition from individual contributor to leader requires intentional development and self-awareness.

Action Items:

1. **Develop Emotional Intelligence (EQ):** Invest in self-awareness tools such as EQ-i 2.0® or 360° feedback to understand how you "show up" and are perceived by others. Reflect weekly on what emotions drove your decisions and interactions.
2. **Cultivate Active Listening:** In meetings, silence your phone and email notifications. Practice summarizing what others say before responding to ensure clarity and connection.
3. **Seek and Give Meaningful Feedback:** Replace generic evaluations ("meets expectations") with specific, actionable insights tied to professional growth. Regularly ask your team, "What's one thing I could do better as your leader?"

Key Takeaway Two

Focus on What You Can Control and Lead with Intention

Much of leadership frustration comes from focusing on what's outside your control—others' reactions, firm policies, or client demands. Effective leaders focus instead on priorities, intentional time management, and taking ownership of what they can influence.

Action Items:

1. **Daily Control Check:** At the start of each day, write down what's in your control (decisions, priorities, tone) versus what's not. Direct your energy accordingly.

2. **Prioritize with Purpose:** Spend five minutes each morning categorizing your to-do list: *Do now, Delegate,* or *Defer.* Schedule the "must do" items into your calendar.

3. **Model Adaptability:** When an uncontrollable event occurs—e.g., staffing changes or client demands—verbalize flexibility to your team: "We can't change this deadline, but we can adjust how we approach it." This models composure under pressure.

Key Takeaway Three

Address Problems Early to Prevent Bigger Ones

Ignoring "people problems" rarely makes them go away. Addressing performance or interpersonal issues early—with empathy, clarity, and structure—builds trust, saves time, and strengthens team cohesion.

Action Items:

1. **Schedule Quick Check-Ins:** Set aside fifteen to twenty minutes weekly for brief one-on-one touchpoints. Address emerging issues before they grow into conflicts.

2. **Use the SBIA Feedback Model (Situation–Behavior–Impact–Action):** When giving feedback, describe the situation, the behavior you observed, its impact, and suggest the desired action.

3. **Reinforce Accountability:** After addressing a problem, follow up within a week to ensure progress. Recognize improvement to encourage lasting change.

Chapter 14

Holding Your Colleagues Accountable for Destructive Behavior

Natalie Loeb & David B. Sarnoff

Dear Coaches:

> **I am a partner in a law firm, and recently two of my colleagues have been rude, disrespectful and making unreasonable demands on associates and legal professionals, and it impacts the mood and civility of the firm. How should I approach my partners?**
>
> ***—Proactive Peacekeeping Partner***

David: Thank you for your question, which is an ongoing issue in law firms and was particularly poignant during the pandemic and the Great Resignation. In my opinion, your question raises several topics, including organizational culture, accountability, leadership, and civility. However, the central issue appears to be management challenges tied to attorney well-being and their downstream impact on the firm and its stakeholders.

There have been multiple studies conducted on attorney well-being, including the ABA/Hazelden Betty Ford Foundation Study in 2016[1] and the National Task Force Report on Lawyer Well-Being in 2017.[2] These studies surveyed over 10,000 practicing attorneys and clearly demonstrate that the legal profession is fraught with mental health issues. The results indicate that approximately 20% of attorneys qualify as problem drinkers, approximately 28% experience depression, and many deal with anxiety and stress. This research was conducted a few years before the COVID-19 pandemic. In my opinion, these mental health struggles have only been exacerbated by the isolation, loneliness, and stress many experienced during the pandemic that were not significantly addressed when people returned to the office. Your colleagues today are not the same people they were in early 2020. We have all experienced various degrees of trauma during the pandemic and its aftermath, and in one way or another it has changed us.

For some attorneys, trauma manifests itself in a variety of behaviors, including being rude, raising their voice, and being intimidating. These behaviors have a corrosive impact on the people on the receiving end, elevating their stress and anxiety, and it is not healthy to the business and culture of the firm. While coaching can be quite useful in modifying inappropriate behavior, it is only effective if the client is a willing participant. There are times when therapy and counseling are appropriate to provide attorneys with treatment and services. However, mental health issues are still looked upon with a degree of stigmatization that inhibits attorneys from seeking the help and resources available to them.

With respect to your specific question, one tactic may be to have a conversation with each of your partners and share your observations about how their behavior is impacting others at the firm. When individuals raise their self-awareness as to how they show up and are perceived by others, they are then able to lead with empathy and understand the discomfort and pain they may be causing others. Fostering

---

1. Patrick R. Krill, Ryan Johnson & Linda Albert, *The Prevalence of Substance Use and Other Mental Health Concerns Among American Attorneys*, J. of Addiction Med., Vol. 10, No. 1 (Jan.-Feb. 2016): 46-52.
2. National Task Force on Lawyer Well-Being, *The Path to Lawyer Well-Being: Practical Recommendations for Positive Change*, Am. Bar Ass'n Comm'n on Lawyer Assistance Programs et al., Aug. 14, 2017.

behavior that builds high-trust workplaces is also clearly a business imperative. If stakeholders in a firm do not feel that they are valued and respected, they will leave. Especially in a climate where there are opportunities nationally and, in some cases, opportunities to work remotely. The cost of replacing associates can easily run in excess of $40,000 in recruiting fees alone. Then, factor in lost business opportunity to interview, select, and onboard. Replacing non-attorney legal professionals can also cost tens of thousands of dollars. Losing multiple employees because of bad behavior can easily cost the organization hundreds of thousands of dollars. Creating an environment of civility, respect, and direct communication is vital to addressing bad behavior in a firm and must be a firm leadership initiative for it to be impactful and meaningful. Logically, the health and well-being of attorneys helps to nurture the health and well-being of all stakeholders at the firm. If a firm tolerates bad behavior, that may be the first symptom that the firm is an unhealthy one. While poor habits and behavior may be overlooked if an attorney is a generator, they may be actually costing the firm money in attrition. On the flip side, attorneys who excel in mentoring and developing associates and contribute to retention, may not be compensated or recognized for those efforts.

Natalie: This is going to require some courageous leadership on your part. First you have to decide if you are ready to communicate with your two colleagues. Remember, you cannot control others and how they react to you. You can only control your own behaviors and how you communicate and respond to others. So, if you decide that the culture of your firm and the impact of toxic behaviors are unacceptable and misaligned with the values and expectations of behavior at your firm, dig deep, harness the passion that makes you a great lawyer and human being, and use that commitment to plan and open a conversation with your colleagues. It's worth it. The ROI described previously by David is clear here.

Next steps:

1. I recommend you speak to each colleague separately. If handling these types of situations is new to you, start with a one-on-one conversation rather than a group discussion.

2. Choose the person whom you think will respond more favorably. Try to remember a time when you noticed this person behaving in a way that was respectful and admirable, modeled the behaviors that your firm values, created trust, and inspired performance amongst associates rather than crushing their morale and distracting them. Hold onto that example so you can offer it during your discussion.

3. Next, think about what you want to accomplish in your conversation. Do you want to help your colleagues increase self-awareness by pointing out the behavior and hoping they will self-regulate? Or do you want to brainstorm ideas on what to do or how to handle some of the frequent challenges that erupt due to stress? Either way, keep this in mind: **Focus on the person's behavior, *not* the person's personality.** Adding some "benefit of the doubt" is often a useful tool.

4. Lastly, stay mindful of your own behaviors—eye contact, facial expressions, and speed and tone of your voice—as you have this conversation.

The best time to open a dialogue like this is soon after someone has come to you or you have observed an inappropriate behavior yourself. It might go something like this:

> *Partner Name, do you have fifteen minutes? I have an observation that I think is important to share with you because it impacts our firm.*

If your Partner agrees, you're good to go. If not, wait for another opportunity. Assuming you receive a yes, the continuing conversation could sound like:

> *I'm concerned about the mood of our office. Yesterday, three associates approached me with examples of behavior you have demonstrated over the past two weeks that causes them concern and adds confusion about whether or not they are meeting your expectations. Are you open to listening?*

Again, if you receive a yes, be prepared to share specific examples of the concerning behavior. For example:

Two associates notified me that you threw some documents at them [use specific examples if you have permission from the associates to do so] and I noticed you raised your voice using condescending language on our recent Zoom meeting. [Be prepared to share the example of the condescending language.] This seems to have become a pattern over the past two months. We all experience working with high expectations and it can be stressful, so we are concerned. Are you ok?

Or:

This pattern over the past two months is adding additional stress to our associates and impacting morale and performance. We need them to know we value their work and want them to be successful. Are you willing to swap ideas with me on how we can avoid adding extra stress, by being mindful of how we communicate, and maximize their performance by providing the kind of coaching, feedback, and support they need right now to keep them feeling inspired and our clients happy? I've seen you do this before, and I was very impressed. Remember when . . . .

Finally, propose mutual discussion and swapping of ideas.

Thank you for your time. We set the tone as leaders of the firm. It's hard to remember how much our behavior matters, and it's these particularly stressful times that test all of us. I'm confident that if we continue to support each other, we can have a positive impact on our associates, firm, and clients. In fact, I'd like to open this conversation with [Partner name]. What do you think?

One never knows how these conversations will turn out until they are had. And like I said up front, these conversations take courage.

Don't expect perfection from yourself. Congratulate yourself for taking an important action to help build the morale and culture of your firm, which are so necessary to thrive today. After your conversation, self-coach yourself. Ask yourself, 1) What did I do well?, and 2) What will I do differently next time? And hold yourself accountable for that! You can do it! And know that by doing this, not only are you demonstrating courage, you are making an impact on the success and mental health of your associates and colleagues.

Key Takeaways and Action Items

Key Takeaway One

Toxic Partner Behavior Damages Culture, Performance, and Retention

Disrespectful and unreasonable behavior by law firm partners has a ripple effect across the organization—eroding morale, increasing stress, and contributing to turnover among associates and legal professionals. Such behavior, especially when tolerated or ignored, signals a broader issue in firm culture and leadership accountability. It can also carry a significant financial cost in attrition, lost productivity, and reputational damage.

Action Items:

1. **Establish Behavioral Standards:** Clearly define and communicate the firm's expectations for respectful leadership behavior in writing (partner handbook, values statements).
2. **Create Safe Reporting Channels:** Provide associates and staff with confidential ways to raise concerns about toxic behavior without fear of retaliation.
3. **Hold Leaders Accountable:** Incorporate cultural contributions and team leadership into partner evaluations and compensation decisions.

Key Takeaway Two

Addressing Bad Behavior Requires Courageous, Empathetic Leadership

We emphasize the importance of proactive, one-on-one conversations that are timely, specific, and behavior-focused. Rather than attacking character, effective peer-to-peer leadership involves naming observable behaviors, sharing impact, and inviting dialogue. These conversations are difficult—but necessary—to model the tone, civility, and values expected in a high-functioning firm.

Action Items:

1. **Train Partners on Feedback Models:** Provide structured frameworks (e.g., SBIA: Situation, Behavior, Impact, Action) for giving clear, constructive feedback.
2. **Model Direct Communication:** Senior leadership should demonstrate what "naming behavior" and having respectful but candid conversations looks like.
3. **Recognize Positive Change:** Publicly or privately acknowledge when a partner makes visible improvements, reinforcing a culture of growth.

Key Takeaway Three

Mental Health and Well-Being Are Core Leadership Concerns

Many attorneys are still carrying trauma, stress, and mental health challenges exacerbated by the pandemic and demanding work culture. Some bad behaviors may stem from unaddressed well-being issues. Leaders must recognize this dynamic and balance accountability with empathy. Supporting peer wellness, modeling emotional intelligence, and destigmatizing help-seeking behavior are essential for creating a sustainable legal workplace.

Action Items:

1. **Train Leaders to Spot Red Flags:** Provide education on recognizing burnout, compassion fatigue, and behavioral changes that may signal distress.
2. **Promote Resources:** Regularly communicate availability of EAP programs, mental health benefits, coaching, and wellness initiatives.
3. **Balance Accountability with Support:** When addressing toxic behavior, explore whether underlying stress, trauma, or health issues may be contributing factors and offer support as part of the solution.

Chapter 15

Preparing to Welcome Your New Associates? What You Should Know

Natalie Loeb & David B. Sarnoff

Dear Coaches:

> **It's that time of year again, late summer, when my firm and I (the Director of Attorney Training and Development) are getting ready to welcome new associates! Our attorneys have had a hybrid work arrangement since this past spring (and were fully remote before then). Like most firms, we managed to get through the worst of the pandemic, but after what we've seen for the last two-plus years, I believe we could use some help with equipping our new class of associates to work in the hybrid model that includes three days in the office and two days remote . . . and with partners who've been outspoken about their preference for working remotely. What advice do you have for ensuring the new associates thrive and get the most out of learning from partners, both in person and remotely, when they start this fall?**
>
> ***—Working towards Warm Welcomes***

David: Thank you for your question, and I believe this is a topic that many firms are continuing to address. A law firm partner recently shared with me that some of his partner colleagues do not want to return to the office more than a couple days a week. He shared that they feel they can function well working from home, avoid a draining commute, and have more quality time in their personal lives. When the topic of associate development came up, some of the older partners said they have spent many hours developing and training associates over the years, but the associates still leave for other firms and positions, so these partners would rather not devote time to developing new associates. In my opinion, this was troubling to hear. I think it is incumbent upon firms to dedicate resources and encourage partners to welcome new associates, establish relationships, and be a resource for them to tap into for their skill and career development.

I believe many partners forget the daunting feeling of starting a position as a first-year associate, with limited knowledge of the practice of law, not knowing the culture or operation of the firm and being given substantive assignments on various matters. I recall from my time as an associate those assignments creating anxiety and stress, especially if the direction from the partner was not clear, expectations were not established, and the partner was not available for follow-up questions. I often hear from junior associates that when they receive an assignment, they do not understand how that assignment fits into the overall strategy of the case or deal. Additionally, sometimes assignments are delegated from senior associates who, in many cases, do not have formal training in how to effectively communicate and delegate. I believe you would be well served to coach partners and senior associates to provide a frame of reference when they give assignments by explaining with clarity what the assignment is and its purpose in the context of the larger case or deal. This makes the associate feel included and part of the team.

Quite often when an associate receives an assignment, the partner will ask, "do you understand the assignment?" Generally, the associate will respond "yes" even if they don't understand, for fear of being judged. I believe a best practice for eliciting an honest response from the associate is to lead with care and empathy. A partner may be better served to say, "I want to position you for success on this assignment, and in order to confirm we are on the same page, please explain to me in your own words what I am asking you to do." By spending that extra time in the beginning of the process, the partner can confirm if the associate truly understands the assignment or if they need to engage in further discussion. Otherwise, the partner may receive a draft that does not meet expectations and causes frustration for the partner and the associate.

It is important for partners to understand that we are in a hyper-competitive environment to recruit and retain high-caliber associates. I regularly hear partners discuss how difficult it is to recruit new associates after an associate gives notice. That is why it is a business imperative for partners to be aware that when associates do not feel they are being developed, mentored, heard, and valued, they will leave. As soon as new associates start at the firm, partners should be engaging them, establishing relationships and setting clear expectations so the associates understand what they need to do. I believe it is helpful to create in-person opportunities for associates and partners to interact, collaborate, or give and receive feedback. I also believe in the power of proximity; it allows for spontaneity, learning, innovation, and communication. That being said, hybrid work environments will be a part of life for the foreseeable future and clear expectations about how associates can seek guidance, feedback, and mentoring is critical to keeping associates engaged and feeling connected to the firm.

It is also helpful to create peer support for associates when they have questions, are struggling or are stressed. For example, associates in a practice group can meet once or twice a month for breakfast or lunch (in person or remote) to discuss best practices, identify common challenges, and cultivate peer relationships. These group meetings tend to lead to smaller group or one-on-one conversations that encourage collaboration and teamwork.

Good luck.

Natalie: As you are about to enter onboarding season, it is important to recognize that associate engagement in our hybrid world is highly impacted by associate onboarding practices. Why care about engagement? According to a leading global consulting firm, McKinsey & Company, "it is well understood that people who believe their job has meaning and a broader purpose are more likely to work harder, take on challenging or unpopular tasks, and collaborate effectively. Research repeatedly shows that people deliver their best effort and ideas when they feel they are part of something larger than the pursuit of a paycheck."[1] Ultimately, these work habits lead to increased client satisfaction. There is huge opportunity for partners to use the onboarding process to set the stage for increased associate engagement. Missing this opportunity can have severe consequences like low morale, less productivity, and higher attrition down the road.

So, assuming your firm isn't going to recall partners to the office full-time, how do you approach associate onboarding in a hybrid workplace to support your firm's associate engagement goals? Whether or not your firm is measuring employee engagement or not, progressive law firm leaders are very much aware of the importance of strengthening the entire associate experience to maximize their newly acquired talent. The old playbook relying on feedback techniques such as "no news is good news" or wholly financial incentives just doesn't work anymore. Associates want to feel connected to their colleagues and be proud of their firm, its services, and its culture. There are little tricks you can share with your partners to ensure a smooth, effective, and engaging transition into your firm:

1. Identify lawyers in leadership roles who are accountable for successfully onboarding new associates. Assess their interest in and ability to build meaningful relationships with your new associates. Build up those lawyers' emotional intelligence and leverage their willingness to spend time with the new associates and cultivate their growth, career development, and success.

2. Offer your lawyers specific action steps with time frames to ensure a highly engaging onboarding experience at the firm. Be clear on who is responsible for what.

3. Support your lawyers with the "Why" and "How" of offering emotional support to the firm's future revenue generators. "Why" includes helping the partners to understand the expectations of today's associates. This often includes associates wanting more personal relationships or at the very least being valued and "seen." Surprisingly to many, over half of employee

1. McKinsey & Co., *Making Work Meaningful: A Leader's Guide* (Oct. 26, 2018).

engagement is driven by non-financial recognition. "How" includes teaching the partners specific skills for building relationships and offering guidance, feedback, and support.

4. Those responsible for onboarding need to prioritize relationship building, which can be as simple as remembering the associate's name and showing interest in the associate as a human being. This includes learning how to pronounce a name correctly if it is an unfamiliar name to the partner. Over and over, we hear from associates how powerful it feels when a partner "notices" them. Using their name, along with showing interest in and remembering small facts about their interests both inside and outside of work, will accelerate the building of authentic relationships; a great start to growing employee engagement in today's hybrid environment.

Remember, talent flows to where it's valued.

Key Takeaways and Action Items

Key Takeaway One

Onboarding in a Hybrid World Must Be Intentional, Structured, and Relationship-Driven

The hybrid work model demands that firms rethink how they onboard new associates. Passive approaches no longer work—firms must provide structure, assign responsibility, and create intentional opportunities (both in person and remote) to build relationships, provide feedback, and set clear expectations. Without this, new associates may feel disconnected and under-supported.

Action Items:

1. **Design a Formal Onboarding Plan:** Map out the first thirty, sixty, and ninety days with clear milestones, learning objectives, and points of contact.
2. **Create Structured Touchpoints:** Schedule regular check-ins with partners, mentors, and professional development staff—both virtually and in-person.
3. **Provide Early Feedback:** Offer quick, actionable feedback within the first few weeks to reinforce expectations and build confidence.

Key Takeaway Two

Associate Engagement Is Tied to Recognition, Purpose, and Connection—Not Just Compensation

Today's associates want to feel seen, valued, and included. Engagement is driven largely by meaningful relationships, non-financial recognition, and feeling like part of something bigger than themselves. Partners play a critical role in this by showing interest, using associates' names, and making time for informal interactions that reinforce connection and belonging.

Action Items:

1. **Model Inclusive Behavior:** Partners should learn and regularly use associates' names, ask for input, and acknowledge contributions in meetings.
2. **Communicate the "Why":** Connect assignments to the broader client matter or firm strategy so associates see the bigger picture.
3. **Create Opportunities for Growth:** Involve associates in client meetings, strategy sessions, or pro bono matters to deepen purpose and engagement.

Key Takeaway Three

Partners Need Support and Accountability to Lead in the Hybrid Era

Many partners are either reluctant or unsure how to engage meaningfully with new associates in a hybrid model. Firms should provide clear guidance, timelines, coaching, and emotional intelligence training to help partners mentor effectively. Identifying and equipping the right people to lead onboarding is crucial for associate development, morale, and retention.

Action Items:

1. **Provide Clear Guidelines:** Offer partners a checklist or playbook outlining expectations for associate onboarding, mentorship, and engagement.
2. **Set Measurable Goals:** Incorporate mentorship and associate development into partner evaluations and compensation metrics.
3. **Gather and Share Data:** Track associate satisfaction, retention, and performance indicators to show the impact of effective onboarding.

Chapter 16

Is There Only One Lane on the Road to Partnership?

Natalie Loeb & David B. Sarnoff

Dear Coaches:

> **An attorney at my firm wants to be a shareholder, but he hasn't brought in any clients. He tries hard by networking, but just doesn't seem to reap any fruits from his efforts. What makes an attorney shareholder or partner material?**
>
> ***—Partner in the Making***

David: Thank you for your question. In my opinion, your question is timely, and it's important to ask, "What qualities should a law firm partner and 'leader' possess?" Historically, associates who were high performers, consistently top billers, and connected to influential partners were promoted to a partner position. However, these newly promoted partners, more likely than not, received little to no management and leadership training on how to drive performance through others. Their points of reference were more senior partners who, likewise, weren't formally trained in leadership and management skills, and modeled the leadership practices they learned but not necessarily best practices. In many cases, the leadership style attorneys experienced was based on instilling fear and intimidation.

While there are certainly partners who have not been formally trained who are still effective leaders, by and large, many are not.

I say this because of my involvement in coaching experienced partners, newly promoted partners, and associates who provide substantive feedback to me that they do not possess or observe effective leadership practices. Historically, partner candidates who have established client relationships and a portable or growing book of business receive preferential consideration for promotion to partner. However, while revenue generators are extremely important to the business of the firm, these partners are not the only partner candidates who add significant value to the firm. Partners who can also be effective leaders—who can motivate, inspire, mentor and develop associates, and build a shared mission culture—add significant contributions to the firm's culture and climate, as well as its balance sheet.

While there are exceptions, law firms give the highest level of reward to partners who generate revenue. Rainmakers or high-revenue generators are vitally important to the sustainability and growth of law firms. However, in many cases, rainmakers are not held to the same standards of acceptable behavior that others in the firm are. They may not be held accountable for being rude and disrespectful or exhibiting bullying and intimidating behavior. These partners sometimes model poor behavior for their teams and subordinates who, in some cases, model the same inappropriate behavior.

I have observed, more so now than in the past, that tolerating bad behavior may cost the firm more in attrition and liability than separating from an individual rainmaker. As millennials and Gen Z continue to fill the ranks of new leaders and associate roles, there is less tolerance for partners who assert power and control and a preference for those who practice high-level leadership skills: leadership that makes people feel valued, mentored, developed, and respected. As a Gen Xer, I tolerated abusive conduct and bad behavior early in my career. However, Millennials and Gen Zers advocate for themselves, and they will leave, even without a job offer, if they are treated poorly. I recently co-facilitated a workshop at a partners retreat for a mid-size law firm. The managing partner said, "When we lose a high performing mid-level or senior associate, it costs the firm between $250,000 and $500,000 in recruiting fees, hours of interviewing, onboarding and lost business opportunity while filling the position." This cost is for each associate, which could add up to millions of dollars in lost profit.

Although still a relatively small percentage, more firms are starting to financially incentivize partners who are effective leaders who demonstrate skills in motivating, inspiring, developing, and mentoring associates and other stakeholders at the firm. Partners who model the behavior they expect of others and hold themselves and others accountable help create a culture where associates feel emotionally anchored to the firm. This typically results in associates extending their employee lifecycle at the firm, reducing attrition, raising associate satisfaction, increasing productivity, and contributing to a shared mission culture.

To directly answer your question, attorneys who are not effective revenue generators can still make a case for being elevated to partnership. Attorneys who are high-performing, as well as demonstrating strong leadership skills, building high-trust relationships, and developing the practical and professional skills of junior attorneys, strengthen the business and mission of the firm. Attorneys who possess these qualities, in my opinion, are as important as the partners who bring in clients. Partners who reduce attrition and inspire associates contribute significantly to the bottom line and culture of the firm.

Natalie: My colleague David makes a strong case for elevating attorneys to shareholder if they can contribute to the firm in ways other than bringing in business. When considering what makes a shareholder partner material, there certainly are a few ways to look at it. I asked my colleague Marc Friedman, a career strategist and executive coach, for his thoughts on this matter. In addition to his forty-five-year law practice, including as a law firm Managing Partner and Practice Leader, Marc provides coaching and strategic counseling to a wide range of people in positions of influence to help them achieve their potential. Marc told me,

> An attorney typically qualifies to be a partner or shareholder by satisfying quantitative and qualitative criteria. The quantitative criteria include their record of profitability that will be a function of revenue per lawyer for them and their associates, and, possibly though not necessarily, originations. Some firms don't emphasize originations. The qualitative criteria include lawyer excellence, teaming ability, client satisfaction, mentoring and training, and overall good firm citizenship.

All businesses always need to keep their eye on the state of their business. Having owners with the ability to grow business adds confidence and certainty to the sustainability of the firm.

I'm wondering about the clarity of shareholder expectations at your firm. Is bringing in a certain amount of business expected at the shareholder level? Are your attorneys aware of it? And if so, to what extent do the associates learn how to develop business and at what stage of their careers? Business development skills can be taught, nurtured, and grown. There are many business development consultants with deep expertise on how to help lawyers grow a book of business.

According to Deborah B. Farone, author of *Best Practices in Law Firm Business Development and Marketing,*[1] too often, lawyers fall into the trap of committing random acts of marketing—sporadic posts, scattered sponsorships, and last-minute event appearances that, while well-intentioned, lack cohesion or lasting impact. Instead, lawyers should take the time to define their "inch"—a focused area of strength and passion that sets them apart from others. This could be a specific industry, type of client, or legal issue they genuinely enjoy and excel at. Once identified, this inch becomes the foundation for a strategic, sustainable plan. Working in tandem with their marketing department, they should build a roadmap that includes SMART goals—Specific, Measurable, Achievable, Relevant, and Time-bound objectives—to ensure that every effort aligns with a broader vision and delivers meaningful results.

Like business development skills, leadership skills can also be taught, nurtured, and grown. Adding shareholders with these types of skills and providing the growth opportunities your talented lawyers need to develop will certainly help the overall growth, recruitment, retention, and organizational health[2] of your firm.

Sometimes a talented lawyer does not favor business development. In that case, our clients often wonder if this lawyer can still contribute to the sustainability and growth of the firm in other ways—leading and

---

1. Deborah B. Farone, Best Practices in Law Firm Business Development and Marketing (PLI 2019).
2. Organizational health refers to a company's ability to function effectively, adapt swiftly to change, and maintain a high level of performance over time. It's about having a workplace that promotes well-being, sustainable growth, and resilience.

mentoring others? Overseeing pro bono efforts? Modeling an inclusive culture? Identifying and recruiting top talent?

Whether it be leadership or business development, today's legal workplaces consistently have new challenges. One of the most notable challenges in all businesses is how fragile communication can be. Communication styles vary amongst all of us. A popular way to describe this is offered through the Myers-Briggs Type Indicator.[3] Some of us lean toward a preference for extroversion (generally, people who prefer to direct their energy outwards—to people, things, situations), while others lean toward a preference for introversion (people who prefer to direct their energy inwards—to ideas, information, beliefs). Extroverts are action-oriented, while introverts are thought-oriented. Understanding one's own preference is the beginning for building effective relationships and determining a proclivity for leading others or building businesses. No matter which preference a lawyer has, the lawyer has to be skilled at reading their audience and adapting their behavior to gain the results they are looking to achieve. In the work of leadership coaching, we know that increased self-awareness with a willingness to adapt behaviors based on the needs of clients or staff members can help lawyers achieve the results they desire.

In short, how do you know if your attorney is shareholder or partner material? On a scale of 1–10, 1 being low and 10 being high, how willing is this attorney to increase self-awareness? How willing is this attorney to learn new skills? How willing is this attorney to adapt? If this attorney scores 8 or higher on this scale, with solid specific examples from the past to prove that score, there is a good chance this attorney can be shareholder/partner material. Whether the success of this shareholder/partner requires leadership skills or business development, clear expectations, along with the firm offering support to strengthen or grow the required skills, will set this new shareholder/partner up for success.

---

3. *See* Myers & Briggs Found., https://www.myersbriggs.org/.

Key Takeaways and Action Items

Key Takeaway One

Partnership Criteria Must Evolve Beyond *Just* Business Origination

Traditionally, partnership has been closely tied to bringing in clients and generating revenue. While these remain important, today's law firms increasingly recognize that leadership, mentorship, and cultural contributions are equally vital for long-term success and retention.

Action Items:

1. **Audit and Update Criteria:** Review partnership criteria to ensure they explicitly value leadership, mentorship, and cultural contributions in addition to business origination.
2. **Communicate Expectations:** Clearly articulate these expanded criteria in promotion materials, town halls, and partner-track conversations so associates understand what is rewarded.
3. **Highlight Role Models:** Share stories or profiles of non-originating partners who advanced due to their leadership, mentoring, and positive impact on firm culture.

Key Takeaway Two

Leadership and Business Development Are Learnable Skills

Not all attorneys are natural rainmakers or leaders, but both sets of skills can be cultivated. A firm that invests in building these competencies not only supports attorney growth but strengthens its talent pipeline and organizational health.

Action Items:

1. **Create Individualized Learning Plans:** Design tailored development plans that include leadership coaching and business development training for high-potential attorneys.

2. **Provide Support and Guidance:** Pair attorneys with mentors, coaches, or consultants to help them identify focus areas and build confidence.

3. **Set SMART Goals:** Establish specific, measurable, achievable, relevant, and time-bound goals to track progress and celebrate growth milestones.

Key Takeaway Three

Willingness to Grow Is a Key Predictor of Future Success

An attorney's openness to self-awareness, learning, and behavior change is often a better indicator of partnership potential than current metrics alone. Growth mindset, adaptability, and emotional intelligence signal long-term value.

Action Items:

1. **Assess Growth Mindset:** Integrate tools like 360 feedback, DiSC, or EQ-i 2.0® into the partnership consideration process to evaluate openness to learning and adaptability.

2. **Initiate Developmental Conversations:** Use assessment results to guide candid discussions about strengths, blind spots, and growth opportunities.

3. **Provide Skill-Building Opportunities:** Offer structured programs, coaching, and leadership development experiences to help candidates strengthen emotional intelligence and leadership capacity.

Chapter 17

Stretched Thin As Summer Associate Season Begins?

Natalie Loeb & David B. Sarnoff

Dear Coaches:

> **Our summer associate program started this month and I'm expected to help with mentoring and overseeing their work. We have fewer summer associates than in previous years, and this isn't my first experience with onboarding and managing summer associates (or full-time associates), but the difference this year is that the firm has fewer attorneys and staff to help manage summer associates because of recent cuts. With more work and competing demands to juggle this summer, what managerial skills should I prioritize and focus on improving when working with the summer associates? What managerial traps should I keep an eye out for?**

—Multitasking Mentor

David: Thank you for sharing your questions. You are not alone in facing challenging circumstances in welcoming the summer associate class. In recent years, law firms experienced an overall increase in revenue and profitability in spite of the fears that the COVID-19 pandemic instigated. However, in the first half of 2023, many law firms across the country, including Am Law 100 and 200 firms, announced layoffs, deferred first-year associate classes, and decreased numbers in hiring. This created a difficult environment in which to recruit and integrate summer associates with the intention of offering them first-year associate positions upon graduation. It is important to be mindful that the business decisions the firm is making during stressful economic times are being watched by the marketplace and, in particular, by employees and potential employees. It is worth emphasizing that firm leadership should factor in how business decisions are received and perceived by the audience they are trying to attract. As the saying goes, "you don't get a second chance to make a first impression."

As you describe the dynamic of having fewer attorneys to manage the summer associates and increased work responsibilities, you should think about *what behaviors you and your team are modeling for the summer associate class.* Does it make more sense to have fewer summer associate events but ones that are more impactful, instead of planning several events that may seem rushed, impersonal, not well attended, and performative? It may be better to have a smaller event with genuine interaction with partners and associates than scheduling another Broadway show or baseball game that has limited personal interaction.

Another question I have is how will summer associates receive assignments and who will be assigned to provide guidance and support? Think back to when you may have been a summer associate and the anxiety, excitement, unknown, and newness you experienced. If summer associates receive substantive assignments that give them a flavor of what the actual associate experience looks like, they should have assigned attorneys to answer questions and provide direction. They will be more productive and engaged with support than if they're delegated assignments with little guidance and expected to figure it out on their own. While the latter may have worked in prior generations, it is not so effective with Gen Z and young Millennials. More on generational differences later.

Another managerial skill that will benefit you with leading summer associates is to create an inclusive environment and set expectations early in the summer associate session. You and your team should be direct and specific as to what the firm expects with respect to being physically in the office and working remotely. Also, confirm expectations that summer associates may be called upon in certain situations to work longer hours to help serve client needs, and communicate the professionalism and behavior that is expected of summer associates.

Additionally, setting expectations as to quality of work product is helpful—relay that the summer associates will receive direct feedback, not as a punishment, but to support their growth and development to elevate their skills with the goal of practicing law at a higher caliber. They should receive the feedback with a growth mindset, understanding that they are not expected to get it perfectly at this stage but to learn and incorporate the feedback into future assignments. It is also important to be mindful as to which of your colleagues will spend the most time with summer associates and whether they have the EQ and social skills to put the firm in its best light. You are not only trying to persuade the summer associate to want to accept an offer at your firm; you also want them to go back to law school and share with their classmates that they had a highly positive experience at the firm.

It is also significant to consult with inclusion professionals at your firm to create an inclusive culture with teambuilding exercises that the summer associates will participate in. Tapping back into the generational themes, Gen Z and young Millennials are broadly tuned into training and programming and in many cases read the values and mission statements on firm websites, and they take note of the answers to questions they may have posed during on-campus interviewing. If the experience they have does not align with the expectations set by the firm, this will generally have a negative impact on the summer associate experience for these law students.

In summary, you have a difficult task ahead to manage a summer associate program in the conditions you are faced with. Your priorities should be set on providing an inclusive culture that builds trust among colleagues, assigning meaningful work, and providing mentoring and direct feedback as well as thoughtfully planned and interactive social events. Good luck.

Natalie: David has offered excellent advice already in his response. You may have already noticed how some of the behaviors he is suggesting are designed to set you up for success as a manager, such as:

- assigning attorneys to answer questions and provide direction;
- being direct and specific as to what the firm expects; and
- providing feedback with a growth mindset.

In addition to being a good manager this summer, you can differentiate yourself by being a good *leader*. I love how David not only offered guidance on being a good manager but also snuck in some excellent advice about being a good leader. David also enumerated the behaviors required for you to demonstrate exemplary leadership during this time, including:

- thinking about what behaviors you and your team are modeling for the summer associate class;
- taking ownership of the fact that you also want them to go back to law school and share with their classmates that they had a highly positive experience at the firm; and
- providing a collaborative culture that builds trust among colleagues.

Here's why I want to differentiate the discussion around "management" and "leadership." They are two different sets of skills. Good managers keep their eyes on the bottom line, getting the high-quality work out the door; leaders keep their eyes on the horizon, paying attention to the work culture, morale, and emotional needs of others in order to engage those around them to willingly give their best efforts. Lawyers who understand the difference have more choices on how to intentionally behave and a better chance of providing a summer associate experience where the summer associates feel highly engaged, motivated, and inspired. If your associates leave your firm feeling this way, there is a much higher chance they will accept any impending offers, and at the very least they will reinforce the reputation of your firm as being a fulfilling and supportive place to work, giving you the competitive advantage of attracting great talent in the future.

In our practice, we use the research provided in a book called *The Leadership Challenge* by Jim Kouzes and Barry Posner.[1] These professors, researchers, and thought leaders have studied leadership for over thirty-five years. From their research, they created a definition of leadership worth mulling over: *"Mobilizing others to want to struggle for shared aspirations."* As you can see from the definition, it's not easy. In

1. James M. Kouzes & Barry Z. Posner, The Leadership Challenge: How to Make *Extraordinary* Things Happen in Organizations (6th ed. 2017).

fact, it's a challenge. However, it's not impossible, it is very doable, *if* a leader knows how to behave. Five practices of exemplary leadership with thirty behaviors of leadership are outlined in their most recent edition of the book.

When working with leaders, one of the strategies I like to suggest for demonstrating leadership is to remind the leader of what their constituents are looking for from them. This is going to sound like common sense. However, repeatedly, particularly with our legal clients, we find it is not common practice. So, in the spirit of wanting to help you model the behaviors of an exemplary leader for summer associates who are with you for a short period of time—with the goal of leaving them with a positive impression of your firm and an eagerness to join you if you make them an offer—here is another suggestion I learned from Jim and Barry to add to David's advice.

A large body of research confirms most people want to know:

- Who are you? (professionally and personally)
- What are you going to do?
- Where are we headed and how are you going to take us there?

Yes, it's that simple. Look for opportunities to share the answers to these three questions as often as possible to as many summer associates as possible throughout the summer associate experience.

- Your summer associates want to know who YOU are. Share a bit about your background with them, both professionally and personally.
- They want to know what you are going to do. Let them know how you can help them grow and develop and become the best lawyers they can be, during this summer and in the future.
- They want to know the direction and culture of the firm and how you and firm leadership will get there. What's the plan? What makes your firm unique? How do they fit in? And what are the potential opportunities they can expect if they receive and accept an offer from the firm?

Creating conversations which address these three simple questions will create memorable and impactful moments for your summer associates. They will remember you. They will admire and respect you. And most importantly, having these types of conversations in a thoughtful and genuine manner will inspire them to want to join your firm and offer the highest and best use of their talents.

It seems simple in theory but not so easy in practice, and many find this is more of a challenge than a cakewalk. Maybe this is why Jim and Barry's book is titled *The Leadership* ***Challenge***. However, it appears from your question that you are up for the challenge. Wishing you much success.

Key Takeaways and Action Items

Key Takeaway One

Balance Efficiency with Meaningful Engagement

With limited time and resources, it's essential to prioritize quality over quantity—especially in interactions with summer associates. Rushed or performative events won't leave a lasting impression. What will resonate are authentic connections, thoughtful feedback, and meaningful assignments.

Action Items:

1. **Prioritize Quality Interactions:** Plan fewer events but make them more intimate and meaningful—favor small-group lunches, shadowing opportunities, or one-on-one conversations over large, impersonal gatherings.

2. **Design Purposeful Assignments:** Give summer associates work that is substantive, developmental, and aligned with their interests to showcase the firm's commitment to their growth.

3. **Provide Thoughtful Feedback:** Build in time to deliver constructive, timely feedback that helps them learn, feel supported, and see a path for improvement.

Key Takeaway Two

Set Clear Expectations and Provide Guidance Early

Summer associates need clarity on work expectations, communication protocols, and firm norms—especially in a hybrid or resource-constrained environment. They perform better and feel more confident when given structure, direction, and feedback framed for growth.

Action Items:

Kick off the program with a brief orientation or check-in that includes:

1. Firm expectations (in-office time, professionalism, hours)
2. Assignment logistics (who to ask for help)
3. Feedback philosophy (growth mindset)

Then assign clear attorney contacts for guidance and mentorship throughout the summer.

Key Takeaway Three

Lead, Don't Just Manage

Beyond overseeing tasks, standout lawyers also model leadership by building trust, creating inclusive environments, and helping others understand the firm's mission and values. Summer associates want to feel inspired by your leadership and see how they fit into the firm's future.

Action Items:

Embrace your role as both manager and leader. Use the three guiding questions from *The Leadership Challenge*:

1. Who are you? (Share your story.)
2. What are you going to do? (How will you support their growth?)
3. Where are we headed? (What's the firm's direction and how do they fit in?)

Addressing these will help associates feel connected and motivated to contribute—and to return.

Chapter 18

Get SMART with Achieving Career Goals

Natalie Loeb & David B. Sarnoff

Dear Coaches:

> **I'm a mid-level associate, and so far in my career I've never started a new year with a plan or set of goals for developing my practice and work pursuits, in part because I'm unsure what I should be mindful of at this stage. My firm has a career management program to help prompt attorneys to develop goals—like mentorship/leadership development and business development. I'm considering joining the initiative but have heard mixed reviews from colleagues and don't know if it will be worth my time. Do you think I should join, or should I plan on my own?**
>
> ***—At the Helm of My Career***

David: First, I would like to congratulate you for taking the initiative of engaging in goal setting and career development as an associate. Far too often, attorneys wait until they are later in their careers to focus on business development, and they find they are behind the curve. I would also like to congratulate your firm for having a career management program, even if some of your colleagues report it may not be ideal. Many firms do not have any formal mentorship programs or career and business development training and associates are expected to just figure it out without guidance or strategies while navigating a full workload of billable hours.

Creating a career plan and setting goals for your own professional development is an important step, to work on improving your skill-set, building the foundation for business development and cultivating substantive professional relationships with colleagues and clients. The decision of whether to join your firm's career management program requires careful consideration of whether you should embark on this journey or undertake your own initiative. As a first step, you may want to do some due diligence on the people who lead the program, their work experience, and how long they have been doing training and development. Also, seeking *substantive* feedback from prior participants is helpful to learn what value they found in the program or where it may be lacking. Detailed feedback is preferable to hearing "mixed reviews."

Firstly, let's discuss the advantages of participating in your firm's career management program. One of the benefits is that it is already established, and it probably has a curriculum, case studies, and training in the areas you outlined. It also may provide an opportunity to advance your internal networks and strengthen relationships with colleagues, some of whom you may not have met yet. The mentorship and leadership development components can be valuable, as they connect you with experienced partners and advisors who can offer insights and guidance based on their own career journeys.

Additionally, being part of a firm-wide initiative can raise your visibility and profile within the firm. Engaging in career development programs demonstrates your commitment to personal and professional growth, which can be noticed by both peers and partners. This increased visibility may help create opportunities for collaboration, mentorship, and higher-level assignments.

Business development is another key aspect that such programs often focus on. Acquiring skills in this area is vital for career progression, as it contributes not only to your personal success but also to your ability to contribute to the overall success of the firm. Learning from experienced professionals and participating in networking opportunities facilitated by the program can boost your ability to attract and retain clients. However, I will caution that business development, in my opinion, is more art than science and there is no one-size-fits-all approach. A formula that may work for one attorney may not work for another because of a variety of factors including whether one is more extroverted or introverted, or whether someone is comfortable in larger social settings or prefers smaller groups or one-to-one interactions. Attorneys also use different practices and strategies when it comes to pitching for business or directly asking for it.

Please keep in mind, the effectiveness of career management programs varies based on individual experiences. Some may find immense value in the guidance and resources provided, while others may feel that the program does not align with their specific needs, interests, or goals.

Alternatively, let's consider planning your own development program. This approach allows for a more personalized strategy; however, it may lack the structure and institutional knowledge of a firm-sponsored program. While creating your own career development plan gives you flexibility, it is important to seek objective feedback in order to have perspective on where you may need to focus on growth and development. Planning independently also enables you to customize goals that align with your vision for career progression. However, I must emphasize that overseeing your personal plan requires effective time management skills and the ability to hold yourself accountable to schedule meetings and attend in-person events, seminars and webinars, etc. You may want to consider inviting a trusted friend or colleague to be an accountability partner and check in with you to ensure you are complying with your plan. You should also consider retaining a mentor or trusted advisor who can provide direct feedback as well as share knowledge and experience.

In making your decision, you should honestly assess your preferred learning and development style. If you thrive in structured environments with clear guidelines and support systems, the firm's program may be the right fit. Alternatively, if you prefer a more personalized and self-directed approach, planning on your own might be more suitable.

At the end of the day, whether you join the firm program or create your own plan, you are going to learn new skills and practices that will enhance your lawyering skills and increase your ability to approach and connect with colleagues and potential clients. In my experience, being authentically curious about people and wanting to learn about their stories and journeys will give you a significant advantage over the people who try to do the pressure sell. I wish you luck in your endeavors.

Natalie: The first thing that comes to mind for me when I read your question is "small steps." You need to consider what kind of steps you want to take. Your firm's internal career program will have programming laid out for you. Taking small steps on your own will require diligence and commitment on your part. There are pros and cons to both approaches; however, as David said, just the act of placing mental energy towards considering your career progression is a great first step. If we don't control the events in our lives, the events in our lives will control us. Without some intention and thought to your career it will not end up where you want to be. Never leave your career in someone else's hands. You must own your own career and decide how you want it to progress. This way you can be sure you will be successful and the creator of your own destiny. That may sound overwhelming—but it doesn't have to be. Depending on where you are in your career and your current level of satisfaction, *you* can decide how much time and energy you want to dedicate to elevating your career.

In your question, you reference an in-house program. And like David, I commend your firm for investing in that type of programming for its associates. Being a bit skeptical of the programming is normal, especially for lawyers. However, I like David's advice of getting some specifics about what the programming looks like and how it is delivered from someone who has experienced it, if possible. I will say one thing that I have learned for sure over my thirty-year career in learning and development: Participants get out of the programming what they put into it. Don't expect to magically absorb and benefit from the programming delivered at your firm. For instance, you may be expected to complete assignments and meet with people. If you don't take that seriously or complete that work, you can bet it will feel like the programming wasn't worth your time. However, if you find yourself prioritizing the assignments and engaging in the content, I am sure you will also reap the benefits.

As the Chief Operating Officer at Fredrikson & Byron, P.A, Ann Rainhart has experience with lawyer leadership development programs. Ann shared these thoughts:

> I commend any firm for investing in the careers of its lawyers, it shows that the firm is focused on the future of the firm and in the future of its talent. As a former Chief Talent Officer and now law firm COO, I have always cared about helping law firms and lawyers find the best way to support the career paths of talent within the firm. Having developed and led several leadership programs and now having the benefit of seeing the long-term trajectory of the lawyers who participated in these firm sponsored programs, I see clearly that those who jumped in and participated reaped many benefits. Every single person who dove in, even with skepticism at the beginning, is now in a significant leadership role in their firm, playing a key role in business generation and/or leading a strong team. Some lawyers decided to depart law firm life after the program and have gone on to other fulfilling steps in their career. Bottom line—if the firm is offering you investment in your career, they are about your career.

As David mentioned, your other option is to consider managing your career on your own; another good decision, as long as you give it some thought and commit to the activities necessary to continue to grow and find opportunities. One of the tools we give to leaders that want to commit to action is to set a goal and make it SMART. I can tell you with certainty that without a goal, there is a very high chance you won't reach it. I can also tell you this: When goals are written and visible there is a much higher chance of them being achieved.

When you take on your own career development, you can also decide what goal you want to set first for yourself. SMART goals provide a roadmap for you to heighten the chance of achieving your goal. The idea behind SMART goals is to articulate the goal in a way that will make you highly likely to achieve it. A SMART goal follows the criteria below:

> **Specific:** What will you achieve? What will you do?
>
> **Measurable:** What data will you use to decide whether you've met the goal?
>
> **Achievable:** Are you sure you can do this? Do you have the right skills and resources?

Relevant: Does the goal align with your career development plans? How will the result matter?

Time-bound: What is the deadline for accomplishing the goal?

For example, let's say you set a career development goal for yourself to "Find a mentor." Leaving your goal as "Finding a mentor" is vague and leaves room for the goal to take a very long time or to happen when it happens. If instead you choose to make this a SMART goal, it would look something like this:

Specific: I want to find someone who has experience or expertise in my field who I will feel comfortable with and is willing to give me some time on a regular basis to answer questions and be a sounding board for me.

Measurable: This goal will be achieved when I have identified a minimum of two people who I can ask to be my mentor.

Achievable: This is achievable. I can look through my contacts and speak to trusted colleagues and friends to gain advice on who may be a good mentor for me.

Relevant: Yes, this goal is realistic and aligns with my career development plan, and the results will matter and make a difference.

Time-bound: I'd like to identify this person or find someone to ask to be my mentor within the next three months.

Making this goal SMART gives you concrete steps you can take to reach this goal. With clarity like this around a goal, there is a much better chance you will be diligent and move forward.

What action steps do you see in this goal? You may notice items such as:

1. *Speak* to trusted colleagues and friends to gain advice on who may be a good mentor to me.
2. *Look through* my contacts to see if there is someone who I may like to approach to be my mentor at this moment in my career.
3. *Identify* a minimum of two people who I can ask to be my mentor.

With some small steps identified, you can now choose *when* you want to take those actions. Remember, your goal is time-based and has a deadline. In this case, you gave yourself three months. Keep that in mind and hold yourself accountable to the SMART goal *you* set for yourself as you attack this goal. With this type of self-diligence, there is a very high chance you will achieve this important career development goal for yourself.

As David said earlier, it is very admirable that your firm is offering career development programming. After doing your research, if you find it will be a good use of your time, it is likely the programming will give you a lot of information and a lot to consider and think about. Spending time to build your own career is always a worthwhile venture.

If you choose to not participate or do not work for a firm that offers in-house career development programming, another option is to be diligent and take some time to identify career goals for yourself. If that is the case, I hope you will find the SMART goal model helpful to you. Making vague goals SMART will help to minimize any feeling of being overwhelmed and instead will give you manageable steps and deadlines to help you see a clear path forward.

Key Takeaways and Action Items

Key Takeaway One

Taking Ownership of Your Career Is Essential—Structure Helps

Whether through a firm program or a self-directed plan, intentional career development is critical. Without a roadmap, career growth is often reactive and less satisfying. Structured programs provide built-in support and visibility, while self-planning offers customization and flexibility.

Action Items:

1. **Choose Your Development Approach:** Decide whether you prefer a structured firm program or a self-directed plan that you manage independently.
2. **Leverage Available Resources:** If you opt for a structured program, speak with past participants, review the curriculum, and clarify expectations.
3. **Create a Personal Roadmap:** For a self-directed approach, build your plan using SMART goals and schedule regular check-ins to stay accountable and measure progress.

Key Takeaway Two

Participation Drives Value—Programs Are What You Make of Them

Career programs are not magic bullets. The value you gain depends on how much effort you put in. Those who engage actively (complete assignments, build relationships, reflect on feedback) are more likely to reap long-term benefits in leadership, business development, and visibility.

Action Items:

1. **Commit Fully:** Approach the program with intention by actively participating in all assignments, discussions, and networking opportunities.
2. **Schedule Engagement:** Block dedicated time on your calendar for program tasks, reflection, and relationship-building activities.
3. **Capture and Apply Learnings:** Track your progress and journal key insights to reinforce learning and translate them into daily practice.

Key Takeaway Three

SMART Goals Turn Ambition into Action

Vague aspirations rarely lead to measurable outcomes. Setting clear, actionable, and time-bound goals increases accountability, reduces overwhelm, and gives you a concrete plan to follow—whether you're in a formal program or not.

Action Items:

1. **Define Your Goals:** Write down one to three specific career development objectives and convert them into SMART (Specific, Measurable, Achievable, Relevant, Time-bound) format.
2. **Break Goals into Steps:** Divide each goal into smaller weekly or biweekly actions to make progress manageable and consistent.
3. **Build Accountability:** Partner with a colleague, mentor, or coach to review progress regularly and adjust as needed.

Chapter 19

Feedback Matters: Creating a Two-Way Street

Natalie Loeb & David B. Sarnoff

Dear Coaches:

> **I'm on the professional development team at my firm, and we're about to start annual performance reviews. While partners and supervisors will be giving feedback to their direct reports, we don't have a system for associates, senior associates, and support staff to evaluate their supervisors and partners. Our partners usually don't ask for input from their direct reports, and direct reports might not feel comfortable being honest without a formal process. I think everyone benefits from feedback, so what do you suggest, and how do we get partners to seek out, listen to, *and* act on feedback?**
>
> ***—Feedback Facilitator Seeking Feedback***

Natalie: You have tapped into one of the most important subjects for building a healthy, high-performing culture at a law firm: Feedback! Over thirty years of experience in the leadership development field have taught me that *feedback is a gift*. In fact, when I prepare a 360-degree feedback[1] report for a leader and can present it in person, I often place the feedback summary in a file folder and wrap it with a ribbon with a large bow. I say to my client, "*This is the best gift you will ever get as a leader. It is a non-judgmental, objective summary of how you are seen as a leader by your direct reports, peers and 'boss(es).'*" Ken Blanchard, author of the *One Minute Manager* and other books on management, is known for saying, "Feedback is the breakfast of champions." In my experience, feedback is a tool to help us grow, develop, and move confidently in the direction of success.

So why is it so hard for many to give feedback and for others to receive feedback? We must take this into account as we prepare to curate a process for building or enhancing a feedback loop.

What gets in the way?

1. **Feedback often gets framed as criticism and therefore feels like a personal attack.**

   Instead, how about thinking of feedback as "information"? It is information that can help someone to be a better lawyer, a better leader, and overall a better person. Wouldn't any of us want to know of something that can help us be better?

2. **Feedback can sting.**

   It's a normal human response to feel an emotional reaction to feedback. Our reactions are greatly influenced by the feedback we've accumulated throughout our lives; however, my cumulative experience has shown me that we can expect what I call the SARA response to feedback. SARA stands for "Shock, Anger, Reflection, Action." When the SARA response is shared up front with someone, it can often defuse an emotional reaction. Like many continuums, some folks start at the beginning and some start somewhere in the middle. Wherever one starts,

---

1. During a 360 process, a leadership coach will interview six to eight stakeholders to gather relevant leadership data about the coachee. The coach will then deliver the feedback and debrief with the coachee in the spirit of growth and development. All interviews are considered confidential, and the coach will maintain the anonymity of the people invited to provide feedback.

it's important to muddle through to the end. Action. This is what feedback is intended to do. Get us to take some sort of positive action.

3. **Many don't realize that feedback can be positive too.**

   More often than not, I find that people assume that all feedback means that something needs to change or be redirected. How about positive feedback? Noticing when someone is doing something right! It is so powerful to notice others doing something well and deserving of hearing about it. That feedback is usually well-appreciated and helps to confirm that the positive behavior is continued. A win-win management technique. Ken Blanchard also likes to say, "Catch people doing something right."

All of the cons listed above happen over and over again. However, it doesn't mean one can't intentionally stop the cycle and instead reframe feedback to initiate a positive pattern.

A feedback culture can take time to build. After taking in all of what is written here, it makes sense that giving and receiving feedback can be difficult. Especially for partners who have already been so successful in their careers. Why would someone who has a senior role at a firm need or want feedback? They usually don't. This is why it is so important to educate people in your firm about the benefits of feedback and look for senior members of the firm who are likeminded and will champion a process for elevating a feedback culture.

Is there anyone at your firm who would be willing to lead by example and perhaps seek some feedback from a few other partners? Perhaps this is someone who may be leading an internal firm committee. Perhaps this partner is interested in receiving some feedback on how the leadership of that committee is perceived. If someone comes to mind, you could seek out that partner and have a discussion around feedback and see if they would be open to leading by example. It would be very powerful to have one of your highly credible partners demonstrate the courage to seek feedback. When it happens, you will be surprised by how it will intrigue others. It may also get others interested in the feedback process overall. Then, you can offer to craft a simple feedback process for all partners. Eventually, you might find that partners are curious about how they are perceived by their associates.

With so many differences in expectations and values and needs in today's intergenerational workplace, it can be helpful for partners to not only hear feedback from each other but also to hear feedback from associates on what is helping or hindering their professional lives.

A process like this must be expertly curated and administered in a way that will highlight all of the benefits of receiving feedback. I realize that much of this type of work can be overwhelming, so like always, I encourage you to meet your firm leadership where it is: To what extent are partners interested in seeking feedback? To what extent is the leadership deeply educated on the value of feedback? Is there anyone at the firm who has the credibility and courage to seek feedback themselves and then share the benefits of receiving it with others?

Sometimes in coaching engagements, a first step is to ask the coachee to identify five people and ask those five people to give them three adjectives to describe them. It is always interesting to see who embraces this assignment and how the assignment turns out. At the very least, even if it goes nowhere, the coach hears the coachee's perspective. At most, the coachee practices "seeking feedback," "listening," "managing emotions," and then putting together a game plan for growth.

Feedback provides a game plan for growth. The question may be: Is your firm leadership ready for growth?

David: Thank you for the question. I completely agree with Natalie that feedback is a gift. How else can we gain alignment connecting our intentions with what is actually happening unless we ask for or are open to receiving direct feedback. For starters, I think it is imperative for you to initiate training or provide education to the partners so that they understand that upward feedback is essential to growth and development and can also impact the bottom line of the firm's economics.

First and foremost, upward feedback can provide observations of a partner's strengths to continue leveraging. However, the feedback can also identify opportunities for growth and development that are impacting relationships, or the experience associates and others are having at the firm or legal department. Developmental feedback can play a large role in reducing attrition or increasing retention, which has a direct impact on the bottom line. Feedback is primarily about raising one's self-awareness about how they show up and are perceived by others. Without this feedback, they truly may not know the impact of their words and actions on members of their teams.

I once had a client participate in the three-words exercise that Natalie described above. I asked my client to describe himself in three words and then ask the members of his team to describe him in three words. Members of his team typed up the words and left them on his chair when he was not in his office. The following is a sampling of the words, which we reviewed together: vindictive, intimidating, micromanager, untrustworthy. My client was taken aback by the feedback but once he had time to process it, he looked at me and said, "I don't want to be that guy." This exercise started a long-term journey of seeking feedback and incorporating it into an action plan. If feedback is not converted into action, it is a wasted opportunity.

When designing an "upward feedback" plan, it is important to communicate to the recipient of the feedback that it is vital to growth, development, and raising self-awareness. It is not punitive. An analogy that I use is spinach in the teeth: If we go to lunch and I have spinach in my teeth, I won't know until you tell me. Someone behaving inappropriately or not effectively managing their team may think that they're doing a great job unless they receive feedback informing them otherwise.

It's essential to communicate to the feedback provider the importance of being frank and honest so the partner can improve their performance and become a better manager and leader. Often, associates and staff are fearful to provide upward feedback for fear of retaliation or retribution. When the feedback is collected in a confidential and anonymous way, participants tend to be truthful and direct; when feedback is traceable, people are less likely to provide honest and direct observations.

I once had the opportunity to break bread with a retired army general who held high-level military and government positions. The general told me that after any mission, event, or activity, he would convene what he called an "after action assessment." During this assessment, the general ordered his officers to give him honest, direct feedback, and they were not allowed to hold back. The general believed that he needed this feedback in order to improve his performance and do better. Without it, he would not have a full understanding of what went well and what needed to improve.

Once the partners receive feedback, they should commit to convert it to action. In order to optimize the feedback, partners should first process and reflect on the upward feedback provided by associates and others. Once they have spent some time with the feedback, partners should incorporate the feedback into a personal development plan and identify SMART goals. Goals that are specific, measurable, actionable, relevant, and time-bound. By creating a list of two or three SMART goals at a time, the partners can integrate the feedback into an action plan and start to elevate their performance.

As partners make progress on the behaviors identified in their development plans, they can then swap in other behaviors from the feedback to focus on. It should be an organic plan that is adaptable to the needs of the partners and advances the goals.

Key Takeaways and Action Items

Key Takeaway One

Feedback Is a Powerful Tool for Growth but Must Be Reframed and Normalized

Many partners view feedback as criticism or a sign of weakness. Reframing feedback as neutral "information" or a gift for professional growth helps overcome resistance. Positive feedback is just as important as constructive feedback, and both should be part of a healthy feedback culture.

Action Items:

1. **Educate and Reframe:** Host a firmwide workshop or campaign to redefine feedback as neutral information and a growth opportunity rather than criticism.
2. **Share Real Examples:** Highlight stories of how feedback has led to professional growth within your firm or in other successful organizations.
3. **Normalize Emotional Response:** Teach the SARA model (Shock, Anger, Reflection, Action) so leaders can process feedback productively and move toward action.

Key Takeaway Two

Upward Feedback Helps Leaders Align Intention with Impact

Many senior lawyers are unaware of how they are perceived by those they manage. Without structured opportunities for associates and staff to share upward feedback, leaders lack insight into the impact of their behavior, potentially harming morale and retention.

Action Items:

1. **Pilot a Program:** Design a confidential upward feedback initiative, starting small with one practice group or a respected partner willing to lead by example.

2. **Use Simple Tools:** Leverage 360-degree feedback instruments or low-barrier approaches like the "three-adjective exercise" to gather input.

3. **Ensure Safety and Trust:** Make the process anonymous and use a trusted third party or professional development team to administer and debrief results.

Key Takeaway Three

Feedback Must Lead to Action to Drive Meaningful Change

Feedback is only effective when it is processed, reflected on, and integrated into behavior change. Creating a feedback loop that includes accountability and goal-setting ensures that the insights gathered are not lost.

Action Items:

1. **Create Development Plans:** Have partners translate feedback into SMART goals and clear action steps for professional growth.

2. **Schedule Follow-Ups:** Build in touchpoints—through coaching sessions or check-ins—to monitor progress and adjust goals as needed.

3. **Foster Accountability:** Encourage leaders to share (at a high level) what they learned from feedback and how they are applying it, modeling growth for others.

Chapter 20

A Path to Partnership Success—Why 360 Feedback and Coaching Matter

Natalie Loeb & David B. Sarnoff

Dear Coaches:

> **I'm a senior associate up for partnership at my firm, and I've been asked to participate in a 360-feedback process and coaching sessions (apparently this is now part of the firm's partnership decision). Is this really necessary? Will it make a difference?**
>
> ***—Can I Skip This Rung on the Ladder?***

David: Thank you for your question, and congratulations on being offered an excellent opportunity for your professional development. Before I respond to your question, I want to make this statement, "Feedback is a gift." Hard stop. How else can we get alignment connecting our intentions with what is actually happening if we don't get feedback? 360 feedback is a chance to get deep and rich insights through a coach conducting multiple interviews with several colleagues who report to you, your peers, and people you report to. These interviews are anonymous and confidential, and you are typically not told who said what; rather, your coach creates a feedback summary report of themes and messages focused on strengths you should continue leveraging and your opportunities for growth and development.

As a senior associate up for partnership, you're at a critical juncture in your legal career, especially in light of the fact that your candidacy is potentially being put to a vote for being elected to the partnership. Your firm's decision to incorporate 360 feedback and coaching into the partnership evaluation process may feel like just another hurdle, but it is actually a gift that can help raise your self-awareness and provide valuable insights into where you need to invest in your management and leadership skills. To be offered this opportunity at this stage of your career is not common across the profession, but it is a growing practice because of the value and return on investment. Many partners with decades of experience haven't received formal leadership and management training. As a result—in my opinion—the legal profession, and especially law firms, has a fairly high attrition rate. This attrition rate, particularly among junior and mid-level associates, creates a substantial cost to the firm's economic bottom line.

The 360-feedback process and coaching sessions can offer invaluable benefits to help you strengthen your leadership skills, refine your professional brand, ensure you are positioned for success, and provide you with transferrable skills that you can take anywhere with you in your career. As I mentioned earlier, 360 feedback is a structured process during which colleagues, supervisors, direct reports, and potentially clients and others provide qualitative feedback in a confidential setting to a coach seeking to learn about your strengths and identify areas for improvement.

Unlike traditional top-down performance reviews, 360s give a holistic perspective of how you are perceived within your firm and the broader legal community. Some qualities that may be addressed during these interviews include communication skills, time management, delegation, feedback, stress management, emotional intelligence, executive presence, and leadership. Throughout my coaching career, I have conducted many 360-feedback engagements of attorneys at all levels, from managing partners to mid-level associates, and each one has been unique and different. I have given feedback to attorneys about how their facial expressions in meetings make others feel dismissed and have a chilling effect on others' participation. I have also provided feedback about how one attorney's "casual presence" impacted how partners viewed their commitment to the firm. In most cases, attorneys participating in the 360 exercise received feedback they had never encountered before. This point is especially important because if people are uncomfortable with providing feedback, you may not be aware that certain behaviors are working against you.

While feedback alone is incredibly helpful, it is only part of the process. You must also *act* on the feedback; if you don't, it diminishes the value of the investment. That's where coaching comes in. A skilled executive coach helps you to actively listen to the feedback with a growth mindset and minimize bias or defensiveness to the feedback. An executive coach can act as a thought partner, helping you identify key takeaways and themes. These insights can guide you in crafting a professional development plan, turning feedback into actionable steps, and ensuring you are held accountable for your progress.

As I mentioned above, you may be surprised or even overwhelmed by the volume and type of feedback you receive and as a consequence have difficulty adhering to your professional development plan. Your coach will help by offering strategies for sustainable improvement. I advise that you start with focusing on two or three goals in your new professional development plan to avoid taking on too much at once and becoming overwhelmed; you can always remove and add goals as you make progress or other priorities arise. In addition to working with your coach, be sure to share your development plan with your direct manager, so that they can support you by providing feedback on your successes and challenges as you implement your development plan.

Many lawyers approach 360 feedback and coaching as just another requirement, another box to check, but those who truly engage in the process gain a competitive advantage in their careers. By embracing feedback and working with a coach, you are not just proving your qualifications for partnership—you're demonstrating leadership, adaptability, and commitment to continuous growth, all of which are qualities that define successful firm leaders.

The choice is yours. You can go through the motions, or you can strategically use this opportunity to strengthen your leadership, enhance your reputation, and build a foundation for long-term success.

I wish you the best on your partnership journey.

Natalie: I share David's enthusiasm for having this opportunity offered to you. As David mentioned, the qualitative 360 exercise is growing in popularity in law firms as firm leadership pay deeper attention to the qualities and skills required for a partner to be successful. In the past, elevation to partner was largely focused on being a great lawyer and potential business developer. Today's partners also need to know how to establish outstanding relationships both within and outside of the firm and how to lead themselves and others. Being a great lawyer is your entry ticket, and being a developer of relationships and/or a business developer will enhance your value to the firm.

Today's partners must also have the ability to foster collaboration and lead themselves and others while developing the next generation of lawyers. If you are skeptical about the need for leadership skills at the partner level, take a moment to notice the type of people law firms are hiring today to lead their operations. Many of these professionals have years of experience at large consulting and other types of professional services firms. And make no mistake about it, many of these operational leaders have experienced leadership coaching and 360 feedback. They are familiar with leadership practices and philosophies and understand the value in strengthening the leadership capabilities of their firm's partners.

David explained the 360 process beautifully. A trained executive/leadership coach with the knack for quickly building trust will discreetly interview colleagues and ask them powerful questions to obtain their feedback and observations (maintaining confidentiality of the respondents is crucial here). This skilled coach will summarize the feedback and deliver it to you, highlighting your strengths (to encourage you to keep building on and leveraging them) and sharing information about any other behaviors or areas you need to pay more attention to, to strengthen your leadership capacity.

Perhaps by now, you are beginning to see the value of the 360 process and how it is an investment in you by the firm. That being said, I would be highly skeptical if you told me that you were "ready to go and dive in." Here's why. As trained coaches, we know that feedback is a gift. However, we also know that feedback can "sting." And there is no doubt that you may be a bit wary of what you may hear. We've noticed that our lawyer clients tend to immediately fixate on feedback about areas for improvement and attempt to "litigate" with the coach about why the constructive feedback is not true. Remember, the coach's only skin in the game is to help their coachee build self-awareness and set themselves up for success. To that end, the coach should discuss with the coachee—you, in this case—what to expect prior to diving in to sharing feedback.

I always prepare my clients for what they may experience as their 360 feedback is delivered to them. Remember, lawyers are trained to be "right." They are often considered to be the "smartest person in the room" and usually they are. It can be hard for professionals with such high IQs to ease into listening and processing the feedback being shared with them, even if the purpose is for their benefit and growth. However, when we properly prepare our coachees to receive feedback, we see a tremendous difference in how they take in and process the information.

I educate my clients about the SARA response and recommend you familiarize yourself with it too. It will prepare you to process the feedback being shared while simultaneously leaving space for emotional reactions you may experience.

The **Shock, Anger, Reflect, Action (SARA)** process is a psychological model that outlines how individuals typically respond to constructive feedback. This model emphasizes emotional progression and the steps needed to address and resolve feelings of shock and anger effectively. Here's a detailed breakdown of each stage:

1. **Shock:** Recognize any initial emotional response.
    - Individuals may feel stunned, confused, or unable to process the feedback immediately.
    - Physical symptoms sometimes include rapid heartbeat, sweating, or a feeling of numbness.

Being self-aware and noticing this reaction in the moment can help a coachee give themselves the space to handle the next stage.

2. **Anger:** Acknowledge the feelings of frustration or anger that arise from the shock.
    - This stage often involves a strong emotional reaction, where individuals may feel wronged, disrespected, embarrassed, or confused.

- Anger can manifest in various ways, including shouting, complaining, or expressing dissatisfaction.

When anger erupts, it means the coachee's amygdala got hijacked. The "amygdala hijack" was coined by Daniel Goleman, a leader in "emotional intelligence" research. The amygdala hijack occurs when the amygdala in your brain responds to stress and disables your frontal lobes. This activates the fight-or-flight response and disables rational, reasoned responses. These emotions are valid and normal but can be managed through breathing techniques; taking deep, slow breaths helps to slow your heart rate, decrease your blood pressure, and helps you respond appropriately, which we discuss in the next stage of the SARA response.

3. **Reflect:** Pause and think about the feedback and consider possible solutions.
    - Reflection involves processing the emotions and beginning to think logically about the issue.
    - Individuals may start to see the problem from different perspectives, including the viewpoint of the firm or colleagues.
4. **Action:** Think through potential steps or actions to resolve an issue or express feelings in a constructive manner.
    - This stage involves deciding how to respond to the situation based on the reflection from the previous step.
    - Actions can include working with someone at the firm or the external coach to think about new behaviors or habits to build, new or existing relationships to cultivate.

The Shock, Anger, Reflect, Action model illustrates the emotional journey that often accompanies a 360-feedback process. Understanding this process can help you manage your responses more effectively, leading you to gain the most out of the experience. Keep in mind, the coach selected to conduct the 360 process for you, whether internal or external, will be trained to help you move through the SARA response and leverage both the positive and constructive feedback you receive.

Like David said, this feedback is a gift. I think you should be excited—even if cautiously so—about the opportunity to grow and increase your self-awareness through the 360-feedback process and coaching. And showing appreciation for those who contributed will demonstrate your enthusiasm for the potential leadership opportunities ahead. Wishing you much continued success in your career.

Key Takeaways and Action Items

Key Takeaway One

---

360 Feedback Is a Gift and a Strategic Career Advantage

The 360-feedback process provides a rare, comprehensive view of how you are perceived by colleagues, supervisors, and reports and helps align your intentions with your impact.

Action Items:

1. **Engage Fully in the Process:** Treat the 360-feedback and coaching sessions as a strategic investment in your leadership growth, not just a "box to check."
2. **Look for Patterns, Not Just Comments:** Focus on recurring themes in the feedback to identify where you are most consistently strong and where your growth opportunities lie.
3. **Share Your Development Plan:** Communicate your key takeaways and goals with a trusted mentor or sponsor so they can observe your progress and provide continued feedback.

Key Takeaway Two

Emotional Processing Is Key to Maximizing the Value of Feedback

Constructive feedback can trigger emotional responses. Understanding and navigating the SARA model (Shock, Anger, Reflect, Action) allows you to respond productively rather than defensively.

Action Items:

1. **Prepare Mentally:** Before receiving feedback, remind yourself that it may be surprising or uncomfortable but is intended to help you grow.
2. **Pause Before Reacting:** If you feel defensive or upset, use breathing techniques or take a short break before responding to ensure you stay thoughtful and professional.

3. **Reflect with Curiosity:** Once emotions settle, revisit the feedback with a growth mindset. Ask yourself, "How might this be true, and what could I do differently to improve?"

Key Takeaway Three

Coaching Turns Insight into Lasting Behavioral Change

Feedback alone isn't enough; partnering with a coach helps turn insight into a clear professional development plan, sustained growth, and accountability.

Action Items:

1. **Co-Create a Development Plan:** Work with your coach to select two to three priority areas to focus on first, so your efforts are realistic and sustainable.
2. **Practice New Behaviors:** Identify opportunities to apply new communication, delegation, or leadership skills in daily work and gather informal feedback to gauge progress.
3. **Celebrate Progress:** Recognize and document small wins along the way, reinforcing motivation and signaling to colleagues that you are actively developing as a leader.

Chapter 21

Navigating the Noise—Dealing with a Difficult Boss

Natalie Loeb & David B. Sarnoff

Dear Coaches:

> **I'm an associate at a law firm, and I'm struggling with my supervising partner's behavior. He gives unclear assignments but then criticizes me (and other associates) when our work isn't what he expected. He's demanding, interrupts us, misconstrues our words, and rants. Sometimes he behaves like this towards clients. It's wearing on me. I'm spending more time worrying about interacting with him than I am on my work. What should I do?**
>
> ***—Lawyer Interrupted***

David: Unfortunately, you are not alone. Coming from someone who was in similar situations early in my associate career, I don't say that to mean you should accept it. Many associates find themselves in challenging situations with supervising partners, particularly in high-stakes, high-stress environments like law firms. What you're describing—unclear instructions, harsh criticism, micromanagement, and emotional volatility—can be unsettling. It doesn't just affect your job performance; it affects your well-being. That's an important aspect to acknowledge, that this experience can be emotionally taxing.

When assignments are vague and expectations are uncertain, it creates a perfect storm for frustration, anxiety, and second-guessing. Your first step is to proactively seek clarification on the instructions. Before starting a task, try to slow the conversation down and ask targeted questions to nail down expectations. Ask questions that address specific deadlines, exactly when the work needs to be completed by. Try to share your understanding of the assignment and ask if it aligns with the partner's expectations. Consider framing these questions as a way to best support the partner's needs ("I want to make sure I'm giving you exactly what you're looking for," or, "I want to make sure we are both on the same page"), which may reduce defensiveness.

Immediately after receiving an assignment, especially if the partner gives it verbally, take time to restate the assignments on a notepad and send a quick summary email to the partner confirming what you understood. For example: "Thanks for walking me through the XYZ issue. To confirm, I'll be drafting a two-page analysis of A, B, and C, using the Smith precedent as a framework. You'd like it by Thursday. Let me know if I've misunderstood anything." This not only documents expectations but also gives the partner a chance to course-correct early. It also provides a record if the partner later insists that they said something else. Importantly, you're not doing this to play "gotcha." It's a responsible way to protect your time and avoid needless delays.

If the partner tends to interrupt or misconstrue your words, consider steering communications toward written formats when possible. If you must meet in person or over the phone, have a written agenda or outline to guide the discussion. It is helpful to come prepared with notes because if the encounter gets stressful, you're more likely to forget to address points without a written reference. Follow up with a written summary which creates clarity, reduces confusion, and provides cover when memories differ.

If you're experiencing truly inappropriate behavior—sustained yelling, personal insults, or discriminatory comments—document it. Save emails and write down dates, times, and summaries of conversations. Keep this documentation private and objective. You may never need it, but if the behavior escalates or if you eventually seek internal support from HR or firm leadership, it provides a chronological record.

You may want to try and find others at the firm who can provide perspective. Ideally, that's someone senior enough to offer guidance but not so close to the partner in question that it would create conflict or get back to the partner. If you have a firm mentor, possibly seek guidance on how to work effectively with a partner who behaves like this, potential coping strategies or different ways to engage or seek feedback.

You mentioned that worrying about the partner is consuming more of your time than doing the actual work. That's a sign of a toxic environment. The amygdala in your brain may sense fear, threat, and stress and pump cortisol and adrenaline into your blood, creating a fight, flight, or freeze response. This physically impairs your ability to think with clarity and focus. It also raises your blood pressure and heart rate and is not a healthy state to be in for an extended time. Needless to say, it also drains your creative and intellectual energy.

Try to create small routines that reset your nervous system after stressful interactions. That might mean a quick walk, deep breathing, listening to a calming song, or talking with a supportive colleague or friend. Don't underestimate the cumulative effect of stress; prioritizing your well-being is not a luxury, it's a necessity if you want to sustain your performance and health in a highly stressful environment.

Finally, consider whether this dynamic is something you can endure, or whether it's a red flag about the firm's culture. If this partner's behavior is widely tolerated or even rewarded, that tells you something about the firm. If, on the other hand, he's the exception and others at the firm are empathetic and supportive, there may be ways to shift your caseload to work with other partners over time.

If the behavior becomes untenable, or if it starts affecting your confidence and sense of self, remember: You have options. Many associates leave law firms not because they can't handle the work, but because the interpersonal environment is toxic. That's not weakness. In many cases, it is doing what's best for you.

Natalie: David offered some excellent advice. He is clearly trying to help you think through what you *can* control versus what you *can't* control. As much as we like to believe we can control someone else's behavior, or even change their behavior, the truth is we can't. Just ask any parent of a toddler. Most of us at one time or another have seen a crying toddler on the floor of a supermarket who seems completely out of control, with the parent or guardian trying hard to control the situation and get the toddler to stop the crying/tantrum. Nothing will do it.

Trying to control the uncontrollable never works. Instead, we have to think about what we can control. Staying focused on what we can control helps us to feel more secure and confident and less stressed. David offered many ideas on aspects one may be able to control, which, as you may have noticed, all pertain to actions *you* can take:

1. Proactively seek clarity of instruction.
2. Ask questions that address specific deadlines, exactly when the work needs to be completed by.
3. Share your understanding of the assignment and ask if it aligns with the partner's expectations.
4. Take time to restate the assignments on a notepad and send a quick summary email to the partner confirming what you understood.

It could be worthwhile to try some of these suggestions and observe if they positively influence the partner's behavior. If successful, continue with the strategies that work.

If not, you have other options. David alluded to those too; the items that are actually in your control. For example, how you respond.

The behaviors exhibited by this partner, as you described, trigger reactions in others. As David mentioned, the amygdala gets hijacked and the cortisol starts to flow. When this happens, "fight, flight, or freeze" arises. In your case, depending on your individual nature, chances are you are noticing an urge to

- "Fight," resulting in an escalation of the situation,
- "Flee," resulting in avoiding the partner at all costs, or
- "Freeze," resulting in accepting the behavior while internalizing the stress that is a result of this behavior.

All of these reactions are completely normal; however, they do not lead to a healthy, productive outcome. And as you mentioned, it is wearing on you.

Let me introduce you to the "power-struggle line." Think of a straight line with you at one end and the partner on the other end. The partner is critical, demanding, and interrupting you when you are seeking clarification, yet you both want the same outcome: Good work for the client. Although you probably don't want to enter into a power struggle, you could be "on the line" if you react with fight, flee, or freeze. You can demonstrate control by choosing to get off the power-struggle line and into a more productive place to produce quality work. In order to intentionally jump off the power-struggle line, you need to use behaviors you can control. Sometimes, when you intentionally jump off, you take the other person with you, de-escalating their behavior as well. Either way, removing yourself from the power-struggle line gives you back the power of choice.

You can choose to do a few things.

- You can take deep breaths.
- You can remain focused on the task and completing it as successfully as possible.
- You can let the partner finish his demands and then calmly acknowledge what you have heard and then ask any questions you may have.
- You can congratulate yourself for choosing to jump off the power-struggle line and not allowing the partner's behavior to significantly impact your stress levels.

Ultimately, remember you do have a choice. As David mentioned: *If the behavior becomes untenable, or if it starts affecting your confidence and sense of self, remember you have options. Many associates leave law firms not because they can't handle the work, but because the interpersonal environment is toxic. That's not weakness. In many cases, it is doing what's best for you.* Find a trusted thought partner to discuss this with so you can make the choice that is best for you and your career.

Key Takeaways and Action Items

Key Takeaway One

Clarity Is Your Best Defense Against Unclear Expectations

When assignments are vague, misalignment and criticism are almost inevitable. Proactively seeking clarity helps protect your time, reduce rework, and create a shared understanding of expectations.

Action Items:

1. **Ask Targeted Questions:** Slow the conversation down and confirm key details—scope, deliverables, and deadlines—before starting the assignment.
2. **Restate in Writing:** Send a short confirmation email after receiving instructions to document what you understood and give the partner an opportunity to clarify.
3. **Guide Discussions with Notes:** Use agendas and written outlines during check-ins so you stay focused even if conversations become tense or derailed.

Key Takeaway Two

Control What You Can Control—Your Response

You cannot change the partner's behavior, but you can manage how you respond. Regulating your emotional state helps you stay productive and avoid escalating conflict.

Action Items:

1. **Recognize Your Triggers:** Notice when you are moving into fight/flight/freeze mode. Pause, take deep breaths, and ground yourself before responding.
2. **Jump Off the Power-Struggle Line:** Respond with calm acknowledgment, clarify next steps, and avoid reacting emotionally in ways that escalate the tension.

3. **Reset After Interactions:** Take a short walk, practice deep breathing, or debrief with a trusted colleague to release stress and prevent it from accumulating.

Key Takeaway Three

Protect Your Well-Being and Evaluate the Bigger Picture

A consistently toxic environment can harm your health, confidence, and performance. It's important to monitor the impact and determine whether this situation is sustainable for you.

Action Items:

1. **Document Problematic Behavior:** Keep private, objective notes of inappropriate conduct in case you need to escalate to HR or firm leadership later.
2. **Seek Perspective and Mentorship:** Talk with a trusted mentor, senior associate, or HR professional for guidance on coping strategies and navigating firm politics.
3. **Assess Cultural Fit:** Reflect on whether this environment supports your growth and well-being. If not, consider ways to shift your caseload or explore other opportunities within—or outside—the firm.

Chapter 22

When the Mentor Needs a Manual: Thriving During Summer Associate Season (Part I)

Natalie Loeb & David B. Sarnoff

Dear Coaches:

> **I'm a senior associate at a law firm. Last summer I was asked to supervise and mentor a few of our summer associates. It was my first time and . . . let's just say it didn't go great. I didn't plan enough, communication broke down more than once, and I wasn't prepared for the fact that some of the summers had never worked in a professional office before—let alone a law firm. There were misunderstandings, some awkward moments, and more than a few "learning experiences" (for all of us).**
>
> **I want to do better this year—for their sake and mine. I'd love any advice on how to make the experience more productive, less chaotic, and ideally even enjoyable. Any advice?**
>
> ***—One Summer Older, Hopefully Wiser***

David & Natalie: Thank you for your question. We applaud you for reflecting on your performance last year and recognizing that it did not go as well as you planned. You demonstrate a high level of self-awareness, an essential leadership skill, and acknowledge that you have an opportunity for growth and development. This is the mindset of a leader. Effective leaders reflect on their own behavior so they can act with intention. By focusing on the only thing we fully control—our own actions—we empower ourselves to make choices that foster positive relationships, engage others, and contribute to their success. In doing so, we also shape our own success and that of the firm.

Supervising summer associates for the first time can feel a little daunting and like you are putting a plane together while you are flying it. You're not alone in finding it awkward, ambiguous, or more challenging than expected—even seasoned supervising and managing attorneys who have decades of experience struggle with leading. You're ahead of the curve simply by seeking guidance at this stage in your career.

So let's talk about how to turn last year's "learning experience" into this year's success story. Here's what we recommend—as your friendly executive coaches and unofficial mentors-from-afar: In order to make this year's summer associate engagement more successful than last year, focus on managing people rather than managing tasks. Ask yourself with each communication and assignment delegation, "How is this summer associate experiencing my behaviors?"

Please keep in mind that summer associates aren't just there to complete tasks. They're there to experience—for the first time for many—what it's like to work in a law firm and learn how to think critically, communicate effectively, receive feedback, and navigate the expectations of law firm life.

Try to approach assignment delegation from the mindset of a coach and think back to your summer associate experience. Ask yourself, if you were back in their shoes, "What would I learn from this task? What context and direction would I need? What skill(s) would this help me to build? How did I solve problems and manage uncertainty?"

Take time up front to explain not just *what* you expect, but *how* the workplace operates. For example:

- Define deadlines for the project and how much time they can reasonably expect to spend on it.
- Specify if they can they come to you with questions. If you don't, they may not believe it is welcomed.
- Outline expectations for communication, e.g., in-person meetings, remote meetings, and emails. Clearly communicate if you want their cameras to be on during Zoom meetings.
- Explain how to own their mistakes (and why doing so earns respect).

Some may say this coddles summer associates or question why they should make this level of effort when no one did it for them. However, by communicating expectations and confirming understanding at an early stage of the relationship, you are more likely to get the work product you want and reduce frustrations.

You mentioned communication broke down last summer. That is not something unique to you and your firm. It is a fairly common occurrence. Often, new supervisors avoid giving critical feedback because they don't want to hurt someone's feelings or are concerned it will escalate into conflict. However, withholding feedback doesn't protect people. In fact, it deprives them of growth.

This year, think about feedback as something that should be a regular practice and remind yourself why it's crucial: It leads to growth and development not only for the summer associate but for you as well. You will get better and better at it as you practice it. Like any other skill, the more you use it, the more competent and confident you will become with it. And giving brief frequent feedback framed in a way that supports development will build trust and motivate summer associates to continue to improve.

One feedback model that provides a general structure is the SBIA (situation, behavior, impact, action) model based on the teachings of the Center for Creative Leadership. To the extent you have time to prepare for a feedback conversation, the SBIA provides an organized and logical way to deliver feedback.

- **Situation.** "In the client call on Tuesday . . ."
- **Behavior.** "You jumped in before the partner finished her thought . . ."

- **Impact.** "That interrupted the flow, and the client looked confused . . ."
- **Action.** "Next time, try waiting for a beat to see if she's done, then add your comment."

Feedback should not be a one-way lecture and is ideally a two-way dialogue. Seek feedback as to how you could have done better. For example, asking, "How's this experience been for you so far?" creates a two-way learning environment and signals trust.

Another common leadership pitfall we see is supervising attorneys assuming the summer associate automatically understands what you are thinking and what you expect. Just because you know what a good first draft looks like doesn't mean your summer associate does. Give clear and unambiguous directions and communicate expectations and specific deadlines. Share examples or give the summer associate access to form files for reference.

Lastly, you are not only supervising summer associates but also have to manage your own workload. This can create stress and test your time management skills. We urge you to focus on being present, focused, calm, and not distracted. If you appear to be rushing or are not maintaining eye contact or interest, you can come off as performative and even disingenuous, which impairs trust and may damage relationships. Bruce Tulgan, founder of RainmakerThinking and author of many books, including *It's Okay to Be the Boss* and *Not Everyone Gets a Trophy*, teaches that when a manager is not highly engaged, low performers will "hide out," mediocre performers will think they are "high performers," and high performers will be "looking for the door."

If you embrace the practices we describe above—act with humility, humor, and empathy—you will be better positioned for success than if you don't. Remember that every manager and supervising attorney are "dinner table conversation." Those that you are responsible for are talking about you when they are not in the office. They are describing what kind of leader you are and how you impact their day and performance. What would you want them to say about you? I wish you the best of luck and look forward to hearing how this summer associate class goes for you.

Key Takeaways and Action items

Key Takeaway One

Lead with Intention and Clarity

Effective supervision begins with clear expectations, structured communication, and proactive planning.

Action Items:

1. **Set Clear Expectations Early:** Explain deadlines, communication norms (e.g., preferred methods, meeting etiquette), and your availability for questions.
2. **Provide Context for Assignments:** Share why a task matters, what skills it helps develop, and what a good outcome looks like. When possible, give examples or model work product.
3. **Confirm Understanding:** After delegating, ask summer associates to restate what they heard, or send a quick follow-up note summarizing assignments to avoid misunderstandings.

Key Takeaway Two

Make Feedback a Regular, Two-Way Dialogue

Frequent, constructive feedback promotes learning, trust, and better work product—for them and for you.

Action Items:

1. **Use a Feedback Framework:** Apply the SBIA model (Situation, Behavior, Impact, Action) to keep feedback specific and actionable.
2. **Give Feedback Often and Briefly:** Don't wait until the end of a project—offer quick course corrections and recognition in the moment.
3. **Invite Their Feedback:** Ask summer associates how the experience is going and how you could better support them to model humility and growth.

Key Takeaway Three

Balance Supervision with Presence and Professionalism

Your demeanor and engagement directly shape how summer associates experience the firm—and how they talk about you afterward.

Action Items:

1. **Be Present and Focused:** When meeting with summers, give them your full attention—put devices aside and make eye contact to signal that their work and learning matter.
2. **Manage Your Time and Energy:** Plan check-ins and assignment reviews when you can be calm and not rushed, so you don't appear distracted or dismissive.
3. **Lead with Empathy and Humor:** Acknowledge the learning curve, normalize mistakes, and create an environment that reduces anxiety and fosters confidence.

Chapter 23

When the Mentor Needs a Manual: Thriving During Summer Associate Season (Part II)

Natalie Loeb & David B. Sarnoff

Dear Readers:

Last month,[1] we responded to a thoughtful question from a senior associate seeking guidance on how to effectively manage summer associates. We offered practical advice on supervision, communication, and mentorship—tools to help senior associates support the next generation of talent.

But that conversation also prompted us to reflect on the summer associate experience itself. This month, we're turning our attention to the challenges summer associates often face as they navigate a new and sometimes overwhelming environment. From managing time and deciphering feedback to understanding workplace etiquette, the learning curve can be steep.

1. *See* chapter 22, *supra*.

We encourage senior associates and even partners to read on—not only to better support their summer colleagues, but also to revisit what it felt like to be in their shoes. A little empathy can go a long way in building strong, supportive teams.

—Natalie & David

Natalie: Congratulations! You are a summer associate! Now what? Navigating the transition from an academic environment to a professional environment can be daunting. You are now a member of a team relying on your enthusiasm, willingness to learn, and ability to deliver results. Ideally, your firm will set some clear expectations of behavior and performance for you, and you will be assigned to a more senior associate who will help you begin to learn the skills that are required for you to be successful at the firm. In terms of legal skills, you are still learning. However, there will be many opportunities to accelerate your learning during your summer employment.

Tip #1: Enter the summer with a learner's mindset. What does that mean? Prepare yourself to stay curious, ask questions and activate your listening skills so you can soak in the knowledge shared with you. Chances are you will be assigned plenty of reading and research that you'll learn from; however, look for opportunities to demonstrate your interpersonal skills. These are the skills that reveal how you positively interact with all personalities and types of people at the firm. Creating the narrative of being someone that others want to be around will not only heighten your chances of being asked to return, but they will make others suspect that you are highly desirable to other firms and/or practice groups.

Tip #2: Show capacity for being a good time manager. While you do that, show that you respect others' time. Time management (or self-management) demonstrates diligence, self-accountability, and results. Those senior to you will immediately start to form positive impressions of you when they notice you value how you spend your own time and the time of others. Simple ways to show you are a capable time manager are:

1. Meet your deadlines and commitments.

   If you can't meet a deadline or commitment, notify your senior associate as soon as possible to provide a "heads up" and brainstorm together on what to do.

2. Learn to anticipate the needs of those around you.

   Always take the initiative to make things better. This small piece of advice can make a huge difference in how you are perceived.

3. Plan daily.

   Look at your calendar the evening before or early in the morning of each workday. Notice if you have any open time. If so, offer assistance to your senior associates or others. If your scheduled is jammed, try to block off "focus time" the following day.

4. Schedule time for "deep work."

   Deep work refers to the ability to focus on a cognitively demanding task without distraction. It allows you to produce high-quality work efficiently and is crucial in a professional environment that requires critical thinking and attention to detail.

   - As a summer associate, tasks often involve in-depth legal research and analysis. Deep work helps you delve into intricate legal issues without getting sidetracked.

   - Creating legal documents requires precision and clarity. Deep work facilitates a focused environment to produce error-free and articulate documents.

   - Mastering the art of deep work can accelerate your learning curve, enabling you to absorb complex legal concepts more effectively.

Diligently applying these habits will set you up for success as a summer associate and excellent lawyer beyond! Wishing you a great summer filled with growth and achievement.

David: I echo Natalie in congratulating you on earning a summer associate position. It's a milestone achievement reflected in all the work you put into law school classes and extracurricular involvement. Now what? For many, the transition from student to professional is both exhilarating and overwhelming. You're suddenly surrounded by brilliant, accomplished people, some of whom you hope will support your candidacy for a full-time offer, and you're navigating not just legal work but also workplace norms, implicit expectations, and varying degrees and quality of feedback.

While your legal skills are still developing, your attitude, work habits, and ability to receive feedback and demonstrate professionalism can leave a lasting impression. In fact, these qualities often carry significant weight in determining whether you're seen as a future associate.

As Natalie writes, entering the summer with a learner's mindset is your foundation. That means staying curious, asking questions, and welcoming guidance, even when it's developmental. Law school may have trained you to develop research skills and advocate, but in practice, humility may go further in career development. In many cases, feedback is not a criticism of your work product, it's an investment in your growth. It is a gift.

When someone takes the time to edit your memo, explain a better approach, or clarify a firm norm, receive it with appreciation. Say thank you and express gratitude. Demonstrate that you possess a growth mindset and are open to learning and adapting. Try and let go of defensiveness which can become an impediment to growth.

Not all feedback will be delivered with finesse and high-level skill. Sometimes a partner's offhand comment is actually a big clue: "Punch this argument up," "Be more concise," or "This took too long." Even if feedback is not delivered with eloquence, there are helpful nuggets that you can benefit from. If something isn't clear, politely ask for clarification. "Can you please give me an example of how you want that structured?"

It is important to receive feedback with grace and equally important to incorporate the feedback into your work product so that your supervisor sees a change and improvement. If you receive substantive feedback and ignore it, that can impact your supervisor's willingness to delegate assignments to you.

We all know that developmental feedback can be uncomfortable and sting. Sometimes it can feel personal, especially when you've put in long hours. But don't let that discomfort paralyze you. The more you practice receiving feedback with openness and curiosity, the more resilient you'll become. Senior associates and partners have all been in your shoes. They're typically not looking for perfection, they're looking for your ability to grow and improve.

I also want to address workplace etiquette. Etiquette isn't just about saying "please" and "thank you," though those go a long way. It's about understanding and respecting the culture of your firm. Every workplace has its own norms. How are people expected to communicate? When do people take lunch? How do people address partners and clients? What's the protocol when you're included in a meeting? Observe carefully and attentively. Follow the lead set by associates and partners. And when in doubt, ask, "Is there a preferred format for submitting research?" or "Would it be helpful if I cc'd you on my follow-ups?"

One of the best ways to show respect in a professional environment is by managing your time effectively and, by extension, others' time as well. As Natalie notes, meeting deadlines, planning ahead, and proactively communicating delays are all marks of maturity and accountability. Anticipate what your supervisors may need and keep them informed. If you're juggling multiple assignments, don't wait until the last minute to raise a flag. Let them know your bandwidth is full early so they can adjust expectations and support you.

Whether you're in a team meeting, on a Zoom call, or walking into someone's office, your presence speaks volumes. Put your phone away. Make eye contact. Nod to signal you're listening. Take notes, not just to help you remember, but to show that you're engaged. And keep in mind, summer associates aren't expected to have all the answers, but they are expected to show enthusiasm, humility, and professionalism. Your attitude can be the tiebreaker between you and another equally talented candidate.

You're not just auditioning for a return offer, you're auditioning to be a colleague that others can trust and work with. That means showing respect to everyone from the managing partner to the receptionist. It means taking initiative without overstepping. It means owning your mistakes and being gracious when others make theirs.

Summer associate programs aren't just about proving your skills, they're about developing your professional identity. By showing that you can receive feedback with grace and curiosity, and that you understand how to conduct yourself with professionalism and empathy, you demonstrate that you're not just a smart law student, you're a future team member and potential leader. I wish you the best during your summer and in your career.

Key Takeaways and Action Items

Key Takeaway One

Adopt a Learner's Mindset

Transitioning from law school to firm life requires curiosity, humility, and openness. A learner's mindset—one that prioritizes listening, asking questions, and engaging with diverse personalities—sets the foundation for long-term success.

Action Items:

1. **Stay Curious:** Ask thoughtful questions about assignments, firm norms, and strategy to show engagement and initiative.
2. **Listen Actively:** Pay attention not only to instructions but also to tone, context, and non-verbal cues in interactions.
3. **Demonstrate Positivity:** Bring enthusiasm and a team-oriented attitude to every task—people remember how you made them feel.

Key Takeaway Two

Master Time Management and Professional Presence

Effective time management signals accountability and respect for others. Balancing multiple priorities and managing focus demonstrates maturity, reliability, and professionalism.

Action Items:

1. **Plan Your Day Intentionally:** Review your schedule each morning, identify "deep work" periods, and allocate time for research, drafting, and follow-up.
2. **Communicate Proactively:** If deadlines are at risk, alert supervisors early and propose solutions.
3. **Show Respect for Time:** Be punctual, prepared, and mindful of colleagues' bandwidth—small acts of reliability build big trust.

Key Takeaway Three

Treat Feedback and Etiquette As Career Accelerators

Feedback—delivered skillfully or not—is a gift that helps you grow. Professional etiquette and emotional intelligence distinguish those who thrive in firm culture from those who merely survive.

Action Items:

1. **Receive Feedback Gracefully:** Listen without defensiveness, thank the giver, and apply what you've learned in future work.
2. **Observe and Adapt:** Notice communication styles, hierarchy norms, and workplace customs; model behavior on trusted role models.
3. **Build Emotional Resilience:** When feedback stings or workloads feel heavy, pause, breathe, and reframe challenges as learning opportunities.

Chapter 24

When the Mentor Needs a Manual: Thriving During Summer Associate Season (Part III)

Natalie Loeb & David B. Sarnoff

Dear Readers:

> **Over the past two months,[1] we've explored the summer associate experience from both sides—offering guidance to senior associates stepping into mentorship roles and to summer associates navigating the early stages of their legal careers.**
>
> **As summer programs wind down, this final installment focuses on what comes next. Whether you're a senior associate reflecting on your leadership or a summer associate preparing to return to law school, there are valuable lessons to carry forward.**
>
> **In this wrap-up, we share key takeaways to help both groups make the most of their experiences—turning a single summer into a lasting foundation for growth, connection, and professional development.**
>
> ***—Natalie & David***

1. *See* chapters 22 and 23, *supra*.

Natalie: As our summer audience of associates and senior associates moves into the next few months, there is an opportunity for each group to reflect on their summer experiences and think about what they have learned about themselves.

I am a big believer in "self-coaching." Upon completion of a coaching engagement, I encourage my coachees to notice their behaviors and reactions in challenging situations and to ask themselves:

- What did I do well?
- What if anything would I do differently next time?

To Our Summer Associate Readers

You had the chance to experience what it is like to work in a law firm. In addition to being exposed to legal work, I hope you were challenged to think critically, encouraged to notice the variety of communication styles—including your own—and had numerous opportunities to receive feedback.

Your legal expertise will continue to grow. Law school and future summer positions will deepen it, as will the supervision and mentoring you will receive—perhaps like the mentoring you received this summer.

Once you begin full-time work at a law firm, you will be practicing your legal skills every day. Those skills will highlight your cognitive intelligence: your ability to learn, reason, solve problems, and understand complex ideas. However, in addition to cognitive intelligence, your future success will depend on your emotional intelligence too. Emotional intelligence is the ability to identify and manage one's own emotions as well as the emotions of others. Emotional intelligence is generally said to include a few skills: emotional awareness or the ability to identify and name one's own emotions and the ability to harness those emotions and apply them to tasks like reasoning, thinking, and solving problems. Another essential part of emotional intelligence is self-regulation, the ability to regulate one's own emotions when necessary, along with helping others to do the same.

Now let's do some self-coaching to prepare you to heighten your emotional intelligence. Working on developing your emotional intelligence through your remaining years of law school will prepare you to enter your full-time legal job with more confidence, setting you up for quicker success. You will become the associate everyone wants on their team, while experiencing less stress as you build and nurture lasting relationships. So let's begin with self-coaching around two behaviors from your summer experience impacted by your emotional intelligence: communication and receiving feedback.

Communication

Certain behaviors are characteristic of specific communication styles. What did you notice about the communication styles of others? What behaviors made others want to gravitate towards someone? What behaviors pushed others away?

What did you notice about your own communication style? What worked for you and helped you to build and deepen relationships. What if anything got in the way of building solid relationships and learning about your peers? If you had a do-over at your summer associate position, what would you want to do differently when you communicated? What obstacle might get in the way of you trying this new behavior? How could you remove that obstacle?

Receiving Feedback

Receiving feedback as a summer associate lawyer is incredibly valuable. It helps you improve your legal skills by identifying areas where you excel and others where you might need more practice. Hopefully you received some constructive feedback from senior associates overseeing your work this summer. If so, chances are they guided you in honing your legal writing, research, and oral advocacy skills, all of which are crucial for your future career.

In addition to feedback on your legal skills, it is important to think about any feedback you may have received on your work style, communication skills, and feedback-receiving skills, all of which pertain to helping you improve your emotional intelligence.

To what extent did I receive feedback on my work? How did I respond to the feedback? What did I learn from the feedback? Did I receive any feedback that "stung" yet ultimately helped me grow? What did I learn? What can I do differently next time to be sure I am seen as someone who graciously receives feedback? Did I find myself seeking feedback? (If so, pat yourself on the back.) If not, what got in my way of seeking feedback?

Any feedback you received was a "gift." It was proof that the senior associate cared enough to direct you towards what's expected and how to be successful and effective at the firm. There is no doubt that feedback can sting at times, yet it is the most powerful way to help us grow. To ensure you get the most out of your feedback and maximize your summer experience, use these three simple yet powerful steps:

1. Be honest with yourself. Look in the mirror and note your strengths and weaknesses. Maximize your strengths and minimize your weaknesses. This increased self-awareness will serve you well as you continue through your studies and career.

2. Reflect on any feedback you receive. Remember, it is a gift. Spend time understanding the feedback and how you can apply it to your work in the future.

3. Use the feedback to set specific, achievable goals for improvement. Think about one or two specific behaviors you can do that will help you move closer to the expectation described through the feedback.

These simple yet powerful reflection tools will help you to build a self-coaching habit. Continue to self-coach yourself and just watch what will happen!

To Our Senior Associate Readers

The question in our June column[2] came from a senior associate who aspired to be a better supervisor and mentor this summer. From experience, this senior associate had learned that in addition to providing direction (the "what to do") it was important to think about how that direction and feedback was delivered (the "how it's said"). Masterful supervising requires intention, increased self-awareness, and attention paid to communication skills.

---

2. *See* chapter 22, *supra.*

Communication

To help you make the most of your summer experience as a mentor and supervisor, here are some self-coaching questions to reflect on:

What did you notice about your own communication style? What behaviors made others want to gravitate towards you? What behaviors, if any, pushed others away? To what extent were you successful when setting expectations? Did you get the type of results you wanted? If so, what did you do well? Is there anything you could do in the future to improve?

Giving Feedback

Did your summer associate(s) graciously accept any feedback you delivered (and to what extent)? Did you notice a positive change in their behavior after you delivered the feedback? If so, why? If not, why not? If the feedback you delivered didn't lead to positive changes, what did you do next?

In Joseph Folkman's book, *The Power of Feedback*,[3] he describes feedback as a transformative force for both personal and organizational success and compares the impact of feedback on performance to "rocket fuel." The rocket fuel propels leaders and employees from good to great performance, and is essential for creating a thriving, strengths-based workplace culture.

Some items to consider to make feedback powerful are listed below:

- Feedback is not just a performance management tool; it is central to professional growth and the improvement of relationships within organizations.
- Most employees desire more feedback, believing it boosts their performance and expands their career possibilities.
- Leaders who actively seek feedback are rated more positively than those who only give it, underscoring the importance of modeling openness and curiosity.

---

3. Joseph R. Folkman, The Power of Feedback: 35 Principles for Turning Feedback from Others Into Personal and Professional Change (Wiley 2010).

- When managers give effective feedback, it raises employee engagement and fosters a culture of ongoing development.

Remember, any feedback you delivered was a "gift." It was proof that you cared enough to take your time to help this summer associate be a better lawyer one day. I am sure that if the feedback was delivered with that spirit in mind, it was accepted as it was intended. Pat yourself on the back for that. And if you still have some room for growth as you learn to deliver feedback, pat yourself on the back for your increased self-awareness! That is a symbol of your heightened emotional intelligence!

David:

From the Summer Associate's Perspective

This summer may have been your first real exposure to the pace and expectations of law firm life. You likely encountered a range of communication styles—some direct and clear, others more ambiguous. As Natalie noted, feedback may have been detailed and helpful, or it may have felt cryptic. Now is the time to reflect on what helped you succeed and what challenged you.

Ask yourself:

- Did I learn to plan my days intentionally, balancing multiple assignments with research, drafting, and meetings?
- Did I clarify deadlines and expectations instead of making assumptions?
- Did I take feedback—however it was delivered—and incorporate it into my next assignment?

Perhaps most importantly, did I begin developing the ability to manage my emotions when the work was stressful or feedback felt personal? The capacity to pause, breathe, and respond rather than react will serve you well—not just during the bar exam, but throughout your career.

Whether you were supervising or being supervised, your summer experience offered a fertile environment for building emotional intelligence. Think back and ask yourself:

- When did I feel most effective, and when did I feel off balance?

- Was I aware of my facial expressions, posture, and tone?
- Did I pick up on others' non-verbal cues—or miss them?

These questions can help you become more aware of how you show up in professional settings. It's an ongoing learning journey.

You also had opportunities to test your time management, planning, and prioritization skills—focusing deeply even when surrounded by distractions. Daily interactions gave you practice in communication and feedback, whether you were asking for clarity, delivering an assignment, or responding to edits. These skills will benefit you in high-stakes moments, including preparing for and sitting for the bar exam.

If you're studying for the bar in the coming year, these same skills will make a difference. Time management is essential—creating and sticking to a study plan, using deep work time effectively, and knowing when to rest. But emotional intelligence is just as important: staying focused under stress, asking for help when needed, and keeping perspective when a practice exam doesn't go well.

Over the last two months, Natalie and I explored the summer associate experience from two vantage points: the senior associate seeking to improve their supervisory and mentoring capacity and the summer associate stepping into the world of law firm practice. In both columns, the common threads were emotional intelligence, time management, communication, and feedback. We tried to express that these qualities aren't just nice-to-have skills but rather are the foundations of a successful career in law.

From the Senior Associate's Perspective

You may have discovered that the role demands more than delegating tasks and reviewing work product. Managing people requires self-awareness and an understanding of how your words, tone, and behaviors are received. For example, reflect on moments when your urgency may not have landed with your summer associates. Did you gauge the listener's frame of reference? Did you fall short on properly conveying the stakes? "We need this by 2 p.m. because the client is waiting for it to make a filing decision today" lands differently than "Get this to me by 2 p.m."

Think about times when you delegated effectively and when you didn't. Were you assigning based on availability or on skill and development goals? Did you provide enough information up front to set your team up for success? And when things didn't go as planned, how did you give feedback?

Looking Ahead

As you wrap up the summer, take time to reflect:

- What moments challenged me the most, and what did I learn from them?
- What will I do differently next year—in law school, bar study, or my first year of practice?

The summer is winding down, but the learning continues. Think through your expectations for yourself and for those you'll work with. Commit to developing the skills that allow you to show up at your best.

Good luck—and keep growing.

Key Takeaways and Action Items

Key Takeaway One

Self-Coaching Fuels Continuous Growth

Both summer and senior associates can deepen their professional development by reflecting intentionally on their behaviors, communication, and learning moments. Self-coaching builds awareness and accountability—core elements of emotional intelligence.

Action Items:

1. **Reflect Regularly:** After each project or milestone, ask yourself: *What did I do well? What could I do differently next time?*
2. **Notice Patterns:** Track when you felt effective versus off balance to identify triggers and growth areas.
3. **Set Micro-Goals:** Choose one behavior to strengthen each month—such as listening actively, managing stress, or clarifying expectations.

Key Takeaway Two

Feedback Is a Gift and a Growth Tool

How you give and receive feedback shapes your professional reputation and relationships. When approached with openness and curiosity, feedback accelerates both skill development and trust.

Action Items:

1. **Seek It Out:** Proactively ask supervisors or peers for feedback on your work style, communication, or client interactions.
2. **Reflect Before Reacting:** When feedback stings, pause, process, and look for the lesson within it.
3. **Apply and Acknowledge:** Implement at least one suggestion from feedback and let the giver know how it helped—this reinforces your growth mindset.

Key Takeaway Three

Emotional Intelligence Distinguishes Great Lawyers from Good Ones

Beyond legal acumen, success in the profession depends on emotional intelligence—awareness of self and others, empathy, adaptability, and communication finesse.

Action Items:

1. **Observe Communication Styles:** Identify which behaviors in others invite collaboration and which create distance; adjust your approach accordingly.
2. **Regulate Under Pressure:** Practice pausing and breathing before responding in high-stress or high-stakes moments.
3. **Model EQ Daily:** For senior associates, demonstrate empathy and clarity when supervising; for juniors, show composure and openness when receiving direction.

Chapter 25

Performance Reviews Should Be a Tool, Not a Chore

Natalie Loeb & David B. Sarnoff

Dear Coaches:

> **Every year around this time, my law firm's professional development committee sends the same email about performance reviews. It's a familiar routine: we fill out forms, have a meeting, and then go back to business as usual. The whole process feels mechanical—like something we do because we have to, not because it leads to meaningful growth. I always walk away wondering, "What was the point of that?"**
>
> **I have financial and professional goals I'm serious about. Shouldn't this process help me move toward them? Or am I missing something?**
>
> ***—Review Fatigued***

Natalie: There's no doubt that the annual performance review process can seem useless sometimes. Whether the process is successful depends on how the feedback is collected and then delivered. Every firm has their own approach. In my opinion, your job is to figure out how to make the process work for you. Let's have a little fun with this.

Do you remember the Charles Dickens play, "A Christmas Carol," with the ghosts of Christmas past, present, and future? Let's take a journey through the "ghosts of performance reviews past" and think about how to transform this seemingly mechanical process into a meaningful growth opportunity.

Take a moment to think back to your previous review experiences. Each one probably left different impressions. There were likely unhelpful elements, like generic feedback that felt copy-pasted, vague comments without specific examples, too much focus on administrative tasks rather than development, and one-sided conversations rather than two-way dialogue. If any of this sounds familiar, you are not alone. This is the feedback we often hear about annual performance reviews. The good news is that no matter how a review is delivered, there will usually be some hidden gems in there. That is where you want to focus. And that is where you can find some helpful tips for growing as a lawyer.

Now let's think about the "ghost of performance review present" and what you can do this year to make the process work for you.

This year, bring a fresh perspective and eagerness to leverage your feedback. Look for specific feedback about your work product, insights about client relationships, comments about your leadership potential, and suggestions for skill development. If you're wary that your performance review may fall short in certain areas, come prepared with a learner's mindset and a list of thoughtful questions.

Instead of viewing the process as a checkbox exercise, try approaching it as a strategic growth opportunity by taking ownership. Here are some tips.

Before the review:

- Review your past work highlights and challenges.
- Identify specific areas where you want feedback.
- Prepare questions about advancement opportunities.

During the review:

- Take detailed notes.
- Request specific examples.
- Discuss concrete next steps.

After the review:

- Create an action plan based on feedback.
- Schedule follow-up discussions.
- Set measurable goals.
- Track progress regularly.

Use this present-day experience to convert your feedback into growth with actionable steps. For example, if you're told:

- "Improve writing," request sample documents considered excellent.
- "Enhance client relations," ask to shadow senior partners.
- "Develop business," seek mentorship in business development skills.

Returning to the suggestion to prepare questions for your review, here are some ideas to get you started:

Career Development Questions

- What specific skills should I prioritize developing in the next six to twelve months?
- Which practice areas do you see growing, and how can I position myself to contribute?
- What differentiates associates who make partner from those who don't?

Financial Growth Questions

- What metrics are used to evaluate associate compensation?
- How can I increase my value to the firm?
- What additional responsibilities would justify a compensation increase?

Client Relationship Questions

- How can I take on more client-facing responsibilities?
- What feedback have clients given about my work?
- Which client development activities should I focus on?

Leadership Development Questions

- What opportunities exist for leading junior associates?
- How can I contribute more to team success?
- What committee work would be valuable for my growth?

Keep in mind that these questions are open-ended, and your reviewer may require time for reflection before responding.

Remember: The most successful attorneys view feedback as valuable data rather than criticism. They use it to refine their practice and advance their careers. Stay present during your review this year. Soak in all of the positive feedback you receive and focus on what you can do to grow and develop. In the long run, this will help you to meet those financial and professional goals you are so serious about.

David: Thanks for your question. It is one that we are often asked in our practice. Natalie addressed many substantive aspects of the review process and best practices. Let me introduce you to the "ghost of performance review future." Close your eyes and imagine yourself one year after your review, after applying Natalie's advice. What would you be proud to say changed as a result of the review process? Focus on what you want to be able to communicate as your areas of growth and development, such as: "I stepped into more client-facing work, supported members of my team and cultivated high trust, improved the quality and speed of my drafting, and contributed to a new matter that expanded our practice." That single sentence becomes your personal vision. It keeps the review from being a one-day event and turns it into a compass for the next twelve months.

Let's go back in time to a day or two before your review. As Natalie adeptly focused on external factors of the review process, I would like to take the time to focus on internal factors such as mindset and emotional intelligence.

When emotions run the show, we often miss the most relevant parts. In many cases, people go into a review expecting the worst-case scenario. They fall into survival mode, and the ensuing chemical reaction impairs the brain's ability to think and act rationally, logically, and clearly. As a result, many people leave the review session and can't recall exactly what was said.

Starting the day before your session, take time to reset a few times. Sit with both feet on the floor and breathe in gently through your nose, then exhale longer than you inhaled. Do this a few times. If your heart is racing, try a box breathing exercise: inhale to a four count, hold for four, exhale to four, hold for four. Do this exercise for three to five minutes at least a few times the day before and day of your review session. When you enter the session, lean into a growth mindset and focus on the fact that the information you will receive is vital to your professional growth and development.

After reviewing your notes and digesting the feedback as Natalie mentioned, take time to prioritize the feedback into actionable steps. Start by focusing on your top three priorities. If you focus on too many, you will likely spread yourself too thin and make less progress overall. By focusing on a smaller amount, you can make incremental changes that stick and become lasting behavior changes. Do a lot of little rather than a little of a lot. For example, if tomorrow you decide to run a marathon, you are more likely to start by running two miles a day rather than twenty.

From there, translate each priority into everyday behavior. What does it look like in practice to improve upon the feedback? If the theme is writing, you might decide that every first draft will start with a one-sentence purpose and an outline to keep it crisp. If the theme is client exposure, you might ask to lead the first five minutes of an upcoming call and send a short summary afterward. If the theme is leadership, you might meet with a junior associate at the start of the week to set expectations and again at the end to close the loop. The point is to make the future observable. People should be able to say, "I can see the change."

Give your plan a simple cadence so it doesn't depend on bursts of willpower. Over the next month, ask for one or two exemplary work products to model your drafting. Schedule a short check-in with a partner or mentor to confirm that you are meeting expectations. Start keeping a journal to track your progress; this can double as a blueprint for your next review. Over the next quarter, identify opportunities to practice the behaviors you've chosen. If something does not go the way you expected, view it as an opportunity to learn, make adjustments, and improve your response going forward.

Finally, close the loop with the people who support your growth. A few times a year, share a concise update with a partner or sponsor: what you've taken on, what changed because of it, and where you want to lean in next. When the "ghost of performance review future" returns next year, you won't be wondering what the point was. You'll have a summary of the prior year, one that began with calm, continued with focus, and ended with meaningful progress toward the financial and professional goals you care about.

Key Takeaways and Action Items

Key Takeaway One

Transform the Review from a Routine into a Growth Opportunity

Performance reviews often feel procedural, but they can be powerful if you approach them strategically—with preparation, curiosity, and ownership of your development.

Action Items:

1. **Prepare Intentionally:** Review past feedback, accomplishments, and challenges; come with specific examples and questions about advancement.
2. **Engage Actively:** Take detailed notes during your review, ask for specific examples, and clarify expectations.
3. **Follow Through:** Create a written action plan with measurable goals, and schedule follow-up check-ins to track your progress.

Key Takeaway Two

Regulate Emotions to Maximize Learning and Clarity

A growth mindset and emotional composure allow you to absorb feedback productively. When stress or defensiveness takes over, valuable insights get lost.

Action Items:

1. **Practice Emotional Reset:** Use grounding techniques like box breathing before and during your review to stay calm and present.
2. **Listen Without Reacting:** Treat all feedback—positive or critical—as data for growth, not as a personal judgment.

3. **Reflect Before Responding:** After your review, take time to process and prioritize the most relevant feedback before creating next steps.

Key Takeaway Three

Turn Feedback into Measurable, Visible Change

The real value of a review lies in how you apply the insights to your daily habits and long-term goals. Small, consistent actions build credibility and momentum.

Action Items:

1. **Set Three Priorities:** Identify your top focus areas for improvement and convert each into observable behaviors (e.g., leading a client call, revising drafts with structured outlines).
2. **Build Accountability:** Share progress updates with mentors or supervisors quarterly to reinforce your commitment to growth.
3. **Track and Reflect:** Keep a brief journal of progress, lessons, and wins—this record becomes the foundation for your next performance review.

Chapter 26

Taking Leave Without Losing Ground

Natalie Loeb & David B. Sarnoff

Dear Coaches:

> **I'm considering taking leave from my law firm. While I don't want to get into specifics, the decision feels high-stakes given the nature of legal work and the expectations that come with it. I'm trying to weigh the personal need for time away against the professional risks. How should I approach this decision, and what factors should I consider to protect my career while prioritizing the need for the leave?**

—Being Intentional About My Career

Natalie: Today's workplaces are very complex. There are high demands in terms of work performance, long hours, and of course, the reward of compensation that comes along with it all. Our lives too are very complex. We are human beings and life happens. Sometimes a leave is required, whether paid or unpaid. No matter the reason or type of leave, it is understandable that it may feel "high stakes."

Here in the United States, law firms are recognized as high-performing work cultures. Highly talented people are sought out, hired, trained, and expected to contribute to the firm's overall success, meaning meeting the expectations of very demanding clients. When one chooses to be engaged in this challenging, innovative, meaningful yet sometimes tedious work, one is usually compensated well and supported by intelligent people (hopefully both intellectually and emotionally). The way in which you are supported reflects the work culture created by the firm. Some firms will recognize the valuable benefits of supporting leaves for employees, while others will stigmatize leaves and attach them to the belief that anyone taking leave is not completely focused on their career and the success of the firm.

Some employees fear that taking time off will make them appear less dedicated, negatively impact performance reviews, or even put them at risk of being fired or laid off. From my experience, this seems to be a concern more particularly acute among younger workers (Gen Z and Millennials). It makes sense to me since many of these workers are newer in their careers and still navigating relationships within their firms and assessing to what extent they can trust their leaders to continue to support their career growth when they return.

Many work cultures in the United States equate long hours and constant availability with commitment and strong work ethic; some work cultures encourage the belief that prioritizing health or personal needs over work is a sign of weakness or laziness. Both of these misconceptions make it difficult for employees to consider disconnecting for a longer period of time.

If you are uncertain of the extent to which a leave may be supported, the best you can do is think about how to approach this leave in a way that will minimize any concerns for the firm. Remember, chances are high that your firm put a lot of effort into recruiting and training you. If the leave is highly important to you, approach your firm with a "plan." You can mutually determine the best way for you to take leave to tend to whatever you need to—without feeling pressure or guilt—and then reenter smoothly. Giving this type of thought to your potential leave will relieve any stress you are feeling about the leave while heightening the confidence your employer has in you and your continued commitment to the firm.

Note also that whomever is in charge of "people" at your firm will be familiar with the FMLA. The Family and Medical Leave Act of 1993 is a United States labor law requiring covered employers to provide employees with job-protected, unpaid leave for qualified medical and family reasons. Be prepared to ask your employer what criteria must be met to qualify for FMLA leave, if you meet them, and what your next steps are if you do. Some firms will have additional firm policies to help facilitate employee leaves. It is critically important that you find if and how your firm supports employee leaves. Armed with that information, you can get to work creating a plan.

Think deeply about the work and client relationships you have pending.

- Who is capable of covering this work for you while you are out?
- Have you covered for others when they are out?
- Can you approach particular people to get a sense if they will welcome some work transitioned from you while you are on your leave?
- Do you need to consider getting additional support from somewhere else within the firm?
- Is there a practice manager or coordinator or talent officer that can help you think this through?

The more preparation you do—laying out a clear plan for your exit, time out, and return—the higher the chance of you receiving the support you need without any negative residual effects when you return. As I mentioned earlier, life is complex, filled with highs and lows, giving us reasons for occasional extended leaves. There may be risks to taking a leave. There also may be risks to *not* taking that leave. Think that through too. If you do indeed decide to request a leave, be prepared. And upon the approval of the leave, accept it with grace, leverage the time out of the office, and return ready to roll.

David: Natalie raised many insightful points about how to position a leave and put a plan in place to minimize disruption to the firm, clients, and colleagues. As I observed throughout my career, in many firms, particularly those led by Baby Boomers and Traditionalist partners, there remains an unspoken mindset that if you ask for a leave, you haven't learned to "play hurt," to use a sports metaphor. The idea is that commitment means pushing through no matter what's happening in your personal life. A partner might say, "I've had my own challenges, but I'm here every day, why aren't they?" That sentiment, while often born of generational norms around resilience and loyalty, can inadvertently create shame or fear for those who need legitimate time away.

Too often, attorneys assume that taking leave signals a lack of grit. Partners may quietly question whether the reason for the leave is "real" or merely a convenient excuse for burnout or disengagement. Ironically, those same people sometimes soften their views only when they learn the leave involves something undeniably serious, such as illness, a family crisis, or mental-health emergency, at which point they say, "Now I understand." But by then, the damage may already be done. Colleagues may have gossiped, judgments have already formed, and the person taking leave feels isolated or guilty for doing something entirely reasonable.

There's also a less talked-about layer: jealousy. Some colleagues resent that someone "gets to step away" while they remain tethered to deadlines and client demands. Others see leaves as incompatible with advancement because they equate presence with performance. The old belief that "you need to be seen in the office to be effective" still lingers, especially among partners who built their careers in eras where proximity and visibility defined success.

Law firms must begin reframing leave not as a break from responsibility but as an exercise *in* responsibility. Knowing when you are depleted, distracted, or overwhelmed and choosing to step back before mistakes or burnout occur is an act of judgment, not weakness. A well-planned leave can protect client relationships, team morale, and ultimately the firm's reputation for quality work product.

When discussing your decision, consider communicating that your leave of absence is driven by responsibility to the firm and a desire to protect client service. Indicate that you have contemplated coverage to ensure as smooth a handoff as possible. This language underscores accountability and foresight, the very traits partners value in future leaders.

If a firm's culture equates constant visibility with value, employees will understandably fear stepping away. Leaders set the tone by how they talk about and respond to colleagues on leave. When partners gossip, question motives, or make comments like "I don't have the luxury of time off," they reinforce stigma and erode trust.

True leadership requires modeling empathy and perspective. Leaders should ask themselves, "What kind of workplace do we want to be? Do we value humanity and sustainability, or do we reward only endurance?" Culture is not what firms say in policies, it's what partners do in practice. Strategy is what we do, culture is how we do it. If a senior attorney undermines the legitimacy of someone's leave, firm leadership must step in. Protecting the leave and return experience is a matter of organizational integrity, not convenience. It contributes to overall retention and affects attrition as well as the firm's reputation and brand in the marketplace.

Firms that want to retain top talent, especially younger lawyers, must hold colleagues accountable when they damage that experience. A single dismissive comment about someone's "commitment" can undo years of progress in creating an inclusive, psychologically safe workplace.

Returning can be just as challenging as leaving. Partners may assume that because you were "away," you'll need to "catch up" to prove commitment again. Counter that perception by scheduling brief re-entry meetings before your return to review active matters and priorities. This demonstrates initiative and reaffirms that you're ready to re-engage. Equally important, leadership should protect the returning attorney from being overwhelmed their first week back. A supportive culture recognizes that reintegration takes time and that successful returns benefit everyone.

Ultimately, the goal is not just to help one attorney navigate a personal crossroads, it's to help the profession evolve. Lawyers, like all humans, are not machines. Life happens, which may include illness, caregiving, loss, or exhaustion. Destigmatizing leave is not only about compassion but also sustainability. Firms that normalize rest and recovery retain healthier, more loyal, and more productive professionals. When leaders support leave without judgment, they send a powerful message.

In the end, the real measure of a firm's strength is not how it operates when everyone's at their desks but how it supports those who need to step away and how it welcomes them back when they return. If your firm makes leave difficult, try not to let that dictate your choice. Listen to your instincts and do what's right for you.

Key Takeaways and Action Items

Key Takeaway One

A Well-Planned Leave Protects Both Your Well-Being and Your Professional Reputation

When a leave is approached with clarity, preparation, and foresight, it signals maturity and judgment rather than disengagement. Taking time away does not hinder your career when it is paired with thoughtful planning that reassures the firm, protects client service, and demonstrates your continued commitment.

Action Items:

1. Develop a thoughtful leave plan before initiating the conversation. Identify outstanding matters, deadlines, and client relationships and outline a seamless coverage strategy to reduce uncertainty for partners and colleagues.
2. Meet proactively with key stakeholders (practice leaders, colleagues, talent/HR) to align on roles, responsibilities, and communication expectations during your leave. This demonstrates professionalism and reduces the perception of disruption.
3. Clarify firm policies, both formal (e.g., FMLA) and cultural, in advance. Know your rights, understand the firm's leave process, and gather information so you enter the conversation prepared and confident.

Key Takeaway Two

How You Frame the Leave Shapes How Others Perceive It; Intentional Communication Counters Stigma

The language you use when discussing a leave influences how leaders interpret your motives. When you position the leave as an act of responsibility to the firm and its clients, you shift the narrative from absence to accountability, reducing the potential for misunderstanding or judgment.

Action Items:

1. Position the leave as an act of responsibility to the firm, your clients, and your own long-term sustainability. Emphasize that stepping back now prevents mistakes, burnout, or diminished performance later.

2. Use accountability-based language when discussing the leave (e.g., "I've considered how to protect client service," "I've prepared a coverage plan," "I'm committed to a smooth return"). This reframes the leave from "absence" to "leadership judgment."

3. Discuss transition support directly with colleagues who may cover your work. Approach them with appreciation and clarity to foster goodwill and reduce resentment or misinterpretation.

Key Takeaway Three

Successful Reintegration Requires Intentional Re-Entry Planning and Firm-Wide Cultural Support

Returning from leave can be just as sensitive as requesting it, and proactive reintegration helps reestablish momentum and credibility. A supportive culture and your own thoughtful re-entry plan ensures that your return strengthens relationships rather than reopens doubts.

Action Items:

1. Before returning, schedule brief re-entry meetings to review priorities, ongoing matters, and client updates. This shows initiative and helps counter any lingering perception that you must "prove" your commitment.

2. Set realistic boundaries and workload expectations for your first weeks back. Advocate for a phased re-entry if appropriate and ensure leadership understands that reintegration takes time.

3. Engage allies, mentors, sponsors, or talent professionals to help monitor workload, messaging, and cultural dynamics upon your return. Their support can buffer unhelpful commentary and reinforce a positive comeback experience.

Case Study

Managing the Mix at Harper & Stone LLP

Background

Harper & Stone LLP is a mid-sized law firm with offices in three major cities. Like many firms, it is experiencing growing pains: a new class of associates has just arrived, client demands are increasing, and several key partners are pushing for improved profitability while maintaining quality of life for attorneys and staff.

The litigation department in the New York office is at the center of several internal challenges: generational differences, workload imbalance, and a partner who is brilliant with clients but demanding with junior attorneys. The firm recently rolled out a 360-feedback and coaching initiative to strengthen its management bench and improve engagement.

Key Participants

- **Sophia Rivera (Partner):** A top rainmaker and trial lawyer. Known for her exceptional client advocacy and creative strategy sessions, she also tends to be impatient and occasionally curt when work doesn't meet expectations.

- **Jordan Lee (Counsel):** Recently promoted from senior associate, now supervising a team for the first time. Shows promise as a thoughtful manager and has begun scheduling weekly team huddles but struggles with delegation and coaching under pressure.

- **Amina Khan (Senior Associate):** Talented, organized, and admired by clients for her professionalism. She is a natural mentor to associates but often overextends herself.
- **Marcus Bennett (Associate):** Smart and diligent second-year associate who values clear feedback. He has shown initiative by volunteering for complex assignments but tends to take criticism personally.
- **Emily Chen (Summer Associate):** A first-generation law student with strong research skills and a growth mindset. She needs guidance on professional norms and expectations.
- **Lisa Tran (Practice Group Administrator):** Known for her diplomacy and problem-solving. Lisa has started using workload tracking software to improve resource allocation but sometimes hesitates to escalate issues to partners.

Scenario

The litigation team is handling a major client matter. Early in the engagement:

- **Positive Examples:**
  - Jordan organizes a kickoff meeting and invites Lisa, modeling cross-functional collaboration.
  - Amina volunteers to run a short "Summer Associate 101" lunch to help Emily and other summers understand the basics of case workflow.
  - Sophia sends a firm-wide thank-you email when the client praises the team's initial research memo, boosting morale.
- **Challenges:**
  - Sophia gives last-minute verbal instructions with no deadlines, creating confusion.
  - Jordan rewrites Marcus's draft instead of giving coaching feedback, missing a development opportunity.

- Emily hesitates to ask questions about a client assignment and later turns in work that is off-target.
- During a tense status call, Sophia raises her voice at Marcus in front of the team. The group is shaken, but no one addresses it directly.

The team is delivering excellent client work, but the pace and tone are creating stress. Leadership sees this case as a chance to model both strong management and professional development.

Learning Themes and Integration of Chapter Insights

1. **Management versus Leadership:**
   - **Positive Behavior:** Jordan uses a kickoff meeting to align the team (management) and frames the matter as a learning opportunity (leadership).
   - **Developmental Opportunity:** Add regular check-ins to clarify shifting priorities and keep morale high.
   - *See* chapter 13, How Can I Better Manage People and Administrative Tasks?
2. **Clarity and Accountability:**
   - **Positive Behavior:** Lisa proactively tracks workloads to spot overcapacity issues.
   - **Developmental Opportunity:** Jordan and Amina can communicate assignment expectations in writing and hold team members accountable for meeting deadlines without micromanaging.
   - *See* chapter 13, How Can I Better Manage People and Administrative Tasks?
3. **Mentorship and Onboarding:**
   - **Positive Behavior:** Amina's "Summer Associate 101" lunch demonstrates proactive mentorship.
   - **Developmental Opportunity:** Create formal peer mentoring and feedback loops so associates like Emily know where to turn for support.

- *See* chapter 15, Preparing to Welcome Your New Associates? What You Should Know, and chapters 22, 23, and 24, When the Mentor Needs a Manual parts I, II, and III.

4. **Feedback Culture:**
   - **Positive Behavior:** Sophia's public praise after the client memo models recognition of good work.
   - **Developmental Opportunity:** Feedback to Marcus should be private, specific, and constructive, avoiding public criticism.
   - *See* chapter 19, Feedback Matters: Creating a Two-Way Street.

5. **Career Growth:**
   - **Positive Behavior:** Jordan shares their own SMART goals with Marcus, modeling transparency.
   - **Developmental Opportunity:** Encourage Marcus and Emily to set their own development goals and check progress monthly.
   - *See* chapter 18, Get SMART with Achieving Career Goals.

Discussion Questions

1. Which positive leadership behaviors in this scenario should the team amplify?
2. How could Jordan and Amina use coaching techniques to turn mistakes into learning moments for Marcus and Emily?
3. How should the team respond to Sophia's public outburst while preserving client service and professionalism?
4. What systems (mentorship, feedback, scheduling) could prevent future breakdowns?
5. How might 360-feedback and coaching support Sophia in becoming more emotionally intelligent and self-aware?

Facilitator's Guide

Managing the Mix at Harper & Stone LLP

This guide is designed to help readers process the case study and extract learning opportunities about management and leadership. It highlights **positive leadership behaviors** that should be reinforced, **developmental behaviors** that require improvement, and **reflection questions** to deepen understanding.

1. **Key Learning Themes**

   - **Management versus Leadership:** Management ensures tasks are clear and completed; leadership inspires, mentors, and sets the cultural tone.
   - **Clarity and Accountability:** Effective managers communicate expectations clearly and address destructive behavior directly.
   - **Mentorship and Inclusion:** Developing junior talent and supporting first-generation or summer associates strengthens culture and retention.
   - **Feedback Culture:** Constructive, two-way feedback accelerates growth and trust.
   - **Positive Role Modeling:** Leaders who show calm, empathy, and recognition foster psychological safety and team engagement.

2. **Positive Leadership Behaviors in the Case Study**

   Highlight these as examples of what "good" management and leadership look like:

   - **Kickoff Meetings:** Jordan brought the team together at the start of the project, including Lisa (administrator), modeling inclusivity and cross-functional collaboration.
   - **Mentorship Initiatives:** Amina held a "Summer Associate 101" lunch, creating psychological safety and accelerating learning for juniors.
   - **Recognition:** Sophia's thank-you email praising the team for a client win reinforced morale and modeled public appreciation.
   - **Transparency in Growth:** Jordan shared personal SMART goals with Marcus, encouraging openness about professional development.
   - **Proactivity:** Lisa introduced workload-tracking software to help manage scheduling, showing administrative leadership.

3. **Developmental Behaviors to Address**

   Areas where leaders in the case study fell short and need growth:

   - **Unclear Delegation:** Sophia gave vague verbal instructions without deadlines, creating confusion.
   - **Micromanagement:** Jordan re-did Marcus's work instead of coaching him, missing a teaching opportunity.
   - **Silence in the Face of Outbursts:** Amina and Jordan did not address Sophia's public criticism of Marcus, weakening trust.
   - **Lack of Confidence from Juniors:** Emily hesitated to ask questions, highlighting the need for clear norms around communication.

- **Stress Spillover:** Marcus took feedback personally, showing the need for resilience coaching and better framing of feedback.

4. **Reflection Questions for Readers**

Use these questions to guide personal or group reflection:

On Management vs. Leadership

- Where in your own practice do you "manage tasks" well, but miss opportunities to "lead people"?
- How do you set both clarity and inspiration for your teams?

On Clarity and Accountability

- Think of a time when unclear expectations led to rework or frustration. How could a written confirmation or check-in have changed the outcome?
- How comfortable are you with addressing destructive behavior directly? What strategies might you use?

On Mentorship and Inclusion

- What intentional practices can you adopt to support junior lawyers or staff in your firm?
- How do you create an environment where first-generation attorneys or summer associates feel safe to ask questions?

On Feedback

- How often do you provide feedback that is both constructive and specific?
- When was the last time you asked for feedback from a junior colleague? What did you learn?

On Role Modeling

- If your associates described your leadership at the "dinner table," what would you want them to say?
- How do you model calm, empathy, and recognition in high-pressure moments?

5. **Suggested Exercise for Readers**

After reading the case study, invite readers to:

1. **List two positive behaviors** from the case study they want to reinforce in their own practice.
2. **Identify one developmental behavior** from the case study they recognize in themself.
3. **Write a SMART goal** for how you will improve that behavior in the next ninety days.

Part III

Emotional Intelligence and Communication

Chapter 27

Using Communication to Defeat Frustration

Natalie Loeb & David B. Sarnoff

Dear Coaches:

> **I am a law firm partner, and we have an understanding at our firm that if you don't feel well, do not come into the office. This understanding was emphasized especially during the COVID-19 pandemic. On a Sunday night, I received a text from an associate who said, "I am not feeling well, should I come in tomorrow?" I became extremely frustrated, especially because it was a text, but felt compelled to respond. Not how I want to spend my Sunday nights. How should I handle this matter?**

—Do Not Disturb

David: Thank you for your question. While your inquiry is specific to this associate's situation, it may be symptomatic of other issues at your firm involving effective communication, mutually agreed-upon expectations, accountability, and feedback. If the "understanding" was communicated to all employees of the firm, then my reaction would have been to respond with something along the lines of: "As has been communicated by the leadership of the firm, please do not come to the office if you are not feeling well. I hope you feel better." However, you may want to have a subsequent meeting when the associate is feeling better to communicate your expectations if a similar event occurs in the future and that you may prefer an email to a text message, especially on a Sunday evening. Clearly and directly communicating your expectations is vital to minimizing any ambiguity or misunderstanding and lets the associate know exactly how you feel. It also gives clear guidance on how the associate should respond in the future.

This exercise can be applied to other aspects of the working relationship, including giving assignments, delegating work, and giving feedback. When you are clear and direct with your expectations, the associate will have a better understanding as to whether they have met expectations. It allows their response to be measured against expectations that you set forth and have been mutually agreed upon. When a partner's thoughts or directions are ambiguous, unclear, or not communicated at all, that creates the perfect environment for misunderstanding, frustration, and conflict.

If an associate returns an assignment that is incomplete or off the mark, the assigning partner bears responsibility as to whether the instructions given were clear, unambiguous, and appropriate for the associate's skillset. It is also important that the partner provide ongoing feedback as to whether the associate is on the right track or if their work product is meeting expectations. Without thoughtful and meaningful feedback, it is difficult for the associate to grow and develop the skills that the partner is looking for the associate to possess. All too often, if an associate hands in a draft document that does not meet the partner's expectations, the associate may never receive another substantive assignment from that partner in the future. In my opinion, this is a disservice to the associate by not giving the direction and feedback that would help them improve their work product and provide an opportunity for professional growth and development.

All too often we hear from senior partners, "no one gave me feedback when I was an associate, and I figured it out." This may be true; however, expecting your associates to do as you did may not be a best practice for building a high-performing, collaborative work environment. Clearly communicating your expectations will remove guesswork from the equation and set you up to encounter less frustration (and fewer Sunday night texts) in the future.

Natalie: When I see this question, I have a question for you: How would you have preferred for this associate to handle this situation?

Think that through, clarify what it would "look like," and then prepare to communicate that expectation directly to the associate in response to that text ***and*** next time you meet to discuss work matters. For example, perhaps you prefer a brief email (rather than a text?) that says, "I do not feel well and will not be in the office tomorrow."

If this is the case, it is crucial for you to set the clear expectation that you prefer an email over a text. It is also important to reiterate the firm's agreed-upon understanding to have those who feel unwell stay at home rather than be in the office.

To echo what David said earlier, this is all about communicating clear expectations in a timely manner. Once the associate is crystal clear on what's expected, the associate can be held accountable for meeting this expectation moving forward.

Something to think about: We all went through a traumatic pandemic together. As a result, many of us learned that communication about health issues exposes our humanity, empathy, authenticity, and patience. Ask yourself; what is the downside of optimizing these qualities? Probably nothing. What is the upside? The associate feeling "cared about." The fact that this associate asked whether or not to come in tomorrow (ignoring the firm's understanding) makes me wonder if the associate truly trusts whether the firm means what it says. The associate may be "testing this assumption" by sending you this text. It seems clear from your question that the firm does indeed mean what it says. That being the case, you can use this example as an opportunity to reconfirm the "understanding" as well as an opportunity to build some trust by delivering an answer with a dose of concern and care.

Setting expectations and holding others accountable for meeting them does not have to be done without humanity, empathy, or concern. For example, your responding text to this associate could look something like this: *"Thank you for letting me know. I hope you are feeling better soon. In the future, please correspond to me by email rather than text when you need to let me know you won't be in the office.* [and if you prefer the associate lets you know on Monday morning, rather than Sunday evening, add that too]. *Please let me know who will be handling "x" while you are out. Get some rest. I look forward to seeing you back in the office when you are feeling better."*

Sending that response is not the final step. As David mentioned above, you may want to have a subsequent conversation during a future work meeting when the associate is feeling better and returns to the office. Remember to remind the associate of the firm's view on staying home when one feels ill, and to reinforce your expectation on your preferred communication mode if and when the associate needs to be out again due to illness, especially if they feel unwell on a Sunday evening. Clearly and directly communicating your expectations with a sense of humanity, empathy, and concern is vital to minimizing any ambiguity or misunderstanding and, at the same time, lets the associate know you care.

These days, talent flows to where it feels valued and cared about.

Key Takeaways and Action Items

Key Takeaway One

Clarity in Expectations Reduces Miscommunication and Frustration

Unspoken "understandings" can lead to confusion. Leaders should communicate expectations explicitly—such as preferred communication channels, timing, and protocols for calling out sick—so that associates know exactly what's expected. This reduces unnecessary frustration (like Sunday night texts) and helps create accountability.

Action Items:

1. **Document and Share Expectations:** Create a written guide outlining communication preferences, response times, meeting protocols, and procedures for time off or emergencies.
2. **Discuss and Align:** Review expectations with associates and staff during onboarding or team meetings to ensure mutual understanding.
3. **Revisit Regularly:** Periodically check in with the team to adjust expectations as workflows, client demands, or technology evolve.

Key Takeaway Two

Effective Feedback and Communication Are Ongoing, Not One-Time Events

One-off responses to behavior are not enough. Partners should follow up with a conversation to reinforce expectations and explain *why* they matter. This approach applies to other areas like delegating assignments and reviewing work—setting clear expectations and providing feedback is critical for associate development.

Action Items:

1. **Follow Up Consistently:** After addressing behavior or reviewing work, schedule a brief follow-up conversation to reinforce expectations and clarify the "why."

2. **Integrate Feedback into Workflow:** Provide real-time feedback during assignments and at completion, making it a natural part of the work process.

3. **Model Continuous Communication:** Encourage partners to use regular check-ins and touchpoints to keep expectations, progress, and development front of mind.

Key Takeaway Three

Empathy and Humanity Can Coexist with High Standards

Accountability does not require coldness. Particularly after the collective trauma of the pandemic, showing concern and care in communications—especially around health—can build trust and loyalty. A simple expression of empathy ("I hope you feel better") alongside a request ("Please email rather than text") can go a long way.

Action Items:

1. **Lead with Empathy:** Begin conversations by acknowledging the person's well-being or circumstances before shifting to expectations or requests.

2. **Balance Care with Clarity:** Pair compassionate language ("I hope you're recovering well") with clear instructions or standards to maintain accountability.

3. **Model Humanity:** Encourage partners and leaders to share small, authentic gestures of care—thank-yous, check-ins, and encouragement—to foster trust and loyalty.

Chapter 28

If You're Happy and You Know It, Let Them Know

Natalie Loeb & David B. Sarnoff

Dear Coaches:

> **I'm a fifth-year associate and, despite the usual challenges over the past few years, really enjoy my work. My firm has a hybrid work arrangement, and I'm happy to be in the office attending client meetings and observing and learning from partners in person during anchor days. But not all of my colleagues are as enthusiastic as I am about working in the office and can be difficult to be around. I'm concerned that this isn't just an "adjustment period" for some but rather the new status quo and am considering applying elsewhere that has better office morale. What do you suggest I do?**
>
> ***—Should I Stay or Should I Go?***

Natalie: As a leadership coach, I often remind leaders that emotions are contagious. If you are a regular reader of our column, you are starting to notice a theme. A great lawyer has a combination of intellectual competence and emotional competence. Intellectual Competence (IQ) results in great legal work. Emotional competence (EQ) results in authentic, high-trust relationships with colleagues and clients.

I commend the fact that you, as a fifth-year associate, notice how others' emotions have an impact on you and/or other associates and staff. I can hear the tone of hopefulness in your question as you describe that you are happy to be back in the office. You sound like someone who is energized by being around other people. Human beings have a fundamental need for inclusion in group life and close relationships. We are naturally social animals and tend to function best when this social need is met. Being around your clients and colleagues in the office certainly helps to meet this need.

However, there are some people who are not energized by being around other people for a variety of reasons, including, but not limited to, personality style, social anxiety, health concerns, and long commutes; and there will always be colleagues around us who don't share the same enthusiasm for being back in an office. Those reasons will impact their emotional state, and, in turn, those emotions can impact others. According to psychologist Dr. Sherrie Bourg Carter, "For centuries, researchers have studied the tendency for people to unconsciously and automatically mimic the emotional expressions of others, and in many cases actually feel the same feelings simply by exposure to emotions in social interactions. Studies have found that the mimicry of a frown or a smile or other kinds of emotional expression trigger reactions in our brains that cause us to interpret those expressions as our own feelings. Simply put, as a species, we are innately vulnerable to 'catching' other people's emotions."[1]

So, what can you do? Apparently, you are energized by a hybrid work experience. Own it and enjoy the flexibility your firm is offering you. As always, you will be expected to meet your deliverables and deadlines. However, in a hybrid workplace you may find you will have more choice on how and when. Being in the office will undoubtedly expose you to a mix of other lawyers, clients, and staff who don't share that same enthusiasm. Like any other situation, you always have a choice about how to respond. To help respond in a *healthy way*, here are some ideas for you:

---

1. Sherrie Bourg Carter, *Emotions Are Contagious—Choose Your Company Wisely*, Psych. Today (Oct. 20, 2012).

1. Recognize that everyone has had different lived experiences throughout the pandemic. Those experiences can be influencing how they "feel" about a new transition to a hybrid work environment. Those feelings may translate into a lack of "enthusiasm" and poor morale in the office. You can't control how others feel, but you can lend an empathic ear if you think it may help. Sometimes people just need to feel "heard." Researcher Brené Brown is known for some excellent work on how to demonstrate genuine empathy.[2]

2. Remember, you cannot control someone else's behavior, only your own. Remind yourself every day of the advantages of being in the office, including the additional learning and relationship-building now available to you. Maintain your enthusiasm and eagerness to be back live with your colleagues. Remember, *your* emotions are contagious too!

3. Do not engage in any negative talk circulating. Hold onto your enthusiasm and use your hopeful approach to model positive behaviors for others. Others will notice, in a good way. I promise you.

4. If you're happy and you know it, let your partners and other senior leaders know. Your leaders will be happy to hear that *you* are indeed happy to be back in the office and around your clients and colleagues again.

5. Remember to take care of yourself. Making time for some self-care is not selfish. It is a priority for a healthy personal and professional life. In order to maintain your energy and enthusiasm, you need to have enough exercise, sleep, and downtime.

David: Thank you for your question. I believe Natalie has touched upon some of the key fundamentals about how to address your circumstance from an emotional intelligence perspective. In my opinion, EI or EQ is, at its essence, about raising self-awareness and recognizing one's own emotions and being able to influence those emotions.

---

2. *See, e.g.*, Brené Brown on Empathy, https://www.youtube.com/watch?v=1Evwgu369Jw (Dec. 10, 2013).

At a higher level, it is a powerful skill to recognize emotions in others and be able to influence their behavior. In many cases, highly effective leaders are able to do just that. They drive performance through others.

While I commend you for your positive mindset and outlook, I am curious to know if there is someone at the firm, be it a peer or partner, that is influencing the way you show up to work and what they might be doing to nurture that. As I like to say, leaders model the behavior they expect of others. When I was a mid-level associate, there were partners who inspired and motivated me in such a way that I looked forward to going to work, being challenged, and learning new skills. However, there were other partners who were not mentoring, blamed associates for mistakes, and made it a difficult work environment when assigned to their matters.

As a fifth-year associate, you are getting closer to the point of being considered for partnership at your firm and becoming a future leader. This may be an opportunity for you to model the behavior you expect of others. As Natalie mentioned in her reply, leading with empathy is a powerful leadership skill. Demonstrating empathy, meaning putting yourself in the shoes of others to try and understand their lived experiences and acknowledging the source of their pain or challenges, allows you to assess if there are ways to influence their behavior. There is a quote that is widely attributed to Dr. Martin Luther King, Jr., "be a thermostat and not a thermometer." Meaning, be the person who sets the tone, enthusiasm, and optimism of the team. However, in order to do that effectively, you must first build trust and cultivate and nurture relationships to understand what the driving force is behind your colleagues' emotions. How you show up impacts how your message is received by others.

As Natalie said, the pandemic created a shared experience that has impacted and traumatized everyone to different degrees. It may be helpful to engage your colleagues and try to understand what is motivating their reluctance to return to the office and if they are struggling from a mental-health perspective. Alternatively, some of your colleagues may simply prefer to work remotely and believe they are more productive and comfortable in that environment.

In my opinion, the legal profession changed more in the years from 2020 to 2022 than in the prior fifty years from an operations, logistics, technology, and practical viewpoint. In January 2020, it was almost unthinkable that the entire legal profession in the United States would be able to function and profit in a predominantly remote environment. However, it did just that. That said, the profession is now searching for balance between how to achieve efficiency, productivity, and growth and trying to meet the needs of professionals who are essential to achieving those goals. Maintaining an agile and growth mindset is helpful for embracing and adapting to change as opposed to resisting and entrenching in the ways things have been done in the past.

From my perspective and experience, associates learn a significant amount of the practice of law by watching and listening to partners interact with clients, strategize, draft documents, and manage teams. Without the power of proximity, there is an added layer of difficulty when trying to observe and participate in real time. Again, you are well positioned to model the behavior and demonstrate the benefits to career and professional development by being in the office. Remember, be a thermostat instead of a thermometer.

I also want to address the other part of your question as to whether you should consider exploring the market to seek a firm that has better morale and more like-minded associates. For some background, I left the practice of law going into my fifth year and spent sixteen years in executive search, coaching and consulting partners, associates, and law firms. I counseled clients that considering opportunities and exploring the market does not obligate you to accept an offer and in fact provides information and market intelligence about what is happening at other firms. That said, you may want to seriously consider how the current dynamic at your firm, as you describe it, may be a significant advantage for you for promotion and advancement.

Your enthusiasm for your work and showing up every day is a distinguishing characteristic separating you from your colleagues in the eyes of the partners who evaluate which associates get elevated. If you are overall happy with the assignments, supervision, and future opportunity at your current firm, it is important to do a cost-benefit analysis about how moving to another firm as a fifth-year associate would benefit your career.

To be honest, in a large percentage of law firms, you will most likely find at least some associates who are unhappy and disillusioned with the demands of practicing law. I see your work ethic and energy as a significant asset in being recognized and positioned for promotion when measured against your colleagues. At the end of the day, you should try to find what will make you happy, and it may be right in front of you. If your associate colleagues are truly unhappy and discontented, there is a strong possibility they will self-select out and leave the firm.

Good luck with your career.

Key Takeaways and Action Items

Key Takeaway One

Your Attitude and Energy Can Influence the Tone and Morale of Those Around You

In a hybrid environment, maintaining a positive and engaged presence can inspire others and increase your visibility with firm leadership.

Action Items:

1. **Capture Positives Weekly:** Write down one positive interaction, observation, or learning experience from being in the office at the start of each week.
2. **Share Intentionally:** Communicate that positive takeaway with a colleague, mentor, or supervisor to model optimism and engagement.
3. **Reinforce Culture:** Use these moments to encourage others, celebrate wins, and contribute to a culture of enthusiasm and professional growth.

Key Takeaway Two

Colleagues May Have Very Different Responses to Hybrid Work Due to Personal Circumstances

Demonstrating empathy, by listening without judgment, builds trust and reflects the kind of emotional intelligence valued in future leaders.

Action Items:

1. **Schedule Weekly Check-Ins:** Set aside at least fifteen minutes each week for informal conversations with colleagues, prioritizing those who may seem disengaged.
2. **Practice Active Listening:** Focus on hearing their perspective without interrupting or rushing to provide solutions.
3. **Validate Their Experience:** Acknowledge their feelings and show empathy, reinforcing psychological safety and trust.

Key Takeaway Three

If You're Generally Happy with Your Firm, Your Commitment, Visibility, and Positive Attitude May Be Positioning You for Promotion

Don't let short-term frustration with office morale outweigh long-term career opportunities.

Action Items:

1. **Initiate Career Conversations:** Schedule a brief meeting with a trusted partner or mentor to discuss your career trajectory and long-term goals.
2. **Express Enthusiasm:** Share your commitment to the firm and highlight what excites you about your work and future opportunities.
3. **Seek Growth Feedback:** Ask for candid input on strengths, areas for development, and specific steps you can take to position yourself for partnership or leadership.

Chapter 29

Is Praise As Important As a Paycheck?

Natalie Loeb & David B. Sarnoff

Dear Coaches:

> **I'm a partner at a large law firm, and we recently began conducting mid-year performance reviews. The firm provided partners and managers with sample agendas and items that should be discussed, including providing specific feedback about employees' achievements, demonstrating appreciation for their efforts, and asking employees about their professional development goals and how we can better support them in achieving their goals. When I was an associate, partners used performance review discussions to tell me areas I needed to improve or that I needed to step up on my billable hours—why do I now need to invest time to coddle associates or tell them they're doing a great job when that is what they are expected to do in the first place?**
>
> ***—Frustrated Over Feedback***

Natalie: "I provide feedback every week . . . it's called a paycheck." If I had a dollar for every time I heard that statement, I'd be a very wealthy coach. I don't. Instead, I've had the chance to have rich discussions with lawyers and legal professionals about the value of feedback. Like everything else today, the necessity for feedback along with how feedback is being delivered has evolved. Here is something to consider: At the time of the writing of this answer, there are five generations in the workplace at the same time. Each generation tends to have its own view of feedback. With an acknowledgment that I may be overgeneralizing, my twenty-five years of working with law firms and observing changes to the workforce make me confident that the below table rings true for most. And a lot of heads nod in agreement when I mention this at conferences:

Generation	Feedback Mantra
Traditionalists (born 1928–1945)	"No news is good news."
Boomers (born 1946–1964)	"Once a year is enough."
Gen Xers (born 1965–1980)	"How am I doing?"
Millennials (born 1981–1996)	"I want it FAST." (Fast, All the time, Specific, Timely)
Gen Zers (born 1997–2012)	"I want it all the time at the push of a button."

As the world changes and new generations assume their roles in our workplaces, they bring with them different values, needs, and expectations. As you can see from the above, the need for feedback is driven by the generational shifts we will continue to experience. It's not unusual for conflict around feedback to arise if different people have different perspectives on the value of feedback.

When working with high achievers, you will find that many of them say they don't need recognition. They are self-motivated and their good work is their reward. However, when you ask those same high achievers, "If someone were to notice your work and let you know it was well done and appreciated, would you like that?" the answer is always a resounding "Yes!" What does this tell us? When we are all working on recruiting and retaining top talent, perhaps one simple strategy for keeping top talent is to recognize the talent and provide some sincere, well-deserved positive feedback.

This leads me to my last argument in this column for feedback. When employees know they are making progress on a meaningful goal, productivity will rise. This is the basis for a book written by

Teresa Amabile and Steven Kramer titled *The Progress Principle.*[1] In this book, Amabile and Kramer note how seemingly mundane workday events can make or break employees' inner work lives. "Inner work lives" refers to consistently positive emotions, strong motivation, and favorable perceptions of the organization, their work, and their colleagues. The best leaders demonstrate behaviors to help build and sustain the *inner work lives* of their direct reports. The worst managers undermine inner work life, often unwittingly.

So how does this relate to your firm providing partners and managers with sample agendas and items that should be discussed, including providing specific feedback about employees' achievements, demonstrating appreciation for their efforts, and asking employees about their professional development goals and how we can better support them in achieving their goals? It seems that your firm is taking into account the generational shift in today's law firms. Your firm has progressive leaders paying attention to the "*inner work lives*" of their attorneys and professional staff. And your firm is giving you the tools to help you help the firm retain top talent. My suggestion is to seek any additional guidance you need as you stretch out of your own comfort zone and try applying these tools. Notice what you learn and observe the impact. If you can be patient with yourself and others, I am confident you will experience a positive difference in the morale and productivity of your associates.

David: Dear *Frustrated Over Feedback*, thank you for the question. Know that you are certainly not alone as a partner in the legal profession struggling with how to deliver effective feedback. At its essence, feedback is a gift. It is a gift that helps each of us get alignment, connecting our intentions with what is actually happening. Without the gift of giving and receiving feedback, how can anyone, including associates and partners, improve their performance? That said, it is not easy. I polled many law firm partners about what prevents them from giving direct and effective feedback. The responses were varied, but the two most consistent were:

---

1. Teresa Amabile & Steven Kramer, The Progress Principle: Using Small Wins to Ignite Joy, Engagement, and Creativity at Work (2011).

1. I am concerned about insulting or hurting someone's feelings by giving critical feedback; and
2. I am concerned about getting into an escalating conflict or argument by giving constructive feedback.

By not delivering effective and direct feedback, partners are doing a disservice to associates who would otherwise not know where they need to do better. In addition to the feedback, partners should also provide specific action items and tools for associates to implement into their performance going forward. Associates also need to receive feedback on work done well so they can leverage their strengths and raise them to the next level.

In the leadership development program The Leadership Challenge, one of the Five Practices of Exemplary Leadership is Encourage the Heart.[2] According to its founders Barry Posner and James Kouzes, Encourage the Heart involves taking time to connect, engage, and celebrate successes. This is an imperative when creating a spirit of community that not only considers achievement and success, but also, the heart. Recognizing associates' achievements and even celebrating small wins has an impact on the firm culture and community, not just one associate.

I believe the sample agendas your firm is providing represent a positive step toward bringing a practice of equity to how associates receive feedback. I don't think your assessments necessarily need to be identical for each associate; however, the firm's agenda provides a framework for all associates in the firm to get equitable depth of developmental feedback. Quite often, partners tend to provide developmental and direct feedback to associates who they have a level of comfort with, who look like them, who are like-minded, or share other commonalities. I believe this practice fails the associates who are left out and marginalized. This is a destructive habit and contributes to firms losing high performers from underrepresented communities because they do not feel included, valued, mentored, or professionally developed.

Partners often share frustrations with having to invest time to teach, develop, and mentor associates, many of whom end up leaving the firm

---

2. *See* https://www.leadershipchallenge.com/five-practices.

anyway. I believe this mindset raises an opportunity to investigate why associates are leaving the firm. Often, HR departments in law firms conduct exit interviews to see why people leave the firm. However, in many cases, the data is not shared with the management committee or practice group leaders. Valuable insights can be extracted from these interviews, and partners should be studying them to learn where to improve their engagement with associates.

I also suggest firms conduct "stay interviews" by asking associates what can be done differently or better to make them want to stay. I believe many partners lose sight of the fact that associates are a major profit center for the business of the firm, and providing feedback, along with action items for the associate to incorporate into future behavior and performance, allows the partner to delegate more effectively and focus on higher-level issues.

I applaud your firm for also incorporating the demonstration of appreciation and gratitude for the associates' contributions and for soliciting the associates' goals and aspirations. This serves multiple purposes, including building trust between partner and associate. This is critical to having a high-performing work relationship. Building trust requires the nurturing and cultivation of relationships that begins with each person learning about the other person. When a partner asks an associate, "What are your goals and aspirations and how can I support you?" the associate feels valued, heard, and a sense of belonging. When they are not asked, associates may begin feeling disconnected and unvalued, which could be the impetus for a job search.

Please keep in mind that there is research to support the premise that associates don't quit firms, they quit managers. If a partner is not effectively leading and developing associates, then they are likely costing the firm significant money in recruiting fees and lost business opportunities. Leading with care and empathy is, in my opinion, a strength and takes courage. An example is as follows: "I care about your career growth and development of skills, and because I care, I need to give you this feedback." That allows you to deliver incredibly direct feedback that will more likely be received in a productive way, even though it may sting. At the end of the day, you need to ask yourself, do you want to be right about your assertion that partners weren't required to provide detailed feedback thirty years ago, or do you want to be an effective leader for today's associates?

Key Takeaways and Action Items

Key Takeaway One

The Evolving Workplace—Shaped by Generational Differences—Has Redefined What Associates Expect from Their Leaders

Younger lawyers view regular feedback, appreciation, and career conversations not as luxuries, but as essential components of development and engagement.

Action Items:

1. **Prepare Intentionally:** Review the associate's recent work and select a specific accomplishment to recognize before the performance conversation.
2. **Lead with Appreciation:** Begin the discussion by acknowledging the associate's contribution to build trust and engagement.
3. **Provide Constructive Feedback:** Transition into developmental feedback and career guidance, framing it as a partnership for growth.

Key Takeaway Two

High-Performing Associates, Especially from Underrepresented Backgrounds, May Receive Less Meaningful Feedback Due to Unconscious Bias or Lack of Familiarity

Inconsistent or vague feedback undermines development, inclusion, and retention—and weakens the firm's talent pipeline.

Action Items:

1. **Standardize the Process:** Use the firm's feedback template to provide structured, consistent input for every associate.
2. **Check for Clarity and Balance:** Review your feedback to ensure it is specific, actionable, and includes both strengths and areas for growth.

3. **Audit for Bias:** Ask yourself reflective questions—such as "Would I deliver this same feedback to someone who reminded me of myself?"—to minimize unconscious bias.

Key Takeaway Three

Partners Who Engage Associates in Conversations About Their Goals—and Show Care for Their Development—Build Trust, Loyalty, and Performance

Feedback isn't just about critique; it's also about connection, motivation, and belonging.

Action Items:

1. **Ask About Goals:** During mid-year reviews, include the question: "What are your professional goals, and how can I support you in getting there?"
2. **Listen Actively:** Allow associates to share without interruption, take notes, and reflect their responses back to ensure understanding.
3. **Follow Up:** Revisit their goals in future check-ins, track progress, and provide opportunities or resources that support their development.

Chapter 30

Don't Let Senior Associates Slip Through the Cracks

Natalie Loeb & David B. Sarnoff

Dear Coaches:

> **I'm a senior associate at a large firm. I have received excellent feedback from clients and, with my goal of making partner, have brought in new clients through business development and networking activities. But in the past year or two, my supervising partner has stopped giving me feedback and appears to be directing opportunities and mentoring to other associates. I'm concerned that the partner's perceived silence in my direction will hurt my chances of making partner. Am I misreading the situation? Should I verbalize my concerns, or should I take the hint and consider looking for opportunities elsewhere?**
>
> ***—Misreading Signals?***

Natalie: Yes, my guess is you are misreading the situation. Don't start looking elsewhere . . . yet. If I could change something immediately in law firm culture it would be to eliminate the emotional connection to the thinking and related behavior of *"No news is good news."* I joined the legal industry in 1988, and at the time I immediately noticed how infrequently constructive/developmental feedback was delivered to both lawyers and administrative staff. I also noticed how unusual it was for someone to receive positive feedback when it was clearly deserved. At the time, I was doing my graduate work in industrial/organizational psychology, and I was learning all about the power of feedback. In fact, we were reading books like Joseph Folkman's *The Power of Feedback*,[1] to help us learn about how to use feedback as a tool to elevate performance and morale.

While learning about the power of feedback, it was completely confusing to me as to why people in supervisory and leadership positions in their firms were not using this performance management tool on a regular basis to grow, develop, and retain the highly talented individuals in their law firms.

As I have dug deeper to satisfy this curiosity, I learned something interesting about generational differences and feedback. Concisely put, here is what I learned about feedback through an intergenerational lens.

Traditionalists, born between 1928–1945, are known for framing feedback as *"No news is good news." Baby Boomers*, born between 1946–1964, are known for framing feedback as *"Once a year is enough."* This is how annual performance reviews came to rise within organizations.

Generation Xers, born between 1965–1980, are known for framing feedback as *"How am I doing?" Millennials*, born between 1981–1996, are known to frame feedback as *"I want it FAST" (Fast, All the time, Specific, Timely). Generation Z*, born between 1997–2012, are known to frame feedback as *"I want it all the time at the push of a button."*

At this moment in time, we can see how there is a lot to consider about how feedback is delivered and how it is received. There is also a lot to consider for maximizing the impact of feedback. In your case, it appears you were receiving feedback regularly and then it stopped. From the way you describe yourself, it appears as though your work performance continues to be high; however, your motivation may be suffering due to the lack of feedback over the past one to two years. Also, you are noticing that the supervising partner is providing feedback to others on a more consistent basis.

---

1. Joseph R. Folkman, The Power of Feedback: 35 Principles for Turning Feedback from Others into Personal and Professional Change (2006).

Don't misinterpret the lack of feedback as though something is wrong. It could be that your supervising attorney frames feedback as "no news is good news." Unfortunately, some lawyers have a reputation for avoiding delivering constructive or developmental feedback when it is actually needed. Don't wait any further for any surprises. Initiate a conversation with your supervising partner. You need to know if the lack of feedback has to do with a change in your performance (from the supervising partner's perspective) or if is it merely that the supervising attorney sees you as self-motivated and self-directed and feels that you no longer need additional feedback. If the supervising partner confirms the latter, please share the following with them:

When performance consultants ask high performers if they need positive feedback, they often say no. We are told that the recognition they receive is a paycheck. However, when high performers are asked, "If you received some positive feedback, would it impact you and your performance?" the answer is always a resounding "Yes." Evidently, high performers benefit from feedback, and certainly positive, constructive, and developmental feedback. High performers that don't receive feedback on a regular basis and instead see moderate and low performers receiving feedback often feel devalued and look elsewhere for employment.

In short, I hope that doesn't happen for you. Instead, I am hopeful that a candid conversation with your supervising partner about the lack of feedback over the past year or so will reset your relationship and the amount and kind of feedback you receive moving forward.

Senior associates are the up-and-coming senior lawyers of the firm. It is a critical time for receiving feedback and honing both lawyering and leadership skills. Good luck with your conversation.

David: Thank you for your question. As I was considering a response, several perspectives and lenses came to mind. Firstly, I agree with Natalie that this may be a miscommunication. If the partner believes you have become more independent and self-sufficient, then the partner may be of the mindset to focus on developing other associates to position them for success and develop their skillset and careers as well. However, I believe it would be prudent to test that theory. If this is not the case, it is important for you to get an objective perspective of your status within the firm, particularly now that you are cultivating client relationships and building your own book of business.

While the current situation may be uncomfortable and unsettling for you, it is important to look at it as a developmental opportunity not only for your own career trajectory but also for evaluating your performance towards others as an aspiring partner and leader. I would like to address these one at a time.

With respect to your situation with your partner, I believe letting a year or two go by without getting feedback or seeing workflow delegated to you is too long of a time frame to not have addressed it. Having worked at a law firm for over nine years, with four of those years as a litigation associate, I understand the stresses and time demands of the practice combined with cultivating client relationships and business. Going forward, if you encounter a similar situation and don't receive feedback for a period of time—capped at approximately two months—I believe a conversation should take place. This may take the form of a status check as to how your work is being evaluated or if there are skills or behaviors that you should be doing more or less of at the firm.

I would also ask you, did you receive a review by this partner or anyone over the past year or two? Was there any indication or information in your review that sheds light on how your performance was evaluated? Have you also discussed your work product with *other* partners and colleagues to get their perspective on the quality of your work for someone at your level? This may be a path to consider before you approach your partner so that you have some data and observations from other partners. If you decide to schedule time with the partner to discuss the lack of feedback and communication, you may also want to consider role-playing the dialogue with a trusted colleague or friend so you get comfortable with your talking points; doing so may also reduce anxiety. I think preparing for a conversation such as this is important, and you should not go into it cold and unprepared. If you have a trusted mentor at the firm, they may be a resource to consider to get insights and advice on how to approach this partner.

The second point I want to communicate is that this is an excellent opportunity for you to take stock, raise your level of self-awareness, assess how you show up, and understand how you are being perceived by others and how your words and actions may impact the junior associates who you may supervise and mentor. We say on a regular basis, *"leaders model the behavior they expect of others."* Ask yourself the following:

1. Am I giving timely feedback to associates?
2. Am I giving them action items to improve and develop skills and performance?
3. Am I delegating with clarity, confirming understanding of the assignment, and providing clear deadlines?

I believe that doing this exercise may prove helpful to you in preparing to have a potential conversation with your partner because it will help you to develop a better understanding of being in their shoes.

Lastly, ask yourself, *"Do I actively seek feedback about my performance and how I impact others?"* Seeking feedback is a vital leadership skill and probably one of the least practiced by leaders. Seeking feedback is important for many reasons, one being that the additional insight will help you to align your behaviors with your intentions, to learn where you need to make adjustments or leverage your strengths, and to be vulnerable to your team. Vulnerability has been identified by extensive research as a high-level leadership behavior. It builds trust and increases your team's commitment to their work and support for you.

Performing the above exercises will ready you for the conversation with your partner and will also help to elevate your communication and leadership skills as you prepare to enter the next phase of your career.

Key Takeaways and Action Items

Key Takeaway One

Lack of Feedback May Be Cultural, Not Personal

In many law firm environments, particularly among senior attorneys shaped by older generational norms, "no news is good news" is still a common mindset. The absence of feedback may not signal dissatisfaction or failure but may instead reflect a belief that high performers do not require consistent reinforcement.

Action Items:

1. **Clarify the Context:** Schedule a conversation with your supervising partner to ask about expectations and the reason for limited feedback.
2. **Use "I" Statements:** Frame the discussion around your commitment to growth (e.g., "I want to ensure I'm meeting expectations and continuing to improve").
3. **Align on Next Steps:** Request specific guidance on performance priorities and agree on how and when feedback will be shared going forward.

Key Takeaway Two

Feedback Is a Two-Way Street and a Leadership Skill

As a senior associate striving to make partner, it's crucial not only to seek feedback but also to model giving it—timely, specific, and constructive—to junior associates. This not only fosters a positive team culture but also demonstrates leadership readiness and emotional intelligence.

Action Item:

Self-assess how you lead others. Ask yourself:

- Am I providing clear expectations and timely feedback?
- Do I delegate with clarity?
- Am I investing in the development of those I supervise?

If not, begin integrating these habits now to demonstrate partner-level leadership.

Key Takeaway Three

Self-Awareness and Preparation Strengthen Your Position

This moment is not just about getting feedback; it's also a valuable opportunity to reflect on how you are perceived within the firm and to build a broader foundation of support. Gathering feedback from other partners and mentors can provide a more accurate view of your standing and help you engage in a more productive dialogue with your supervising partner.

Action Item:

Before approaching your partner:

- Reflect on recent reviews and gather informal feedback from trusted colleagues or other partners.
- Consider role-playing the conversation with a mentor or peer.
- Identify a mentor or sponsor within the firm who can provide insight into firm politics and help you navigate the path to partnership more strategically.

Chapter 31

De-escalating Tensions in the Office One Kind Gesture at a Time

Natalie Loeb & David B. Sarnoff

Dear Coaches:

> **I was hired as a lateral partner and still feeling things out at my new firm. Recently, a colleague (an associate) I've worked closely with since starting here has been over-reactive and short-tempered. I've considered asking why but don't want to overstep or pry—not to mention I'm still relatively new at the firm. Should I concern myself with my crabby colleague or keep my head down and do my job?**

—Cautious Newcomer

Natalie: When I started my career, I spent ten years as part of a human resources (HR) team in a large law firm. I had the opportunity to get involved in various functions of HR and found that I was interested in what is known as "employee relations." The main purpose of employee relations is to foster and improve positive relationships among employees. Successful employee relations helps to increase retention and productivity while also encouraging a highly engaged and pleasant workplace culture. In the employee relations role, one is often asked to be a sounding board, guide, or mediator when two or more professionals in the firm are in some sort of conflict. This was a new role for me, and, like you, I was "feeling things out in this role."

Part of my training for this role was to observe the head of human resources conduct disciplinary discussions. These discussions took place when team members were not meeting performance expectations, were behaving "unprofessionally," or were engaging in unproductive conflict. As I watched the head of HR share candid observations and deliver sensitive feedback, I remember thinking I would never be able to have these types of conversations. I couldn't see myself opening a conversation with someone who may react defensively or become upset.

I share this story because I learned an important lesson while *feeling* uncomfortable. As I watched the head of human resources have multiple conversations with various people over time, I observed that the outcomes were rarely negative. In fact, nearly every conversation I witnessed ended with the employees feeling relieved, "heard," and less stressed, and often thanking the head of HR for her support. My observations taught me to "reframe" my approach to having employee relations discussions and lean into using my communication and interpersonal skills. It didn't take long before I found the confidence in myself to open these important conversations.

I sense you too are experiencing some fear about the potential outcomes if you open a conversation with your colleague. This is more common than you may think. And often it is this fear that gets in the way of taking advantage of an opportunity that could most likely lead to a better result. I applaud you for noticing a behavior that is not contributing to a pleasant work environment. If you are noticing it, chances are that others are too. And for the person displaying the behavior, there is a good chance, if it continues, that it will impact how that person is embraced by the firm and perhaps evaluated in terms of client service and performance. Being crabby occasionally is understandable. Being crabby consistently will impact one's career.

What the person really needs is someone who cares enough to share feedback while inquiring if the person is ok. More often than not, there is a reason for crabby behavior. Offering your colleague the opportunity to share their story and to be heard will likely defuse the crabbiness and set the stage for forward-thinking problem solving. And with that comes a sense of relief, a feeling of being supported and a willingness to behave differently. This is what I learned from observing my head of HR.

What does this mean for you? It means you have a choice to make. Leave things be and wait to see if the behavior stops. Or leverage your own communication and interpersonal skills and see if you can influence some change. Showing care, concern, and compassion will never backfire on you. Instead, it will humanize you and foster trust with those around you.

We no longer live in the "leave your emotions at the door" era. Our work lives are an integration of both life and work. This means we need more "real" relationships with our coworkers. Some of us, particularly in law firms, need to unlearn the "proper" etiquette that used to prevail at firms and build up our capacity to be brave and have courageous conversations with our colleagues, other associates, direct reports, and even our bosses—including about how we are *feeling*.

In his book *Speak-Up Culture,*[1] Stephen Shedletzky suggests that by fostering a genuine sense of care, leaders set the stage for innovation, collaboration, and significant organizational development. People lead from every seat. We can all contribute to fostering a genuine sense of care. The longer people's pain and frustrations are ignored, the more they feel isolated and resentful.

As colleagues and leaders, we can make a difference. However, many people still feel awkward and shy to do so. Challenging this feeling and flexing empathy will work.

Brené Brown, a thought leader in empathy and the author of *Daring Greatly,*[2] reminds us that we can demonstrate empathy by offering reassurance from an objective place. Demonstrating empathy does not mean you need to take on someone's emotions to the extent that it becomes a burden; instead, you can use some short phrases and your listening skills to show the other person you care.

In summary, praise yourself for noticing someone's behavior, which may benefit from an empathetic ear. Next, consider courageously

---

1. Stephen Shedletsky, Speak-Up Culture: When Leaders Truly Listen, People Step Up (2023).
2. Brené Brown, Daring Greatly: How the Courage to Be Vulnerable Transforms the Way We Live, Love, Parent, and Lead (2012).

opening a conversation with this person. Be prepared to practice your empathy and listening skills. Overall, you will be sending a message that you care. And when someone leads with care, they can *feel* confident about what they are doing. And YOU will make a difference.

David: Thank you, Natalie, for sharing your experience. Entering a new role as a law firm partner comes with multiple challenges, both professionally and personally, and may involve dealing with a colleague who may be short-tempered and overreact. Such dynamics can potentially interfere with collaboration and create an unhealthy work environment. As a new partner, you do not want to be identified as a complainer; however, you may want to consider addressing it with the associate or, as Natalie suggests, with an HR professional who is trained to facilitate a dialogue and work towards resolution. Whichever approach you choose, it is important to approach the situation with empathy and effective communication, which will help set the stage for a positive outcome.

As Natalie mentioned, we all bring our lived experiences and emotions to the workplace. Personal and professional stressors impact how we show up and how we behave in our work environment. Taking the time to empathize and connect to your colleague's situation may foster greater understanding and provide key information to help you work towards a resolution. This does not necessarily mean that you agree with how your colleague is behaving but rather helps you better understand why they are behaving in this way. I believe it is also important to be aware of a perceived power differential in how you, as a partner, deal with the behavior of the associate. It may require additional thought to engage in a way that can de-escalate defensiveness because of your title and role.

Communication and cultivating trust are the foundation to any healthy working relationship. If you choose to initiate a dialogue with your colleague in the spirit of creating mutual understanding about how their behavior is impacting you and your work life, ideally, the conversation should occur in a private setting, free from interruptions or distractions. In my opinion, it is meaningful if you express that your intentions are also inspired by a level of care for your colleague and to understand if they are dealing with a difficult professional or personal challenge that is impacting their behavior. It is typically less helpful to criticize their behavior and motives than to start from a position of care. They may rebuff your engagement even though your approach to and investment in the conversation are authentic.

You also may want to consider using "I" statements to express your feelings and observations, avoiding "you" statements that come across as accusatory or judgmental. For example, say, "I've noticed that there have been instances where our interactions seem tense, and I want to understand if there's anything I can do to support you better." This style may encourage more engagement and less of a defensive posture from your colleague.

As Natalie expressed, active listening is an impactful practice to reduce workplace conflict. After you communicate your perspective and feelings, create space for your colleague to process, respond, and share their perspective. Even if there is initial silence, my suggestion is to sit in that silence and not try to fill the void with talking. Try to avoid interruptions or speaking over one another, maintain comfortable eye contact, and try to maintain open and relaxed body language and not cross your arms or have a closed posture. Demonstrate genuine interest by nodding, making eye contact, and paraphrasing their statements to show that you understand their perspective. By actively listening, you create a space for your colleague to feel heard and respected, fostering a more positive atmosphere for addressing the underlying issues.

One suggestion that is practiced by one of my colleagues is to start the dialogue with breathing exercises, such as box breathing, to reduce stress and tension before you start the dialogue. This is also a healthy practice during the course of the day that may help in better managing emotions and stress and may reduce overreactive behavior.

If the overreactive behavior persists despite your efforts, consider involving a neutral third party, such as a mediator or HR professional. Mediation can provide a structured and impartial environment for both parties to express their concerns and work towards a mutually beneficial resolution. Having an objective perspective can often uncover underlying issues that may not be apparent to those directly involved in the conflict.

Navigating a workplace environment with an overreactive and short-tempered colleague, particularly as a new law firm partner, requires a delicate balance of empathy, communication, and proactive problem-solving. By understanding the root causes, initiating open communication, implementing active listening techniques, encouraging stress management strategies, establishing boundaries, and seeking mediation when necessary, you can contribute to a more positive and collaborative workplace culture. As a new partner, your leadership in addressing such challenges can not only improve your working relationship but also set a precedent for a healthier and more harmonious professional environment going forward.

Key Takeaways and Action Items

Key Takeaway One

Caring Conversations Build Trust and Influence Culture

Displaying care and empathy—especially in a firm culture still adapting to more human-centered leadership—signals strong interpersonal awareness and helps create a supportive work environment. What might feel like overstepping could instead be seen as modeling emotional intelligence and collegial concern.

Action Items:

1. **Initiate with Care:** Approach your colleague privately and choose a calm, respectful setting to start the conversation.
2. **Ask Open-Ended Questions:** Use curiosity-driven language (e.g., "I've noticed some tension and wanted to check in—are you okay?") to invite dialogue.
3. **Listen Without Judgment:** Give space for them to share, validate their experience, and express support to build trust and model emotional intelligence.

Key Takeaway Two

Active Listening and Thoughtful Framing Matter More Than Having All the Answers

You don't need to solve your colleague's problems—but you *can* make them feel seen and heard. That alone can shift a difficult dynamic. Using "I" statements and active listening helps reduce power imbalances and keeps the conversation constructive.

Action Items:

1. **Prepare Your Approach:** Plan your tone and language in advance, using "I" statements (e.g., "I've noticed our interactions have felt strained lately, and I wanted to check in with you.").

2. **Practice Delivery:** Rehearse with a friend, mentor, or coach to build confidence and ensure your words come across as constructive and calm.

3. **Listen Deeply:** During the conversation, stay present, allow pauses, and use silence as a tool to encourage openness and reflection.

Key Takeaway Three

As a New Partner, Modeling Emotional Intelligence Builds Leadership Credibility

Even though you're still adjusting to the firm, addressing a colleague's behavior thoughtfully signals emotional maturity and leadership potential. Avoiding the issue may preserve short-term comfort but risks long-term tension or missed opportunities for connection and culture shaping.

Action Items:

1. **Have a Private Conversation:** Address the behavior directly and respectfully, using "I" statements and open-ended questions to invite dialogue.

2. **Model Emotional Composure:** Stay calm and curious during the discussion to set a tone of professionalism and constructive engagement.

3. **Monitor and Follow Up:** Acknowledge positive change if it occurs, or involve HR/firm leadership if the issue persists to ensure support and accountability.

Chapter 32

Distinguishing Bickering from Bullying

Natalie Loeb, David B. Sarnoff & Fritz Galette

Dear Coaches:

> **My law firm continued with a hybrid work model this year but lessened the number of days we can work from home. We're now in the office four days a week and have more in-person meetings and face-to-face time with one another. I've observed interactions between colleagues that are making me uncomfortable and seem to be negatively affecting some of my co-workers. I'm unsure whether these interactions are normal workplace conflict or if I'm witnessing workplace behaviors placing unintended pressures on some who are more vulnerable even by well-meaning leaders and co-workers.**
>
> **How do I know if I'm blowing things out of proportion?**
>
> ***—Hang Back or Help?***

Natalie: Recently, I was with a group of law firm leaders, and we were talking about how the legal workplace has changed. One leader mentioned how he was waiting for the workplace to go back to "business as usual." By that, the leader meant no more hybrid work and an expectation that all lawyers and staff return to their offices five days a week. Only time will tell if law firms will eventually require this. However, in the meantime, we all remain in a huge change management process.[1] Covid disrupted our workplaces, accelerated the use of technology for day-to-day virtual work, and impacted how we communicate, lead, build relationships, give and receive feedback, use our time, and service our clients. I think it's safe to say none of us were prepared for this change completely, and even today we see leaders struggling to craft a clear vision for hybrid work policies and new behavioral norms for how we interact with each other as we all settle into our firm's expectations.

With clarity for you and others on being in the office four days a week, apparently you are noticing a commitment to that expectation. What you also seem to be noticing are unsettling behaviors, which, as you described, are uncomfortable to witness and negatively affect some of your co-workers.

Workplaces are comprised of a variety of personalities and work styles. Behavior that is "unsettling" to one person may be "comfortable" for someone else. For example, direct and blunt communication is usually welcomed by someone who is eager for clarity and quick results, whereas someone who prefers a more methodical approach and needs time to analyze information can be rattled by direct and blunt communication. On the other hand, someone who demonstrates tactful, patient, moderately paced behavior may ignite impatience in those that want direct, candid feedback. And those with a similar work style will appreciate the more moderate thoughtful pace. Here, I am talking about normal style differences in the workplace that with increased self-awareness can be addressed and handled productively by well-meaning leaders.

How can you gain comfort or be helpful when noticing adverse impacts on your co-workers versus knowing if you're blowing things out of proportion when interactions seem more intense? Begin with finding time to check in on your colleague "one on one" in private. Language like, "I noticed your reaction to yesterday's interaction with [Name]. Are you ok?" can go a long way. Your colleague will either

---

1. For further discussion of the change management process, see Harvard Business School Online, *5 Steps in the Change Management Process*, https://www.youtube.com/watch?v=wxVgd8h1svU.

show appreciation for you noticing and following up or dismiss the interaction. Either way, you have made the workplace a better place by showing some care and concern.

If your colleague opens a conversation with you, let them talk. Be a sounding board. Set your boundaries so as not to be pulled into any drama. However, showing empathy can be helpful. According to Brené Brown, a leader in empathy, empathy is *connecting to the emotions that underpin an experience.* Acknowledging frustration, anger, disappointment, or confusion can go a long way. If your colleague feels the behavior experienced is demeaning, condescending, or inappropriate, encourage your colleague to speak to a leader at the firm who can help defuse those types of situations. Sometimes leaders are not aware of how their comments, behaviors, or actions land on others. A seasoned human resources professional, professional development leader, or partner with a knack for offering feedback to those leaders in a constructive way can be hugely helpful to those well-intentioned leaders.

It's unlikely that by showing empathy you will be "blowing things out of proportion." Instead, you are showing that you noticed, that you care, and that you want to invest in a healthy culture at your workplace.

David: Thank you for sharing your question. I agree with Natalie's analysis that the workplace is in constant flux trying to find balance managing hybrid and in-person work structures. Some of the challenges that come along with that may include managing workplace conflict and addressing behavior that may be inappropriate. As employees spend more time in person, they may experience increased conflict because these interactions happened less frequently in a hybrid environment. Some people have more difficulty addressing conflict in person than dealing with it from behind a device. As Natalie points out, it can be highly effective to communicate directly, actively listen, and lead with care and empathy. However, I think it is important to note that if the behavior or conflict is ongoing or escalates, it may be considered an example of workplace bullying.

Workplace bullying is pervasive and can be extremely damaging to an employee as well as the organization. According to the Workplace Bullying Institute (WBI), "workplace bullying is repeated, health-harming mistreatment by one or more employees of an employee: abusive conduct that takes the form of verbal abuse; or behaviors perceived as threatening, intimidating, or humiliating; work sabotage; or in some combination of the above."[2] According to WBI, about 30% of all employees in the United States experience workplace bullying at least once. That equates to over forty-eight million employees. Workplace bullying can take the form of yelling, engaging in spreading rumors and lies, sabotaging work product, unfairly placing blame, withholding information, or physical behavior intended to harm and/or intimidate. In many cases, bullying behavior goes unreported and can persist over long periods of time and has a significant impact on the victims of bullying, which in turn impacts colleagues throughout the company.

I believe it is important to be mindful of behavior that may rise to the level of bullying and report it to HR or leadership. Bullying in the workplace also takes a significant toll on productivity and organizational culture and greatly increases attrition. Additionally, it can expose the organization to liability for creating a hostile work environment and causing harm to the victim(s). Individuals who suffer the effects of a bully often take medical leave or are more likely to utilize sick time. They can suffer from depression, damage to reputation, and diminished self-esteem. Eventually, it leads to employees quitting and potentially taking legal action against their employer.

It is vital that the person engaging in bullying behavior be confronted with their behavior and the impact it is having on others and presented with action items that they will be held accountable for to change their behavior. If a bully does not receive any feedback or is not held accountable, they will likely continue engaging in destructive behavior that can turn a workplace into a toxic culture, and there is a high likelihood that high-performing and talented stakeholders will leave. Even if a stakeholder is not the target of bullying, witnessing the impact of this behavior could be a factor as to whether that person decides to stay or leave.

As Natalie stated, workplace conflict may be caused by a misunderstanding or a dispute over personal preferences and can be resolved through dialogue and listening. However, if it is determined that conduct rises to the level of workplace bullying, the organization should have systems in place to support the victim of the conduct as well as

---

2. *See* https://workplacebullying.org/defined/.

address the aggressor in order to act with equity and send a message to the organization at large that this type of behavior will not be tolerated.

Dr. Fritz Galette: The quarantine abruptly disrupted our way of life, causing adjustments in how we live and work. We were reminded that not all of us were impacted the same. For some, remote and hybrid work schedules allowed for better handling of personal responsibilities, while for others it led to decreased productivity and isolation. For some, it facilitated some protection from daily office interactions laced with microaggressions and insensitivity. For others, it impacted career progressions as in-person interactions diminished, slowing the transfer of knowledge and experience through mentorship. Now, as we continue to return to in-person work, after a period of volatile, uncertain, complex, and ambiguous change (aka VUCA), we are a *changed workforce.*

During times of change, it is normal for there to be an extended period of adjustment and readjustment where we question and challenge the norms of the past. This includes daily office interactions and how they are affecting people. It is also normal for there to be a period of recovery and healing. Our continued growth and development require it. I agree with Natalie that there needs to be a greater awareness of the diversity of personalities, lived experiences, and workplace styles. We also need to be more mindfully aware of workplace interactions and more curious about how those interactions are affecting our people. I agree with David that we need to be alert to take action if those interactions rise to the level of bullying.

Unfortunately, workplace bullying is pervasive in places where we are not asking these questions. We need to build into our workplace culture the practices, policies, and procedures that result in inclusive safety, trust, and genuine interaction. We won't know if we are overreacting or under-responding in a given situation unless we are in a community with the very people who may be impacted. If we are intentionally working towards creating a culture of connection/community, we will know each other better and have a more informed sense of whether we are "overreacting" or being good fellow citizens of the workplace, responding appropriately and collaboratively whenever possible.

Key Takeaways and Action Items

Key Takeaway One

Empathy and Curiosity Are Powerful Tools for Cultural Health

Noticing discomfort or unsettling behavior in the workplace—and choosing to check in—demonstrates care and builds trust. Rather than fearing you're "overreacting," framing observations with curiosity can open up space for connection and support.

Action Items:

1. **Initiate a Caring Check-In:** Privately approach the colleague and gently share what you observed, using language like, "I noticed yesterday's interaction seemed tense—are you doing okay?"
2. **Practice Empathetic Listening:** Focus fully on their response, reflect back what you hear ("That sounds frustrating"), and validate their experience without judgment.
3. **Stay Curious, Not Reactive:** Avoid speculation or taking sides—ask open-ended questions to understand, not to solve, and keep the conversation constructive.

Key Takeaway Two

Know the Difference Between Conflict and Bullying

It's important to distinguish between typical workplace tension or style differences and conduct that crosses into bullying or hostility. Workplace bullying—when left unaddressed—can cause serious harm to individuals, erode firm culture, and even expose the organization to legal liability.

Action Items:

1. **Recognize the Signs:** Learn to distinguish normal conflict from bullying by watching for repeated patterns of verbal abuse, humiliation, exclusion, or sabotage.

2. **Document and Support:** Keep objective notes of incidents and encourage affected colleagues to share their experiences with HR or a trusted leader.

3. **Take Timely Action:** If harmful behavior persists, escalate by reporting it yourself—early intervention protects individuals and the firm's culture.

Key Takeaway Three

In a VUCA World, Culture Must Evolve Intentionally

The shift to hybrid work has fundamentally altered workplace norms, expectations, and emotional dynamics. With greater in-person presence, there's also a renewed need for cultural mindfulness, inclusive leadership, and community building to help people readjust—and feel safe.

Action Items:

1. **Create Space for Connection:** Build in regular informal check-ins or team huddles to support open, honest conversation and help people readjust to hybrid work.

2. **Champion Inclusion and Safety:** Advocate for policies and practices that promote psychological safety, belonging, and equitable participation.

3. **Model the Culture You Want:** Demonstrate respect, empathy, and constructive communication in every interaction to set the tone for others.

Chapter 33

Navigating Political and Social Tensions in the Legal Profession

Natalie Loeb & David B. Sarnoff

Dear Coaches:

> **I'm a managing partner overseeing several offices in my region and other areas of the country.**
>
> **Our attorneys and staff have diverse backgrounds and various points of view on hot-button issues. It has been brought to my attention that colleagues' differing opinions are creating conflict and tension in the office and interfering with client work. We've worked hard to create an inclusive, safe culture—what can I do to prevent this from eroding and reinforce respectful interactions within the firm?**
>
> ***—Feeling the Tension***

David: Thank you for your question and for being proactive in addressing the tensions within your firm. For what it is worth, you are not alone. Law firms and companies across the country are dealing with varying degrees of divisiveness or contentiousness among stakeholders, mostly revolving around politics, social issues, or internal rivalries. With respect to election results, I know that some firms issue statements to stakeholders to please not gloat to colleagues if their candidate wins and asking people to act with humility. Likewise, they ask stakeholders whose candidate loses to accept the result with grace and be prepared to move forward. While communicating these expectations is helpful, it is probably not enough at this stage. However, it can be a start to move forward in an inclusive way that promotes civility.

Addressing conflict and tension within a law firm requires a multipronged approach that leverages emotional intelligence, active listening, empathy, and effective conflict management strategies. As a managing partner overseeing several offices, you are in a unique position to lead by example and reinforce a culture of respect, inclusivity, and collaboration. I share the following with all leaders that I coach: Leaders model the behavior they expect of others. Hard stop. If the leaders are not willing to set the example for everyone else, it is highly unlikely their strategy will be successful. However, if leaders are going to lead from the front, there are several practices and strategies that can be socialized throughout the firm that will go a long way to communicate the expected behaviors and how they impact organizational culture. If the leaders of a firm are not willing to invest the time and resources to model the way, then they should rethink their plan.

Demonstrate Emotionally Intelligent Behaviors

First and foremost, leaders have to model emotionally intelligent behaviors. When I say emotional intelligence, I mean having the self-awareness to understand how you show up, how you are perceived, and how your words and actions impact others. I often quote Maya Angelou, who sums up this concept in a quote attributed to her, "People will forget what you said, they will forget what you did, but people will never forget how you made them feel."

Emotional intelligence also includes the ability to recognize, understand, and manage your own emotions as well as recognizing the emotions of others. For managing partners like yourself, this is a critical skill when navigating office conflict and reinforcing a respectful culture. If tensions are high and you recognize that you may be in an elevated state, e.g., your breathing is rapid and there is a tightness in your stomach, recognize that may not be the best time to move forward with a discussion that may escalate; if possible, adjourn to a later time when calmer heads can prevail.

Once you are aware of your emotions, managing them becomes key. Leading by example in this regard—remaining calm, composed, and acting equitably when faced with tension—sets the tone for the rest of the firm. If your team sees that you handle conflict with a level head, they are more likely to emulate this behavior. There is another saying, "Calmness is contagious."

Build Inclusivity Through Empathy

Empathy, or the ability to understand and share the feelings of others, also plays a crucial role in creating an inclusive and respectful workplace. Being aware of the interactions among your team members, especially those arising from differing perspectives, will help you address concerns before they escalate. Strong relationships are at the core of high-performing teams. By fostering open dialogue and providing an environment where everyone feels heard, you can defuse potential conflicts at an early stage. Establish yourself as a leader who is approachable, fair, and willing to listen to all sides before making decisions.

Be Present and Practice Active Listening

If you commit to hearing others' perspectives, it is important that you are present, focused, and tuned in and not distracted by email or devices. If your attention is elsewhere while someone is trying to share their feelings or perspectives, you send a message that what they are saying has little importance to you. To avoid being distracted, practice active listening, an effective strategy for staying focused. Active listening is a powerful tool for preventing misunderstandings, and it de-escalates conflicts. Active listening is an exertion that requires you to resist the impulse to be distracted and to ask follow-up questions for clarity or to confirm your understanding. In a legal setting, where the stakes are high and tensions can rise, ensuring that all voices are heard can help mitigate friction. One of my clients works at a company where the mantra is, "Disagree But Commit." Everyone on the team can contribute to the decision making, but when the leader makes a final decision, everyone commits to following through on the final decision, even if they disagree with it.

Given the diversity of viewpoints in your offices, it is essential to provide a forum where employees feel safe to express their thoughts without fear of retaliation or judgment.

Ensure a Judgment-Free Forum for Employees

Encourage meetings or informal discussions during which team members can voice concerns or opinions constructively. However, if you commit to this practice, it is important to clearly communicate your expectations that colleagues proceed with civility and respect; if anyone acts outside the expectations, you must hold them accountable.

The accountability piece is where most firms stumble, and the lack of accountability typically exacerbates the situation.

Advocate for an Inclusive Workplace

Promote a culture of inclusivity where different opinions are respected, even when not agreed upon. Sometimes conflict arises because people feel left out or feel that their opinions were not given consideration. By making inclusivity a norm, you can help prevent conflict from arising due to perceived slights or exclusion. Help your team understand that disagreement is natural, especially in a diverse workplace. However, the focus should be on disagreeing respectfully. Establish guidelines for discussions around controversial topics, emphasizing respect and understanding over winning an argument. This can reduce the likelihood of discussions spiraling into personal attacks.

Minimize Disputes and Maintain Organizational Culture with Communication

An effective way to prevent conflict from damaging your firm's culture is to address it as soon as it arises. Avoid letting tensions simmer and go unresolved as this can lead to resentment, low morale, and finger pointing. Conduct regular check-ins with team leaders to gauge the atmosphere in each office and identify potential flashpoints before they become full-blown issues. Provide your attorneys and staff with training on conflict resolution and effective communication skills; in my opinion, this is an underutilized tool that's effective for addressing conflict that's destructive to the firm. Empowering your team with the tools to manage their own conflicts can reduce the burden on leadership to intervene in every dispute. Moreover, training ensures that everyone in the firm understands the importance of respectful interactions and has the information to handle difficult conversations.

In situations where conflicts between colleagues become particularly heated, consider offering mediation or facilitated dialogue with an impartial third party. I have conducted multiple mediation sessions between stakeholders. In one case, I facilitated dialogue between an executive director and a general counsel. By our third session, there was a breakthrough when the executive director said, "I didn't know that's why you did that. Had I known that, I would not have reacted as I did." Simply put, the conflict could have been resolved at an early stage if there was direct communication between the parties. If you don't explain your actions, others will interpret with their own emotions and reasoning, which will typically go to a dark place. A neutral third-party mediator can help both sides understand each other's viewpoints and guide them toward a resolution. This helps maintain relationships and prevents conflicts from escalating and causing wider harm.

Reinforce the values of respect, collaboration, and inclusion by setting clear behavioral expectations. Create or update the firm's code of conduct to reflect these values, and make sure that everyone—regardless of position—is held accountable for upholding them. Make no mistake. Holding anyone, let alone firm leaders, accountable is always difficult; but firms distinguish themselves by having impactful accountability practices, which significantly improves behavior. Leaders who model these behaviors create a ripple effect throughout the firm, setting a standard for all employees to follow.

In a law firm, hot-button issues such as politics, race, gender, and other societal concerns can trigger strong emotions. While it is important to foster open dialogue, you must also create boundaries that prevent these discussions from becoming toxic.

As a managing partner, your role in fostering emotional intelligence, empathy, and active listening within your team is crucial to preventing conflict from eroding your firm's culture. By promoting respectful interactions, addressing conflict early, and leading by example, you can maintain an inclusive environment where differing perspectives are valued rather than feared. Ensuring that your attorneys and staff are equipped to manage stress and conflict effectively will reinforce the firm's commitment to respect, inclusion, and collaboration.

Natalie: I completely concur with everything David shared. When a culture of divisiveness exists and is nurtured, it takes courage, and the skills David described, to intentionally change it. Ultimately, you, as the leader and managing partner of the firm, get to decide what culture you want to prevail at your firm. If you decide it is a culture of inclusion and safety, you must be intentional about modeling those behaviors and holding others accountable when others display behaviors that are not consistent with what you expect.

One of my favorite parables is *Two Wolves*. I think of it often as I navigate the internal conflicts I experience when interacting with others with differences of opinions. The story of the *Two Wolves* is a memetic legend of unknown origin, commonly attributed to Cherokee or other indigenous American peoples in popular retelling. The legend is usually framed as a grandfather or elder passing wisdom to a young listener; the elder describes a battle between two wolves within one's self, using the battle as a metaphor for inner conflict. One inner wolf has "destructive" traits like manipulation, arrogance, deception, envy, and greed, while the other embodies "good" traits like empathy, compassion, curiosity, active listening, integrity, and honesty. When the listener asks which wolf wins, the grandfather answers, "whichever one you feed." As managing partner, your behaviors "feed" the culture of your firm. It is why it is so important to be self-aware, self-reflective, and diligent about addressing your own and others' behaviors.

Other behaviors come to mind in addition to what David shared. I found them very useful and positively impactful when I found myself in a divisive situation. After September 11, 2001, I struggled with the attack on our country and the backlash on many of our citizens. I feared for the safety of my family, community, colleagues, and friends. There was much discussion around how to respond to the attack on our soil. I was surrounded by divisiveness, and it was highly stressful.

One of my colleagues noted this, and I was invited to participate in an "Israeli-Palestinian Dialogue Group." It was not necessary to be Israeli or Palestinian to be a member, but it was necessary to bring myself to the multi-cultural group with a learner's mindset and a sense of curiosity. I committed to do that.

If you are a regular reader of our column, you are familiar with the word "dialogue." David and I use it often. The definition we like to refer to follows: **Dialogue** demands our ability to participate effectively in a way in which everyone aspires to win together. We must be prepared to question our assumptions, which takes effort when many, including the most powerful among them, are often held unconsciously.

This practice of dialogue meant I had to be prepared to question my own assumptions and unconscious biases. I had to bring "curiosity," not "conflict," to our meetings. This intentional curiosity meant I had to heighten my listening and empathy skills (as David mentioned), while challenging and checking for biases that were contributing to conflict. This was hard work. However, I learned a lot and it paid off. On Holocaust Remembrance Day (I am Jewish), I was asked by the leader of the group to light one of the remembrance candles. I will never forget when one of the Palestinian members stood up and asked to light it with me. We both had committed to curiosity, dialogue, challenging our assumptions, and choosing a learner's mindset. This moving moment has helped me to navigate other divisive situations. It reminds me to keep the aspirational goal of inclusion and safety in mind; and with a commitment to intentional behaviors that foster inclusion, it is possible.

Like David said at the beginning of this column, *thank you for your question and for being proactive in addressing the tensions within your firm.* We hope we have given you a few things to think about and act upon as you foster the culture of inclusion and safety you so clearly value at your firm.

Key Takeaways and Action Items

Key Takeaway One

Culture Change Starts with Emotionally Intelligent Leadership

Managing partners must model the behaviors they want to see—empathy, composure, active listening, and accountability. Emotionally intelligent leadership sets the tone and has a ripple effect across the firm.

Action Items:

Practice and model emotional intelligence by:

1. Checking in with your own emotional state before entering difficult conversations.
2. Demonstrating empathy and curiosity when colleagues express concern or frustration.
3. Holding firm leaders, not just staff, accountable for behavior that undermines culture.

Start each leadership meeting with a reflection: "What behaviors are we modeling, and how are they being received?"

Key Takeaway Two

Proactive Dialogue and Listening Prevent Escalation

Creating spaces for dialogue—before tensions escalate—is essential. When employees feel heard in safe, judgment-free environments, misunderstandings can be resolved and divisions softened. Silence or avoidance often deepens the divide.

Action Items:

1. **Create Regular Dialogue Opportunities:** Host structured forums—such as roundtables, town halls, or facilitated discussions—so employees can voice concerns in a safe, constructive way.

2. **Set Clear Behavioral Norms:** Establish expectations for civility, respectful engagement, and confidentiality to encourage open participation.

3. **Equip Leaders to Respond Well:** Provide training in active listening and conflict de-escalation, and make mediation or coaching resources available when issues arise.

Key Takeaway Three

Intentional Inclusion Requires Curiosity, Not Certainty

In times of heightened division—political, social, or interpersonal—leaders must bring curiosity rather than judgment. Choosing dialogue over debate and adopting a learner's mindset can foster surprising moments of connection, even across deep divides.

Action Items:

Encourage a "dialogue mindset" across the firm:

1. Provide training on unconscious bias, perspective-taking, and inclusive communication.

2. Incorporate curiosity-based questions into team check-ins (e.g., *"What's something you've changed your mind about recently?"*).

3. When facing divisive topics, model humility and share your own learning experiences.

Use the *Two Wolves* parable shared in this chapter to reinforce the idea that culture is fed by intentional behaviors—and leaders choose which traits to nurture.

Case Study

Reading the Room—Even on Zoom: Managing Emotions and Communication in High-Pressure Deals

Background

Harper, Lane & Marks LLP is a full-service firm with a thriving Corporate/M&A practice. The group just landed a major cross-border deal with an aggressive timeline. The deal team includes partners, senior and junior associates, client executives, and outside advisors spread across multiple time zones.

With pressure mounting to meet deliverables, communication missteps and frayed emotions are beginning to show up—and risk undermining team cohesion at a critical moment.

Key Participants

- **Daniel Cho (Partner, Lead Deal Counsel):** Exceptionally skilled at negotiating, admired by clients for his precision and calm. However, he tends to be emotionally reserved and can seem unapproachable to associates.
- **Rachel Perez (Senior Associate):** Highly capable and trusted by Daniel for drafting and managing diligence. Recently, she's felt overlooked and undervalued, as her ideas are often not acknowledged in meetings.

- **Tom Watkins (Mid-Level Associate):** Known for his speed and wit. His humor sometimes drifts into sarcasm, which junior associates find intimidating.
- **Jade O'Connell (Junior Associate):** New to M&A work. She is eager to learn but hesitant to ask "basic" questions in front of partners and clients.
- **Anita Shah (Transaction Coordinator):** Manages closing checklists and liaises with specialists across offices. She is observant and diplomatic but often becomes the unofficial "therapist" for team frustrations.

Scenario

During a virtual all-hands deal update, Rachel flagged that the diligence review was running behind because of last-minute requests. Daniel acknowledged the comment briefly but quickly moved to the next agenda item.

Later that day:

- **Tom** made a sarcastic remark on a group chat: "Guess we'll just pull an all-nighter (again)." Some laughed, but Jade felt uneasy and worried she was missing something.
- **Rachel** privately vented to Anita that she feels her input is ignored and that she's carrying too much of the workload.
- **Daniel** sent a late-night email thanking the team for "grinding through" but gave no specific recognition.
- The next morning, a miscommunication about a client's requested closing deliverable led to a sharp exchange between Rachel and Tom on a group call, with Rachel criticizing Tom's lack of attention to detail and Tom audibly sighing and cutting his camera.

Morale is declining. Jade is quietly considering whether M&A is the right path for her. The group is still meeting deadlines, but the emotional tone is tense—and deal fatigue is setting in.

Learning Themes and Application of Emotional Intelligence

1. **Emotional Self-Awareness and Regulation**
   - M&A deals are stressful by nature. Leaders must monitor their own tone and emotional state to avoid unintentionally spreading anxiety to the team.
   - *Key Link:* Chapter 27, Using Communication to Defeat Frustration—slowing down to respond thoughtfully, not reactively.
2. **Recognition and Engagement**
   - Public, specific acknowledgment of contributions prevents burnout and attrition.
   - *Key Link:* Chapter 29, Is Praise As Important As a Paycheck?—recognition is a powerful motivator.
3. **Psychological Safety**
   - Juniors like Jade need explicit permission to ask questions and learn without fear of embarrassment.
   - *Key Link:* Chapter 30, Don't Let Senior Associates Slip Through the Cracks—if seniors feel invisible, the next generation sees that as a warning sign.
4. **De-Escalation and Civility**
   - Tension between Rachel and Tom needs to be reset before it poisons the group dynamic.
   - *Key Link:* Chapter 32, Distinguishing Bickering from Bullying—leaders must model calm and create constructive channels for disagreement.
5. **Two-Way Feedback Culture**
   - Associates need space to share concerns and ideas safely.
   - *Key Link:* Chapter 19, Feedback Matters: Creating a Two-Way Street—leaders should actively seek feedback on their communication and management style.

Positive Leadership Behaviors Present

- Daniel's email, though lacking specificity, shows that he notices the team's hard work and wants to encourage them.
- Rachel's willingness to raise concerns shows commitment to deal success and team well-being.
- Anita is quietly building trust by listening to frustrations—an important foundation for psychological safety.

Developmental Opportunities

- Daniel could increase psychological safety by acknowledging comments during meetings and inviting follow-up.
- Rachel and Tom both need to manage conflict more constructively, focusing on facts, not personal frustration.
- The team needs a system to celebrate "small wins" along the way to keep motivation high during long deals.

Facilitator's Guide

Reading the Room—Even on Zoom: Managing Emotions and Communication in High-Pressure Deals

Key Learning Themes

- **Emotional Self-Awareness and Regulation:** Leaders set the tone. Monitoring your own emotional state helps keep the team grounded during deal stress.
- **Recognition and Engagement:** Timely, specific praise is a key driver of motivation and retention, especially in M&A where long hours can erode morale.
- **Psychological Safety:** Creating space for questions and contributions from junior team members improves quality and reduces avoidable errors.
- **Constructive Conflict Management:** Healthy debate should focus on issues, not people, and leaders must model calm, respectful resolution.
- **Two-Way Feedback:** Communication is strongest when feedback flows up as well as down, allowing leaders to adjust their style and improve team culture.

Positive Leadership Behaviors in the Case Study

- **Team Recognition:** Daniel's late-night thank-you email (while not specific) demonstrated awareness of the team's efforts.
- **Raising Concerns:** Rachel flagged a staffing issue, signaling engagement and commitment to team success.
- **Quiet Listening:** Anita checked in with team members and offered a safe space for venting, laying groundwork for psychological safety.

Developmental Behaviors to Address

- **Missed Opportunities for Acknowledgment:** Daniel did not validate Rachel's input during the meeting, sending an unintended message that concerns are secondary to speed.
- **Unconstructive Conflict:** Rachel's criticism of Tom and Tom's sarcasm undermined collaboration and damaged psychological safety.
- **Vague Recognition:** "Thanks for grinding" lacked specificity, leaving associates unsure of what behaviors to repeat.
- **Silenced Voices:** Jade's reluctance to speak up indicates the need for explicit permission to ask questions and contribute ideas.

Reflection Questions for Readers

Emotional Self-Awareness and Regulation

- How do you personally notice when deal stress is affecting your tone or communication?
- What practices help you "cool down" before responding under pressure?

Recognition and Engagement

- When was the last time you recognized a specific contribution on a deal?

- How can you make your recognition more timely, precise, and meaningful?

Psychological Safety

- What signals do you send—intentionally or unintentionally—that either encourage or discourage questions from junior lawyers?
- How do you ensure that all voices are heard in a high-stakes deal call?

Conflict and Civility

- How do you intervene when tension between team members becomes personal or public?
- What behaviors model respectful disagreement for others?

Two-Way Feedback

- How do you invite associates to share feedback on your communication or leadership style?
- How do you respond when the feedback is difficult to hear?

Application

- **Calm Is Contagious:** Your emotional regulation sets the climate for the entire deal team.
- **Specific Praise Drives Retention:** Associates are more likely to stay engaged when they know exactly what they are doing well.
- **Psychological Safety Improves Quality:** Explicitly invite questions and contributions from junior team members.
- **Address Conflict Early:** De-escalate tense moments before they damage trust or derail collaboration.
- **Feedback Must Flow Both Ways:** Make it a routine practice to ask, "How am I doing at keeping communication clear for you?"

Suggested Reader Exercise

After reading this case study, reflect and write down:

1. **One behavior to amplify** from the positive examples (e.g., acknowledging input in real time, creating a closing checklist celebration ritual).
2. **One developmental area to work on** (e.g., giving specific praise, modeling constructive disagreement).
3. **One concrete step** you will take in your next deal cycle to strengthen team communication and emotional intelligence.

Part IV

Well-Being and Inclusion

Chapter 34

Is a Lack of Equitable Feedback Hindering Your Path to an Inclusive Workplace?

Natalie Loeb & David B. Sarnoff

Dear Coaches:

> **I am a partner in a law firm and happen to be a white male in my early 50s. While I view myself as a mentor, I have struggled with giving effective feedback to associates who are people of color and/or female for fear of saying the wrong thing or being perceived as ignorant. I find giving feedback even more difficult in a remote setting on Zoom. How would you advise me?**
>
> ***—Mentor in the Making***

David: I appreciate the question and believe this is a widely held sentiment among law firm partners when it comes to giving feedback across differences. While law firm partners giving equitable feedback to associates who are different from themselves has been a long-term issue, I believe this issue has been exacerbated by remote working environments created by the COVID-19 pandemic. For background, as remote working has become ingrained in the law firm work model, law firms continue to be quite successful in carrying on operations and providing service to their clients under extraordinarily difficult circumstances. I think this success is due in large part to the contribution of business service professionals and administration support professionals who showed up in person during the pandemic when many colleagues were working remotely; and many of these employees are people of color and from underrepresented communities. That being said, Loeb Leadership's research throughout the pandemic indicated that attorneys and legal professionals experienced high levels of anxiety, stress, isolation, and loneliness. Long-term issues involving diversity, equity, and inclusion were also spotlighted as being negatively impacted by remote working and the lack of in-person contact. While law firms have been able to effectively operate their businesses for the most part, cracks appeared as the Great Resignation in 2021 picked up steam, and the legal profession was not immune.

During that time, many attorneys and legal professionals were hired over Zoom and did not meet colleagues in person. Onboarding procedures were adapted and modified to meet the needs under the circumstances. However, when the market began to return to the office, attorneys began to seek other opportunities where there was more inclusion, flexible schedules, mentoring, and practical skills development. Data from exit interviews and surveys that I reviewed clearly illustrate that associates in particular did not feel connected to the culture of their firms, were required to work for the same people, were lacking variety of assignments, did not receive effective feedback, and did not feel mentored. Through conversations, I found this to be particularly true with attorneys from underrepresented communities who did not feel included as members of the team and, specifically, did not receive feedback with equity. For example, an attorney in the audience of one of my feedback presentations, a woman of color, shared that she did not receive the same depth of feedback as her white colleagues did; however, she was held to the same standards of skills and performance for promotion.

Law firm leadership and partners should focus greater attention on how associates receive feedback and ask, "is it being done equitably?" While it is not unusual for individuals to gravitate to like-minded colleagues, people who went to the same school, or people who are from the same place, it is a disservice to the associates who are denied the same quality of feedback because they may look different or have different backgrounds than the partners they report to.

While it may be difficult for you to engage in this feedback dialogue, I believe that if you approach it with genuine and sincere motives to improve the performance of your associates, your feedback will be well received. Giving feedback should be a dialogue, and I recommend that you communicate to associates that your feedback sessions are a two-way conversation. Associates should be cognizant that you encourage them to ask questions and react to your feedback and that you expect them to provide *you* with feedback about how you can better support them.

Try setting up the dialogue from a spirit of care that communicates you are trying to elevate the performance of the associate receiving your feedback. While the words "care" and "empathy" may make law firm partners uncomfortable, it is highly effective to say to an associate, "I care about your career path and professional development. And because I care, I need to give you this feedback." In my opinion, setting up the dialogue this way allows you to deliver direct feedback, and the associate will focus more on what you are saying as opposed to how you are saying it. The best practice for delivering feedback is to specifically describe the situation involved, the objective behaviors that were observed, the impact of those behaviors, and action items for the person receiving the feedback to incorporate into their work.

Partners and leaders also need to raise their self-awareness and identify their biases in how they deliver effective feedback. Investing the time and effort toward creating an inclusive culture goes a long way to implementing these practices. Firms often set out to hire more women, people of color, and people from underrepresented communities and believe they can subsequently figure out how to meet their needs. This strategy is unlikely to position them for success. Firms should first do some homework to understand the general needs of a diverse workforce and create an environment that welcomes and anticipates the needs of new hires, particularly people from underrepresented communities. Additionally, these practices should not only apply to attorneys; implementing these practices for all employees will create an inclusive culture and positive workplace for everyone.

In January 2022, I moderated a panel for a Loeb Leadership public dialogue session[1] about creating an inclusive culture. Some of the key takeaways included:

1. Consider creating mentoring programs, a robust onboarding process lasting up to six months with regular check-ins, and providing resources to make people from underrepresented communities feel valued and included.

2. Use exit interview data to make real-time adjustments and modifications to the firm's practices. This data should be shared with firm leadership and practice group leaders.

3. Don't wait until employees leave. Conduct periodic surveys and focus groups to keep your finger on the pulse of the firm.

4. Spend time to truly understand the exorbitant cost of replacing an employee compared to the cost of training and development.

5. An inclusive culture needs to be designed by the stakeholders of the organization instead of with an off-the-shelf process.

The development of a truly inclusive culture where employees receive feedback with equity will benefit everyone in the organization.

Natalie: Thank you for this question. Let me begin with congratulating you on your demonstration of leadership by asking such a brave question. It takes courage, vulnerability, and strength all at the same time. Your question is courageous because you are saying something "out loud" that other people have asked me quietly over the years. It also combines vulnerability with strength because you are aware that you have more to learn—and have the strength to ask for help. You are also modeling behaviors that the brave people of color/women working for you will respect and admire. Keep in mind, our firms are filled with diverse talent who show bravery and courage every day. And they are looking for those same behaviors in their leaders.

---

1. *See* Loeb Leadership Safe Space Workshop (Jan. 24, 2022), vimeo.com.

As a white woman in a leadership role, I am continuously on my own journey to learn. Like you, I want to be seen and experienced as a good mentor to others. Also, like you, I have struggled with giving effective feedback to people of color and/or to those that identify differently from me for fear of saying the wrong thing or being perceived as ignorant. At the same time, intellectually, I know that withholding feedback is not good. It removes the opportunity for others to learn, grow, and develop. I marvel at the bravery and courage shown by the diverse talent I am surrounded by every day. I have had to push through my fear of saying the wrong thing and learn to place the growth and development of others first.

Unfortunately, if you let this fear get in the way of providing critical performance feedback, you are limiting opportunities for learning and success. Most damaging, it diminishes any chance of you building authentic relationships of trust with your associates.

All of your associates deserve:

- The benefit of feedback so they can strengthen their skills to be the best lawyers they can be.
- The benefit of the wisdom, experiences, and lessons you have learned over the years. This experience includes your learnings about the influential people inside and outside of your firm.
- To be led by someone they can trust, by someone who shows they care about them enough to listen to them, learn about them, and lead them.

Brené Brown, a researcher from the University of Texas, wrote: "When we spend our lives waiting until we're perfect or bulletproof before we walk into the arena, we ultimately sacrifice relationships and opportunities that may not be recoverable, we squander our precious time, and we turn our backs on our gifts, those unique contributions that only we can make."[2]

---

2. Brené Brown, Daring Greatly: How the Courage to Be Vulnerable Transforms the Way We Live, Love, Parent, and Lead (APA 7th ed. 2012).

Simply put: you need to walk into the arena. When you walk into the arena, there is a chance you will get knocked down. Getting knocked down is one of the privileges of being in the arena, because you then have the choice to get back up again. Getting back up again is the resilience, grit, and strength required to navigate the issue you have brought to us. Accept that you will most likely get "knocked down." It is how you recover that matters.

As an example, I was stunned when, five years ago, my Black niece asked me the day after our annual Thanksgiving dinner, "Aunt Nat, how come we have been having Thanksgiving dinners together for twenty-four years and we have never talked about the fact that my father is Black and my mother is White at the dining table." For twenty-four years, none of us entered the arena. This event made me think about the risk of *not* entering the arena, both personally and professionally.

Since this time, my niece and I have had many conversations. Some go better than others. All result in new learnings that we can take with us into further conversations. We are both entering the arena. It is moving us forward to a better place.

I realize now that I was waiting all that time for my niece to begin the conversation about herself and her family because I didn't want her to feel like she was in any way different than the rest of our family. When in fact, my niece was very aware that she looks different than many of us and, as a result, has had a different life experience than many of us. After the killing of George Floyd, my niece invited our entire family to a dialogue group. She skillfully facilitated it, beginning conversations we all wanted to have yet no one initiated in the past. My niece is very brave and courageous. In retrospect, I wish I had initiated more conversation rather than waiting for her to do it. Just yesterday, my niece told me having these conversations has made her feel closer, safer, and more a part of the family.

> *Expecting a person of color to navigate a conversation that humanity has been woefully unskilled at, while managing their own racial trauma, borders on cruelty.*[3]—Dr. Tiffany Jana

---

3. Tiffany Jana, *How to Lose a Chief Diversity Officer in 6 Months*, Medium (Apr. 22, 2021), https://index.medium.com/how-to-lose-a-chief-diversity-officer-in-6-months-6db0dfba6169.

Dr. Jana's comment above reminds me, as a White woman, that it is *my* responsibility as a leader to do what I can to enter into conversations with people of color and different lifestyles than my own. And Brené Brown's words are crystal clear: We all need to enter the arena. Fear cannot keep us out. We may risk getting beaten up, but if we enter the arena knowing there is a possibility of getting knocked down, we can be prepared for it, know how to brush ourselves off and get up again, and keep going.

1. How to enter the arena: Come from a place of curiosity.
    - "I'm not familiar with how you came to this conclusion. Please share your thinking with me."
    - "I realize we may be looking at this situation from two different perspectives. May I share mine and then I'd like to hear yours?"
    - "Please help me. What am I missing?"
    - "Tell me more. I'm interested in what influenced your thinking."
    - "How can I be most helpful/useful to you?"
2. How to get up after getting knocked down: Be brave and remember your goal is learning how to be the mentor they need you to be.
    - "That comment wasn't received as it was intended. Can I try again?"
    - "Please help me understand."
    - "My intention is to provide you with the feedback and support you need to be successful. If it doesn't seem like that, please help me understand. What am I missing and what could I do differently?"

All of the prior suggestions require exhibiting courage, vulnerability, and strength all at the same time. You have already demonstrated those qualities by asking this question. Now go get in the arena. Do it with a sense of curiosity and watch what happens.

Overall, human beings have an intense desire to be seen and heard. When you step into the arena with respect and an understanding you are being an excellent leader, you are demonstrating that you are seeing the other person and want to listen. My niece told me, “A real leader doesn’t mean you hold all the knowledge or power. Instead, a real leader makes space so that others feel connected to the environment and like they are being offered clear direction.” She is brave, courageous, and also very smart.

Key Takeaways and Action Items

Key Takeaway One

Inclusion Means Everyone Gets Feedback

Avoiding feedback conversations out of fear—especially across race, gender, or other differences—can unintentionally deprive associates of growth, mentorship, and advancement. True inclusion means ensuring everyone receives timely, honest, and actionable feedback.

Action Items:

1. Reframe feedback as a gift and a sign of care. Begin with statements like, "I'm sharing this because I want to support your growth and success here."
2. Practice a structured feedback model: describe the situation, identify observable behavior, explain its impact, and outline specific suggestions for improvement.
3. Ensure feedback is given equitably by regularly reflecting on your own habits—track whom you're mentoring, how often, and what kind of feedback you're providing.

Key Takeaway Two

Feedback Across Differences Takes Courage, Curiosity, and Repair

Giving feedback across differences requires courage to step into discomfort, curiosity to learn from others' experiences, and vulnerability to make mistakes and recover. Avoiding the conversation is often more harmful than saying the wrong thing.

Action Items:

1. Use curiosity-driven language to foster dialogue: "Tell me more," "What am I missing?," or "Can I try again?"
2. Normalize imperfection: If a comment lands poorly, acknowledge it, apologize, and recommit to the relationship. Model resilience.

3. Initiate rather than wait—don't place the burden on associates to bring up identity-based issues or feedback needs.

Key Takeaway Three

Build the Infrastructure for Inclusive Feedback

To sustain inclusive feedback practices, law firms must build systems that support equity and connection, especially in hybrid or remote environments. This includes creating safe spaces, mentorship infrastructure, and proactive check-ins.

Action Items:

1. Advocate for formal mentoring programs, extended onboarding, and ongoing inclusion dialogues tailored for underrepresented attorneys.
2. Encourage firm leaders to review exit data, pulse surveys, and focus groups with an inclusion lens to identify blind spots in feedback and support.
3. Lead by example: share your own learning journey and mistakes publicly to normalize vulnerability in leadership and signal that feedback across differences is a shared responsibility.

Chapter 35

Advocating for Your Attorneys' Mental Health

Natalie Loeb & David B. Sarnoff

Dear Coaches:

> **I'm a senior associate at a law firm and also serve on the firm's wellness committee. Many, if not all, of the associates I oversee are burned out after working endlessly through the pandemic. They're reluctant to use their vacation/time off because they notice partners forgoing or working through vacation. I care about these associates and know that in order to remain at their best they need some time to themselves to reenergize. I'm seeking advice for ideas I can present to our wellness committee that will help my associates (and others at the firm) sustain their performance while remaining emotionally and mentally healthy.**
>
> ***—Prioritizing Wellness to Impact People and Performance***

David: Thank you for this question. It is one that applies to everyone in the legal profession. We often hear from our clients or attendees at our programs that they are stressed out, burned out, and do not take time off from work. They do not feel like their best selves. This is a common theme, especially in the legal profession where there is high stress, deadlines, emphasis on billable hours in many firms, and lack of time to disconnect and reduce stress.

What I find contributes to this lack of self-care is that partners do not model the behavior that they expect of others. If a firm is communicating to its associates that there is an expectation that vacation time and personal time should be used, then partners need to model it as well. If they don't, they are sending mixed messages and sowing confusion in the ranks of associates. For example, I have coached senior leaders who are workaholics, sending emails late at night and on weekends. However, these same leaders tell members of their teams that they don't have to work as hard as they do. When I interview the members of the team, they are skeptical that that message rings true. One associate told me, "I was told I don't have to work as hard as the partner. However, I have not seen anyone get promoted who has worked less."

Additionally, when that same associate had taken time off, there were no set boundaries, and they were receiving calls and emails while they were on vacation. I think it is vital that the wellness committee at your firm discuss what is actually being communicated to not only associates at the firm, but all partners, directors, managers, and individual contributors throughout the firm. When it comes to wellness and self-care, there should not be one standard for attorneys and another one for non-attorneys, or one standard for partners and another for associates. A firm that has a consistent and substantive wellness program, that holds people accountable to practice self-care, will generally have a more rested, happy, and productive workforce.

There is significant research on the toll of stress in the legal profession that leads to destructive behaviors, self-harm, substance abuse, and suicide. Burnout behaviors such as lack of sleep and rest and working late hours manifest into physical and psychological health issues and illness. There are two prominent studies that come to mind that I highly recommend. The first, which was commissioned by several organizations, including the ABA, is "The Path to Lawyer Well-Being: Practical Recommendations for Positive Change,"[1] published in 2017 by the National Task Force on Lawyer Well-Being. The release

---

1. Inst. for Well-Being in Law (formerly Nat'l Task Force on Lawyer Well-Being), *The Path to Lawyer Well-Being: Practical Recommendations for Positive Change* (Aug. 2017), https://lawyerwellbeing.net/the-report/.

of this report resulted in a national movement among stakeholders in the legal profession to take action to improve well-being. In December 2020, the Institute for Well-Being in Law (IWIL) was formed to carry on the movement launched by the National Task Force.

The other study is the ABA-Hazelden Betty Ford Foundation's "The Prevalence of Substance Use and Other Mental Health Concerns Among American Attorneys,"[2] which was published in the Journal of Addiction Medicine in 2016. More than 12,000 lawyers were surveyed, and the study yielded eye-opening figures on lawyers suffering from mental health afflictions.

These studies document the impact and long-term effects on attorneys and legal professionals working in the industry and highlight the need for intervention by firm leaders and experts to address this issue in an empathetic and public way within the firm.

Some ideas to bring back to your committee would be to require employees to utilize vacation time and hold them accountable by an agreed-upon measure. Partners and firm leadership need to play an active role in messaging and modeling the behavior by using their own vacation time and refraining from contacting associates and colleagues who are out of the office. There are also activities such as fitness groups within the firm that commit to walking a certain number of steps a day or commit to a cardio activity multiple times a week. Many firms also bring in experts to perform and teach guided meditation, yoga, and box-breathing techniques. These are all helpful practices to reduce stress, rest the brain, and rejuvenate the body.

When a firm is responsive to addressing its employees' burnout, fatigue, stress management, and wellness, employees will feel valued.

Natalie: First, let me congratulate you for making wellness a priority and serving on the firm's wellness committee. Right there, you are sending the message that you believe wellness should be part of the fabric of the firm. You are demonstrating leadership by stepping up,

---

2. Patrick R. Krill, Ryan Johnson & Linda Albert, *The Prevalence of Substance Use and Other Mental Health Concerns Among American Attorneys*, J. ADDICTION MED. 46–52 (Jan./Feb. 2016), https://journals.lww.com/journaladdictionmedicine/fulltext/2016/02000/the_prevalence_of_substance_use_and_other_mental.8.aspx.

getting involved, and exploring options to help the members of your firm live mentally healthy and productive lives.

David mentioned some important studies that prove the necessity for prioritizing wellness. "The Path to Lawyer Well-Being" emphasizes that "well-being is a team sport." The messaging on the IWIL site where the report can be found reminds us that "The contexts in which we live and work such as organizational and professional cultures can play a powerful role in helping or harming individual well-being. Each of us contributes to our workplace and institutional cultures and each is affected by it. What this means is that we're all in this together."[3]

Many of our clients tell us how the loneliness of working remotely affected them. This is coming to the forefront as we ease back into the workplace with hybrid work arrangements. With a renewed emphasis on the importance of wellness in the workplace, these same clients now have research and support to help them overcome some of the stressors that came along with working through a pandemic and what seems to many like continuous change. For some, change is exciting. For others, it is uncomfortable. For all of us, it creates some sort of stress.

In Dr. Fritz Galette's article, "How Change Changes Us,"[4] Dr. Galette says, "Going forward, organizations have to evolve to meet the demands of the times. Systems are composed of humans and thus need to operate as living organisms whose survival depends on flexibility, adaptation, and growth." Your role on your firm's wellness committee will require you to model flexibility, adaptation, and growth. Some ideas for you:

- Test the waters and offer bold ideas on how to improve wellness and observe and measure the responses.
- Use available research to appeal to those that rely on data.
- Acknowledge that it is common to see resistance as your committee makes recommendations to support increased health and well-being of your associates and staff; however, since

3. *See* https://lawyerwellbeing.net/the-report/.
4. Fritz Galette, *Leadership Take Note: How Change Changes Us*, PLI CHRONICLE (Jan. 2022).

well-being is a team sport, you all must come together to provide resources and model the use of the resources to gain a collective positive result.

Personally, due to my interest in self-management, I have spent more than twenty years practicing many of the habits shared in Steven C. Covey's book, *The 7 Habits of Highly Effective People.*[5] The following two habits are foundational for living a healthier personal and professional life.

- Habit 2: Begin with the End in Mind; and
- Habit 3: Put First Things First.

A commitment to these two habits from your wellness committee and those they need to gain support from will help you to shape the wellness culture you desire. For example, "begin with the end in mind" by asking your committee members: If we were the type of firm that prioritizes wellness for all, what would we be doing? What would that look like? What do we need to get there? And who needs to help us?

Next, "put first things first": Where can we begin? What change would make the biggest impact for us all? How can we start to make a difference?

This brings me back to some of David's suggestions. Perhaps partners need to reevaluate their messaging and modeling around time off/vacation time. Perhaps a new protocol can be established where all leaders are mindful of when they send emails and to whom—or perhaps leaders could learn to use the "delay delivery" option in Outlook.

Steven C. Covey reminds us in the classic "Big Rocks" video[6] how we need to make room in our lives for placing our wellness first. This is a timeless lesson for all of us, especially as many of us continue to reevaluate our priorities and how to live our lives in today's world.

---

5. Steven C. Covey, The 7 Habits of Highly Effective People: Powerful Lessons in Personal Change (FranklinCovey 2019).
6. *Big Rocks*, FranklinCovey (Aug. 24, 2017), https://www.youtube.com/watch?v=zV3gMTOEWt8.

Key Takeaways and Action Items

Key Takeaway One

Walk the Talk on Wellness

Mixed messages from firm leadership—saying wellness matters while consistently working through vacations or sending late-night emails—erode credibility and discourage associates from prioritizing their well-being.

Action Items:

1. Encourage the wellness committee to develop a "Wellness Leadership Pledge" where partners commit to taking vacation, refraining from contacting others on leave, and limiting after-hours communication.

2. Train firm leaders to use tools like email delay delivery and set clear out-of-office boundaries to reinforce a culture of rest.

3. Spotlight leaders who visibly prioritize wellness as role models to normalize these behaviors.

Key Takeaway Two

Wellness Is Everyone's Responsibility

Burnout and mental health struggles are pervasive across all levels of law firms—not just among associates. Addressing wellness requires firm-wide accountability and systemic support, not ad hoc initiatives.

Action Items:

1. Propose a firm-wide wellness policy that applies equally to partners, associates, and business professionals—emphasizing fairness, consistency, and accessibility.

2. Create cross-functional wellness ambassador groups to ensure programming is informed by voices across departments and demographics.

3. Use data (from IWIL, ABA reports, and internal surveys) to demonstrate both the human and business case for investing in well-being.

Key Takeaway Three

Culture Change Requires Iteration, Not Perfection

Transforming wellness culture doesn't happen overnight—it requires thoughtful planning, bold experimentation, and regular feedback loops to learn what works.

Action Items:

1. Use Covey's "Begin with the End in Mind" to guide a visioning session with the wellness committee: *What would a truly well firm look and feel like?*
2. Choose one "Big Rock" priority (e.g., protected time off, structured reentry after vacation, no-email weekends) and pilot it with a group.
3. Measure impact via anonymous surveys or check-ins and iterate based on feedback, demonstrating responsiveness and momentum.

Chapter 36

Prioritize Belonging and Accessibility in Your Next Position

Natalie Loeb & David B. Sarnoff

Dear Coaches:

> **I'm an attorney gainfully employed in a firm but exploring other opportunities. When researching firms to apply to and interviewing for open positions, how do I gauge (or assess) whether I'll feel a sense of belonging in the new firm that will help me thrive as a lawyer, maintain my morale, and perform my best?**

—Identifying Cues from Interviews

Natalie: I am no longer surprised by resignations. What does surprise me is how open lawyers are to exploring new opportunities. The re-evaluation of how we work, accelerated by the COVID-19 pandemic along with a generational shift in thinking driven by Millennials and Gen Zers, continues to impact a marketplace where talented lawyers are looking for workplaces where they feel they can contribute, make a difference, bring their authentic selves to work, and be part of a community accomplishing goals. A June 2018 American Bar Association article titled *A Millennial Explains How Law Firms Can Attract and Keep His Generation of Lawyers* reminds us "that Millennials bring to the workplace an enthusiasm to contribute and make a real difference early in their careers. It is imperative for law firms to take advantage of this eagerness and ramp up their efforts to mentor and train young attorneys."[1] Harnessing this enthusiasm and energy early on makes a difference. And providing mentoring and support when the work experience proves more challenging than originally thought is the critical difference in retaining and developing this talent.

In your case, it appears you are ready for a change and are seeking a workplace that will provide this support, training, mentoring, and work culture to maximize your contributions and sharpen your lawyering skills to be the best lawyer you can be. Moving to a new firm can be a big decision. I wonder to what extent you have sought feedback and asked for opportunities at your current firm. If you haven't tried this strategy yet, you may be pleasantly surprised when you seek out some guidance and support. However, there are some firms where providing feedback and new opportunities and encouraging lawyers to bring their whole selves to work is not woven into the DNA of the firm. From your question, it sounds like you are intrigued by a workplace that has an intentional culture designed to help you learn and perform at your best. What you are describing is the need for belonging. Belonging means feeling comfortable in bringing your whole self to work without the threat of being marginalized or minimized; feeling like your contributions matter and are valued; and feeling like you're an integral member of your organization rather than just another cog in the wheel.

While the onus to reshape firm culture rests squarely on firms and firm leadership, our focus here is on you and what steps you can take to ensure organizational fit and that you're getting the most from your current or next employer.

If exploring other options is indeed your next step, here are some things to think about:

1. Be intentional about the questions you ask when you're interviewing. In addition to asking questions about the practice groups within the firm, the compensation, the work you'll be

---

1. *A Millennial Explains How Law Firms Can Attract and Keep His Generation of Lawyers*, Am. Bar Ass'n (June 2028), https://www.americanbar.org/news/abanews/publications/youraba/2018/june-2018/a-millennial-explains-how-law-firms-can-attract-and-keep-his-gen/.

assigned, and the flexibility offered to the lawyers, don't shy away from asking questions about the firm culture.

2. Ask those you meet with at the firm to describe the firm's culture in three words.
3. Might they be able to provide an example of a team on a client matter that works in a way that aligns with this culture?
4. If they could change anything about the firm, what would it be?
5. What are they most proud of as a member of the firm?
6. In what way do lawyers show their individuality at the firm?
7. How does the firm leverage the individual differences lawyers bring to the firm?

These are not easy questions. Be prepared to wait for an answer and remain silent to allow time for your interviewer(s) to reflect on your questions. Ultimately, it will be up to you to assess the answers you receive. Do the answers seem to be delivered with transparency and confidence? Do you like what you are hearing? Can you envision yourself being successful in the culture the interviewers are describing? Do you find yourself energized by what you are hearing and eager to be a team member of the teams being described?

Only you will know if the answers you are receiving are generating an internal sense of enthusiasm and eagerness to join this firm. Allow yourself to listen to your instincts and use that data too as you decide whether or not this firm is the right next step for you in your career. In addition, you can obtain more information from a variety of viewpoints by talking to anyone you know who is currently at the firm or familiar with the firm and its culture. It is always worth that extra time to learn as much as possible from those who have experience at the firm on how the lawyers are truly led and what growth and development really look like at the firm.

I have learned from over fifteen years of leadership coaching that "Talent flows to where it's valued." It is for this reason that many of today's law firms are paying particular attention to their workplace cultures. They aspire to create workplaces where their lawyers feel valued.

You do important work. Your work deserves attention, as do your work style and leadership capabilities. Together, all of these skills will help you develop into the best lawyer you can be.

Ask powerful questions about workplace culture and listen to your instinct. Do your research and talk to as many people as possible that know about the firm you are considering. Take all this data into consideration and you will make a sound decision on whether to stay where you are or move on to your next opportunity. Wishing you much success as you "explore."

David: Thank you for your question. As Natalie has addressed the notion of belonging and intentional cultures above, I will focus on the practice of accessibility, which is becoming a more prevalent topic in law firms because of growing demand for more fulfilling and accessible work environments.

Over the past several years, I have become more involved with inclusion and allyship issues, particularly in law firms. I have been involved in panel discussions, workshop facilitations, and, as of September 2022, served as Co-Chair of the Diversity, Equity and Inclusion Committee of the New York City Bar Association. However, while I have dedicated efforts toward increasing inclusion, I have not been as well versed in the practice of *accessibility*.

In December 2022, I attended the National Association of Legal Placement (NALP) Professional Development Institute, and one panel in particular, led by Haley Moss, Esq. and AJ Link, enlightened me to the importance of accessibility. Mr. Link is the founder of the National Disabled Law Students Association and the National Disabled Legal Professionals Association. Ms. Moss is an attorney, neurodiversity expert, author, artist, and speaker. Ms. Moss also said she was diagnosed with autism. I left this panel with a newfound understanding and appreciation of accessibility and a recognition that I had much more to learn about this topic.

In my opinion, accessibility at its core is about making programs, policies, events, technology, devices, and more available to the widest possible audience within an organization without waiting for someone to say they have a disability or are in need of an accommodation. It requires anticipating needs, seeing with multiple lenses and perspectives, and including others in planning and decision-making to be as inclusive and accessible as possible. Practicing accessibility requires empathy and trying to understand how others experience the environment. It ranges from planning a happy hour or professional development to designing furniture and offices to choosing technology programs and devices. When planning to be accessible, leaders should try to accommodate the widest possible audience, which in turn will have a positive impact on a greater number of people (and ideally everyone) within an organization.

Here are some concrete examples of accessibility. The first is one that I have seen impact firms along generational lines: In many law firms, social interaction revolves around happy hours and events with alcohol. However, not everyone, particularly Gen Z, wants the focus of professional social gatherings to involve drinking, and there are generally few non-alcoholic alternatives at these events other than water or soft drinks. If the event planner was practicing accessibility, there would be mocktails and non-alcoholic beer and wine to help non-imbibing people feel included without them having to consume alcohol. When planning these types of events, it takes a team to understand and address the needs, abilities, and perspectives to create accessibility, which in turn benefits everyone by encouraging maximum participation.

Another example of accessibility involves using technology to make workspace and events more inclusive and user friendly: When a firm has a guest speaker or webinar, are there closed caption options for people who may be hearing impaired or for people who process better visually than by audio? Is there an option for large-type print for visually impaired colleagues? Typically, when one person is planning an event or trying to solve a problem, they are doing it from their perspective and how they think the problem should be solved, and are not necessarily thinking about how the result will impact others.

Inclusive organizations and thoughtful planners practice "universal design." According to the Centre for Excellence in Universal Design, "Universal Design is the design and composition of an environment so that it can be accessed, understood and used to the greatest extent possible by all people regardless of their age, size, ability or disability." They go on to state that "by considering the diverse needs and abilities of all throughout the design process, universal design creates products, services and environments that meet peoples' needs. Simply put, universal design is good design."[2]

Law firms that practice accessibility will create cultures that are high trust, interactive, and benefit not only people with disabilities or special needs but everyone. As you go through the interview process, be mindful and aware of whether the firm practices accessibility by making the work environment as inclusive as possible.

2. *See* https://universaldesign.ie/.

Key Takeaways and Action Items

Key Takeaway One

Belonging Is Central to Thriving in a New Firm

A sense of belonging, feeling valued, seen, and able to bring your full self to work, is essential for professional fulfillment and high performance. Belonging extends beyond visible diversity to include psychological safety, cultural alignment, and inclusive mentorship.

Action Items:

1. In interviews, ask intentional culture-focused questions (e.g., "Describe the culture in three words," or "How does the firm support individuality?").
2. Follow up with people in your network who have worked at or with the firm to learn how inclusion and mentorship play out in practice.
3. Reflect on your instincts during interviews—do you feel energized and respected, or hesitant and uncertain?

Key Takeaway Two

Accessibility Is a Core Indicator of Inclusive Culture

Truly inclusive firms proactively design environments, physical, social, and digital, that support all individuals, not just the majority. Accessibility is about anticipating a range of needs rather than waiting for people to request accommodations.

Action Items:

1. Observe whether the firm offers things like captioning for webinars, flexible workspaces, and inclusive social events (e.g., non-alcoholic options).
2. Ask how the firm incorporates feedback from individuals with different abilities and needs into decision-making.

3. Evaluate whether accessibility appears integrated into the firm's operations—or treated as an afterthought.

Key Takeaway Three

Evaluating Cultural Fit Requires Both Data and Intuition

Firm websites and interviews often showcase idealized versions of culture. The key is to probe deeper and trust both what's said and how it makes you feel. Enthusiasm, transparency, and alignment are critical indicators.

Action Items:

1. Use interviews to assess not only what is said but *how* it is said—do answers seem rehearsed or genuine?
2. Ask "What would you change about the firm?" to reveal honesty and self-awareness in culture.
3. Keep a journal after each interview to track your gut reactions and overall enthusiasm—it's a valuable form of data too.

Chapter 37

Why Partners Shouldn't Ignore Associates' Mounting Stress

Natalie Loeb & David B. Sarnoff

Dear Coaches:

> **I'm a partner at my firm, and over the past few months I've noticed a marked change in the associates I manage. My firm has laid off staff and associates because of slowing work demands and ongoing talks of an economic downturn. Not only has workflow been affected but associates are also now expected to work in the office three to four days each week. I've overheard chatter that associates feel strained and am concerned that work quality and client satisfaction will decline. How can I get them refocused and quash negative sentiments about recent changes?**
>
> ***—Help Me Get My Team Back***

David: Thank you for the question. Based on what you describe, there seems to be significant change occurring at your firm all at once. Change can be difficult for anyone to adjust to, especially associates, particularly when layoffs are involved. How changes are communicated to the stakeholders of the firm can greatly impact how that message is received. While there is no easy way to communicate associate layoffs, it is important that it be carried out with care and empathy. Is the firm providing outplacement services for the affected associates? Are they receiving the opportunity to engage a career coach? Do the associates have at least a three-month runway to keep their firm email and stay on the website while they conduct their job searches? Services like these communicate that the firm is not just cutting people to fend for themselves and their bottom line; it shows a level of care that the firm is interested in giving associates who lose their jobs the opportunity to land on their feet.

While it is important to demonstrate a level of care for the associates who have lost their jobs, it is equally important to address the needs and concerns of the associates who avoided layoffs. Is the firm communicating the "why" of the firm's decision to retain these associates and putting forth clear and unambiguous expectations for the associates who remain? Quite often we hear about feelings of guilt from associates who were not laid off. This feeling is then compounded with a sense that they will soon be overloaded with work because there are fewer associates to handle the workflow. Some partners believe that associates who were not on the layoff list should be grateful for having a job. However, that mindset does not contribute to a healthy and high-trust culture. Partners should be aware that associates are concerned about being overwhelmed and not having support to manage cases and deals. By not addressing these concerns, partners run the risk of making associates feel that they are on their own, and some of the remaining associates may start to look for other jobs. The firm may want to consider sponsoring programs and events around team building and improving culture that do not revolve around happy hours and may include an offsite retreat day. I also think it is important for the firm to be cognizant of how layoffs will impact their reputation and recruiting efforts in the market.

This feeling of being overwhelmed may be reinforced because of your firm's added requirement that associates must return to the office three to four days a week. Are partners also required to comply with this directive? If not, this may create a feeling of inequity between partners and associates and communicates that *"we are not all in this together."*

Has the firm explained why associates are required to come into the office three to four days a week? Is it just for face time, or is the firm being strategic about bringing associates back to the office to collaborate, team build, and have dedicated professional development opportunities? If the decision was made to have associates be in the office with no added strategic purpose, associates may react negatively to this decision.

In addition to the stress over layoffs, increased days in the office, which generally include added commuting time and changes to personal scheduling, can add to associates' stress levels.

Is the firm providing programs around stress management, mindfulness, and meditation? As Natalie and I have discussed in prior columns,[1] there is significant research and reporting about the higher rate of depression, substance abuse, and self-harm in the legal profession compared to many other professions. In my opinion, it is the right thing to do and a good business practice when a firm provides resources and programs to address mental health and wellness issues. Even having a program that teaches breathing exercises, such as box breathing, can help all stakeholders manage stress in a more effective way. It is widely reported that breathing exercises have many benefits, including lowering blood pressure and reducing anxiety and stress. Providing these resources to firm stakeholders will contribute to greater associate health and building trust and culture at the firm, generally leading to higher retention rates and improved work life satisfaction.

Natalie: You started your question with two important words: "I've noticed." I know that may be surprising to hear; however, we have observed that, more often than not, leaders who are in the midst of major events or changes at the firm choose to keep their heads down and remain focused on the outcomes for the firm instead of "noticing" the changes' impact on themselves and their colleagues. Thank you for writing to us and thank you for *noticing*. It is the first step in taking ownership of an issue.

Now you have two choices:

1. to continue business as usual; or
2. to lean into new actions to address your concerns.

---

1. *See* chapter 35, Advocating for Your Attorneys' Mental Health.

David's answer above gives you much to consider if you choose to lean into actions to address your concerns.

Another suggestion is to gather a cross-section of other partners and administrative leaders with similar concerns to swap thoughts on specific actions for your firm. There may already be resources available to your associates that you are unaware of. For example, does your firm contract with an Employee Assistance Program (EAP)? And if so, how can that organization help your firm during this challenging time?

In addition to specific actions, there is some "inside" work you can do here to help yourself *and* those associates being impacted by these changes. Have you ever personally been affected by a downsizing or reduction in force or perhaps a recession? How did you handle it? What helped you get through it? What lessons did you learn? And what silver linings did you find?

My guess is that both you and some of your colleagues have answers to those questions. In addition, you are probably not the only one who has noticed the change among associates. With self-reflection and a willingness to be vulnerable, you and a small group can share your stories and wisdom with others. This will provide an act of caring that your associates and staff really need right now and could help lift morale or, at a minimum, one individual associate's spirits.

Never minimize the impact one person or a small group can have on others. It was Margaret Mead that said, "Never doubt that a small group of thoughtful, committed citizens can change the world; indeed, it's the only thing that ever has."

You can use this same playbook for the associates who seem less than enthusiastic about returning to the office three to four days a week. You have a valid concern about the impact of additional stress and strain on performance along with service delivery to clients. At the core, our law firms are made up of people, and people are "human." Humans perform best and deliver the highest quality of work when they are socially and emotionally healthy. Chronic stress and strain diminish social and emotional health and in turn can cause poor performance and burnout.

All of this being said, firm leaders are responsible for setting the expectations for the associates and staff in their firms. If the leadership requires their people to be present in the office three to four days a week, this is at the discretion of the firm. David's question is a good one to ask yourself: "Has the firm explained why associates are required to come into the office three to four days a week?" Providing the "why" will help others to understand the thinking behind this decision. It will also, most likely, help your people accept or even buy into the decision. The manner in which this message is communicated is important. If you have a "Communications" team or a "Human Resources" team, perhaps they can help you with the messaging.

Another suggestion that I urge you to consider is to be intentional about making in-person work collaborative. If attorneys and staff come into an office where they are the only one there or doing work completely independently while they are in the office, it will be hard for them to continue to be supportive about being in the office three to four days a week. Remember, the world of work continues to evolve, with an increased appetite for flexibility. That train has left the station or, as they say, "the horse is already out of the barn." Those of us in leadership roles have to embrace change, model it for others, and provide the added emotional support to our associates and staff to keep our firm culture healthy and our clients happy.

Key Takeaways and Action Items

Key Takeaway One

Transparency and Care Are the Antidotes to Uncertainty

Layoffs, return-to-office policies, and economic concerns are triggering uncertainty and anxiety. Failing to communicate clearly or show care toward both laid off and remaining associates can breed distrust, disengagement, and attrition.

Action Items:

1. Clearly communicate the "why" behind layoffs and return-to-office mandates, including business rationale and any anticipated benefits (e.g., collaboration, mentoring).
2. Demonstrate empathy for laid-off colleagues by ensuring the firm offers outplacement resources, coaching, and transition time—and share that support with remaining staff to ease survivor guilt.
3. Hold listening sessions or check-ins with remaining associates to hear their concerns and offer reassurance and direction.

Key Takeaway Two

Model Fairness and Humanize Leadership

Uneven expectations between partners and associates (e.g., who must return to the office or who receives support) erode morale. Associates may feel expendable or disconnected when leaders don't acknowledge their emotional experience or model inclusive behaviors.

Action Items:

1. Ensure all leaders comply with return-to-office policies to reinforce unity and fairness.
2. Make in-office days intentional and collaborative by scheduling team-based activities, mentoring, or professional development opportunities rather than solitary desk work.

3. Host storytelling sessions where partners reflect on their own experiences with career uncertainty or stress—modeling vulnerability and resilience while humanizing leadership.

Key Takeaway Three

Prioritize Wellness to Restore Trust and Performance

Chronic stress, anxiety, and lack of clarity undermine performance. Offering tangible wellness programs and stress-management resources can rebuild trust and help associates re-engage with their work.

Action Items:

1. Launch or expand wellness initiatives such as breathing and mindfulness workshops, mental health programming, or access to Employee Assistance Programs (EAPs).
2. Work with HR or communications to deliver messaging that promotes well-being and emotional support, not just operational updates.
3. Propose a culture and morale task force to gather associate input, recommend improvements, and plan non-alcohol-centered team-building opportunities.

Chapter 38

Am I a Change Embracer or Change Resister?

Natalie Loeb & David B. Sarnoff

Dear Coaches:

> **I'm a junior partner and am feeling more stressed than usual. There have been several changes at my firm recently. New leadership, new technologies, colleagues leaving and being replaced by new attorneys and staff, and summer associates starting their programs. Everyone's workflow has been affected, and more projects are being assigned outside of client work. In theory, I like the direction the firm is heading in, but I'm having a hard time dealing with the short-term effects of the changes and feel like I've reached my tipping point. Why am I having such a hard time coping? What can I do to alleviate some of the stress?**
>
> ***—Overwhelmed by Change***

Natalie: You are not alone. Change is running rampant and quickly in our law firms and in our lives. We are living and working in times where the pace of change is overwhelming and unfortunately, the human element is getting lost. To keep innovating, moving forward, and providing excellent service to our clients, we must be able to build workplace cultures that inspire each of us to embrace change and bring our best selves to our workplaces.

There is no one way to do this. Instead, we must pay attention to our own individual needs and our reactions to change. I have met lawyers that embrace change, and I have met lawyers that resist change. Some people find change invigorating and inspiring while others find it threatening and uncomfortable. Based on your question, I am wondering how you would describe your initial reaction to change. In order to lead others through change, you must lead yourself through change first. So let's begin with thinking about your own individual reactions to change. Do you consider yourself a change embracer or a change resister? Or perhaps you are somewhere on a spectrum between the two and are reacting to the fact that there seems to be *too* much change happening *too* fast for you at your firm. Does it feel like you want to say, "Stop the merry-go-round, I'd like to get off"?

As you think about this, please know that there is an abundance of research about how human beings adapt to change. Perhaps you are familiar with the change management theory brought to us by Elisabeth Kübler-Ross. The Kübler-Ross model reminds us of the five stages of grief.[1] When experiencing change, we are actually moving through a grieving process where we feel the emotions of what it is like to let go of the old ways of the past and find comfort in something new and/or different. Elisabeth Kübler-Ross' research summarizes this experience as a pattern of grieving behaviors known as the five stages of loss. They are:

Stage 1—Denial:

> This is the initial reaction when one denies the change and prefers to cling to the status quo. (*No way! A new billing system?*)

Stage 2—Anger:

> At this stage, the individual realizes that denial cannot be continued and becomes angry and frustrated, often resisting the change. (*I can't stand this new system! Here's why it's not a good idea. I'm not going to do it.*)

---

1. Originally explained in her 1969 book, ON DEATH AND DYING: WHAT THE DYING HAVE TO TEACH DOCTORS, NURSES, CLERGY AND THEIR OWN FAMILIES.

Stage 3—Bargaining:

> As one moves along in the grief process, one may acquire a false sense of hope that the change can be avoided. Often this is exhibited in the form of trading off something to maintain status quo. *(If you let me use my old system, I'll get my hours in on a timely basis—guaranteed.)*

Stage 4—Depression:

> In this stage, individuals are no longer refusing the change but are becoming acutely aware of the downside (and potential upside) of the change. (*I'll try it, but it is never going to work, and it will take way too much time to learn.*)

Stage 5—Acceptance:

> In this last stage, individuals embrace the inevitability of the change. They come around to accepting the new way forward by letting go of their emotional connections to the past and staying focused on adopting the change and the future. (*I see the benefit. I can get on board.*)

It's not unusual for someone to get stuck in a certain stage. Or perhaps move along what is known as the "Change Curve," making some progress and then reverting to a former stage as change continues to come along. The important part is to recognize that humans have this natural reaction to change and stay mindful of the stage you may be in. If you find yourself angry or frustrated, it is normal. However, continuous chronic anger and frustration is going to wear you down and perhaps make you unpopular or unpleasant to be around. It will also impact your ability to lead others through change. The chronic stress caused by being stuck in an earlier stage along the continuum can also negatively impact your health. There are numerous reasons to stay aware of your reaction to change and to be open-minded and curious about how to move forward and gain comfort embracing new ways of living and working.

If you find yourself getting stuck in an undesirable stage, challenge yourself. Ask yourself, what actions can you take to move past this stage? One suggestion to help you get unstuck is to refer to Robert Kegan's and Lisa Lahey's work, summarized in their book *Immunity to*

Change.[2] Kegan and Lahey are well known thought leaders in the field of change and have conducted extensive research showing how our individual beliefs—along with the collective mindsets in our organizations—combine to create a natural yet powerful immunity to change. To move past this immunity, we must be specific about what we want to achieve. Being intentional about identifying what specific behaviors or actions we can take to help us move forward or achieve a new goal makes the change process easier. If someone is not ready to take action or commit to new behaviors, they can at least challenge themselves to identify what is getting in the way of making an effort to *try*. Once identified, that obstacle can often be managed or eliminated. And with that obstacle gone, acceptance becomes easier and satisfying.

You mentioned you like the direction your firm is heading in. This is a positive sign. Try to reframe the changes you are experiencing from "problems" to "opportunities." Try to notice if you are getting stuck in an earlier stage on the change curve and, if so, how it is affecting your mood or health. Remind yourself that you need to be patient with yourself and others. Be curious. Give yourself some slack if you are feeling overwhelmed or uncomfortable. When you are tired, overwhelmed, or uncomfortable, you can think of what you are grateful for, including the interesting work and good friends, colleagues, and clients you interact with at the firm. Remember, we are all in this change together. Showing yourself and each other a little grace while you navigate the change curve will certainly offer you some surprisingly pleasant rewards. Try it. And let me know how it turns out.

David: Thank you for sharing your story and for your pertinent questions. It certainly sounds like there is significant change happening in your orbit, and as Natalie said, you are not alone. As technology, AI, and smart machines become ever more present and integrated into our work life and personal space, the only constant is change. Change is not always easy, and for many, it can be quite difficult to adapt to and maintain an agile mindset. Possessing a growth mindset that embraces change and recognizing that you will not always get it right and are a work in progress will help you to see failures, obstacles, and mistakes

---

2. Robert Kegan & Lisa Laskow Lahey, Immunity to Change: How to Overcome It and Unlock the Potential in Yourself and Your Organization (Harv. Bus. Rev. Press 2009).

as opportunities to learn. For more on growth mindset, I highly recommend the book *Mindset* by Carol Dweck.[3]

Practicing law in and of itself is a stressful occupation just by the nature of the work. Now add to your practice organizational change and your managerial and leadership responsibilities and that is quite a workload. Managing change typically includes *managing stress*. One practice to alleviate that stress is to set boundaries and hold yourself accountable for enforcing those boundaries. In the legal profession in particular, showing vulnerability and not always saying, "yes, I can do it," may be seen in some circles as a weakness. While this stigma is changing as younger generations assume more leadership roles, it is a widespread challenge in the legal profession to create personal space to practice self-care, mindfulness, and healthy behaviors. As we have shared in previous columns, the legal profession has an inordinately high rate of depression, substance abuse, and self-harm compared to other professions. In many work environments, there is a mandate to do more with less, which increases the stress and personal impact both emotionally and physically. This is not a sustainable model for a healthy workplace. In my opinion, burnout, which is evidenced in lack of sleep, hydration, and nutrition, takes a significant toll on individuals' health and is counterproductive to a healthy workplace culture.

When an attorney is grinding it out on a trial or working on an M&A deal, the stress and pressure will reach a threshold that will have a disproportionate impact on the manifestation of the stress on the body and mind. What I mean by this is aptly described by my colleague Joy Stephens. Joy is a chemical engineer by training and illustrates this phenomenon by using a glass of water. Picture a glass of water filled to the rim of the glass. Now take an eye dropper and keep adding a drop of water until the water breaches the rim of the glass. As you will see, that last drop of water to breach the rim causes a stream of water over the rim. It is not a drop out for a drop in, rather it is a stream of water significantly greater than that one drop. It is not unlike the stress and pressure that builds up in our bodies and our emotions. Once that threshold is breached, the impact is disproportionate to that last

---

3. Carol S. Dweck, Mindset: The New Psychology of Success (Ballantine Books 2007).

stressful act that set it in motion, and the impact on the body and mind can be debilitating and lead to destructive behaviors.

Also, as a leader, you are being watched and observed by the people who report to you and your peers. Emotions are contagious, and how you show up impacts the way that you and your communication is received. I regularly use a quote by Dr. Martin Luther King, Jr., when coaching clients to "be a thermostat, not a thermometer." A thermostat sets the climate, a thermometer reacts to it. Set the climate and tone in the room, don't react to it. To do this requires a competent level of emotional intelligence to raise your self-awareness, understand how you are showing up, and recognize the impact of your words and actions on others.

Setting boundaries as to when you are disconnecting from work, taking vacation time or personal time, or using small breaks during the day to practice mindfulness, meditation, or exercise is vital to maintaining emotional and physical health. I also strongly suggest working breathing exercises into your daily routine. Breathing exercises have been shown to lower blood pressure, stress, and pulse rates. These practices are also likely to improve one's outlook, optimism, and resilience in order to persevere through adverse conditions and lead others through that adversity. Saying "yes" to yourself is important to be mentally fit enough to support others. As you hear when you fly on an airline, put your air mask on first before you help others. When you practice these behaviors and incorporate them into your daily routine, you not only serve to improve your work life and well-being, but you also model the way for others who are looking to you to lead by example. It is important to note that if you are feeling stress and burnout, it is not uncommon for members of your team to be feeling the exact same thing.

Key Takeaways and Action Items

Key Takeaway One

Normalize the Emotional Journey of Change

Adapting to change often involves a cycle of emotional responses, including denial, anger, bargaining, depression, and ultimately, acceptance. Understanding these stages can help normalize your feelings and prevent burnout from unchecked frustration.

Action Items:

1. Reflect on which stage of the change curve you may be in (e.g., anger, bargaining, depression) and journal how it's affecting your energy, mindset, and leadership.
2. Reframe changes from "disruptions" to opportunities for learning and growth, especially if you believe in the firm's overall direction.
3. Read or revisit resources such as *Immunity to Change* (Kegan & Lahey) to identify internal resistance and begin intentionally shifting your mindset.

Key Takeaway Two

Address the Burnout Cycle with Intentional Recovery

In high-pressure professions like law, the accumulation of stress without relief can result in physical and emotional exhaustion. Burnout builds slowly, like water filling to the rim of a glass, until a single drop causes an overflow.

Action Items:

1. Set clear personal boundaries: Define non-negotiable times for disconnection (e.g., no emails after 9 p.m. or protected lunch breaks).

2. Prioritize daily wellness practices: Try breathing exercises, movement breaks, or brief meditation sessions, even five minutes counts.
3. Schedule intentional recovery time (personal days, mini-breaks, or social connection) to interrupt chronic stress and recharge your system.

Key Takeaway Three

Lead with Emotional Intelligence and Grounded Presence

As a junior partner, how you show up affects your team's morale, engagement, and resilience. Demonstrating vulnerability, emotional intelligence, and healthy coping strategies helps others do the same.

Action Items:

1. Embrace Dr. King's concept of being a thermostat, not a thermometer, set a grounded, calm tone rather than reacting to others' stress.
2. Check in with your team: Ask how they're managing the change and share what's helped you. Normalizing the conversation can reduce isolation and anxiety.
3. Lead by example: When you visibly model boundaries, self-awareness, and adaptability, you empower others to follow suit—creating a healthier, more resilient culture.

Chapter 39

How to Prepare for Your Law School Journey

Natalie Loeb & David B. Sarnoff

Dear Coaches:

> **I'm starting law school this fall—the first in my family to attend. I'm excited but have no idea what to expect or how to prepare, and I don't have any relatives or family friends I can talk to or get advice from. Google search results for "what to expect in law school" range from generic responses about heavy course and workloads to blog posts and articles about how attending law school was the worst mistake of someone's life! Did I make a mistake by choosing to enroll? Will I be woefully underprepared because I don't come from a family of lawyers?**
>
> ***—First-Generation Fearful***

David: Beginning law school is an exciting and challenging experience that can be daunting to incoming students, especially students who are first-generation law students or from underrepresented communities. Students who have a family legacy of attorneys tend to receive more insights and guidance on what to expect; however, it can be challenging for these students as well. In my opinion, the most difficult part of the transition from my undergraduate experience was the intensity and volume of assignments that required significant amounts of time reading cases—sometimes very old cases that I had to read multiple times to fully comprehend.

For many students, the rigor of law school contributes to the stress and pressure to excel and requires a regimen of self-care and mindfulness practices to maintain balance and reduce stress. To create a positive and sustainable transition to law school, it is helpful for law students to establish practices and strategies early in their law school career, focused on academic performance and wellness, that become habits going forward. These strategies should be built around time management, studying techniques, cultivating relationships, seeking feedback, and physical and mental fitness.

Time management is a critical skill to be successful in law school because the magnitude of reading assignments and stress of exams and extra-curricular activities can easily overwhelm someone who is not intentional about protecting and managing their time effectively. First, it is vital to utilize a calendar and enter assignments, exams, and events as soon as possible so a strategy can be planned to manage the workload. Without utilizing a calendar, things may fall through the cracks, assignments may be missed, and less than ideal time for study is allocated. Once you have calendared everything, it is important to prioritize a strategic plan. One method is called the Eisenhower Matrix or Covey Model (see below):

In my opinion, using the matrix is more effective than a vertical "to-do" list because a to-do list can become overwhelming, and entries get lost or overlooked. The matrix breaks down the tasks into priorities and creates a mechanism for triaging tasks by importance. As you can see, the upper left quadrant is for tasks that are "urgent" and "important." This box should ideally contain the three to four most urgent priorities that need to be completed. The quadrant to the upper right is "important" but "not urgent." These are tasks that need to be completed, but not immediately, and can be scheduled. For these, I suggest entering them into your calendar when due and setting reminders to alert you to complete prior to the due date. The lower left quadrant is for tasks that are "urgent" but "not important." These are tasks that other people may present you with that are urgent and important to them but not to you. Try not to get caught up in the emotion of other people's urgency because these are the events that can infringe on your time unnecessarily. It is helpful to set boundaries with other people to protect your time. Finally, the lower right quadrant is "not important" and "not urgent." These are tasks that can clutter your calendar and distract you from more important things. Delete these tasks from your calendar and matrix as soon as possible. Keep in mind that the matrix is organic, and the list can change from week to week.

For me, law school also required a different mindset and skill-set compared to my undergraduate experience. Possessing a growth mindset, as discussed in prior columns,[1] is crucial to being productive and managing stress. In your first year, you may need to read cases, statutes, and regulations multiple times before you fully understand the legal issues at hand and the reasoning of the court. At first, I found this process frustrating and defeating. Over time, I embraced it and approached it as part of the process in learning and understanding various legal principles and concepts. I also highly recommend developing a process and technique for taking notes during class and outlining cases when you are studying. By developing an efficient process, you will be more prepared to review and study for exams than if your strategy is haphazard.

It is also crucial to develop relationships with fellow students and form study groups, to have dialogues and ideate with a small group of four or five students and work through understanding cases and concepts. It is important to establish at the beginning of each group session that everyone is responsible for participating and preparing material to contribute to the shared mission of the study group. If members do not act responsibly, they should be held accountable.

As a first-year student, I did not take full advantage of the resources and programs offered at my school, particularly seeking an upper-class mentor, attending legal writing seminars, and utilizing professor office hours to ask questions. Students, me included, did not want to appear vulnerable or lacking in intelligence and struggled alone instead of demonstrating a growth mindset and benefiting from others' input and guidance. Forming relationships and rapport with upper-class students and members of the faculty will be beneficial during your law school journey and beyond.

Law school is also an optimal environment to start nurturing a professional and personal network of students, faculty, and experienced attorneys. There will be opportunities to attend social and professional events, panel discussions, guest speaker presentations, and student

---

1. *See* chapter 38, Am I a Change Embracer or Change Resister?

organization meetings and events. Make every effort to attend one or more events on a monthly basis. It is easy to neglect them because of the student workload. However, relationship-building is a key component to a successful and fulfilling career in law. These efforts can play a role in developing mentorship relationships and creating job prospects in the future.

Lastly, but equally as important, dedicate time to self-care and wellness. Schedule time in your calendar to listen to a meditation app, go to the fitness center, take a walk, or listen to music. Do something to disconnect from your studies, even if for a brief time. Also be mindful to get as much sleep as you can. Sleep deprivation is a trap that is easy to fall into if assignments and study are left to the last minute and pulling all-nighters becomes routine. Under these conditions, it is hard to be your best self, manage stress, and get appropriate nutrition and hydration. Recognize if you are experiencing burnout and exhaustion and rely on your personal network and professional services to manage your stress and improve mental health. I wish you good luck.

Natalie: David has offered excellent practical advice. Incorporating the habits he suggests around time management, wellness, and relationship-building will certainly set the foundation for you to be a highly successful and happy lawyer. David also mentioned a *growth mindset.* As leadership coaches, we use this term frequently when working with our clients. In fact, a coaching engagement is only successful when the client enters the coaching engagement with this type of mindset. Carol Dweck's book, *Mindset: The New Psychology of Success,* reminds us that when using a "growth mindset, people believe that their most basic abilities can be developed through dedication and hard work—brains and talent are just the starting point. This view creates a love of learning and a resilience that is essential for great accomplishment." This type of mindset will allow you to enter new situations without the pressure of being "perfect." It will set the stage for you to enter your new profession with a "learner's mindset," one where you are curious about your new work, colleagues, and clients. One where you can frame new experiences, not as "I have to," but "I get to." And you "get to" because you belong where you are. Like everyone else around you, you have completed the work successfully; to be at your firm, in your office, and working with your fellow lawyers and clients.

I have had the honor of coaching many newer associates who were first-generation lawyers. In fact, many of them were the first in their families to go to college and then law school. Each one of them told me wonderful stories about their journeys. Those journeys required self-determination, creativity, intelligence, empathy, and resilience. These are not qualities normally taught in law school. However, they are the qualities that will make you a great lawyer and trusted advisor to your clients. They are also the qualities that will one day make you a great leader of others. As you lead teams or perhaps contribute to a committee at your firm, those qualities will help you to influence others in a way to get the best results for you and the firm. These are the qualities that make you "overprepared" to be a great lawyer, not woefully underprepared.

What you are probably noticing is the necessity to make the powerful choice to believe in yourself. Once you choose to do that you become capable of building the confidence you need to be the successful lawyer already within you. Here are some suggestions to help build your confidence and unleash that successful lawyer within:

1. **Remember your successes.** Think about all the accomplishments that got you to where you are today.

2. **When feeling uncertain about your lawyering capabilities, contact a friend, mentor, or colleague from your past.** Ask them for a "pep talk." It's okay to let others know you need a little help to be reminded of your own potential and strengths.

3. **Find an opportunity to train, teach, mentor, or coach someone else.** Helping someone else learn will remind you of how much you have learned and what you have to offer.

4. **Do something differently and watch what happens.** Commute differently, try a new coffee flavor or place, read a new author, watch a movie you would normally not watch. Continuous learning will always increase your knowledge and make you more interesting to others.

5. **Take opportunities to WAIT (Why Am I Talking?).** Be an intentional active listener. Being an active listener will make others gravitate towards you. Everyone loves to be "heard."

And if you allow yourself to remain silent, giving others space to speak, you will find yourself building strong relationships and earning trust.

6. **Protect your time.** Be mindful of how you use your time and prioritize items that need to get accomplished every day. Don't be afraid to set boundaries. Learning to say "no" or "not now" is a critical skill for remaining focused on using your time wisely.

Starting your career with a growth mindset and a strong belief in yourself will help you to establish a sense of belonging and confidence. Next, you can try out a few of the action steps above. My last piece of advice is to be patient with yourself. Make the commitment and give yourself time to practice some new habits we suggested. Over time, I am sure you will spend less time thinking about being woefully under-prepared and will instead find yourself feeling confident and prepared. Remember, a learner with a growth mindset will always turn a "failure" into an opportunity for learning. With continuous learning part of your approach to lawyering, I have no doubt you will soon be a sought-after associate, and if you choose to keep going, a sought-after senior associate . . . and perhaps one day, a partner. Wishing you much success!

Key Takeaways and Action Items

Key Takeaway One

You Belong Here

As a first-generation student, your path may look different, but your qualities of perseverance, resilience, and adaptability are powerful assets. You are not underprepared, you are *differently* prepared.

Action Items:

1. Build confidence by remembering your journey: Reflect on what it took to get here—your achievements, sacrifices, and strengths. Keep a running list of accomplishments to revisit during moments of doubt.
2. Ask for support when you need it: Reach out to a trusted mentor, peer, or faculty member and don't hesitate to ask for a "pep talk" or guidance.
3. Practice intentional listening (WAIT—Why Am I Talking?): Build strong relationships by being present and curious. Listening well is one of the most effective ways to earn trust and build credibility.

Key Takeaway Two

Build Systems That Support Your Success

Law school requires strategic time management, new study habits, and emotional regulation. Without systems in place, burnout can quickly follow.

Action Items:

1. Use a calendar and prioritize tasks with the Eisenhower Matrix to manage reading assignments, class prep, and extracurriculars in a clear, balanced way.

2. Establish and maintain wellness routines: Schedule time for rest, exercise, meditation, or joy. Sleep, movement, and hydration aren't luxuries—they're necessities for high performance.

3. Be proactive with academic support: Visit office hours, attend workshops, and form or join a study group early—don't wait until you're struggling.

Key Takeaway Three

Embrace Growth, Not Perfection

You don't have to know everything. Success in law school—and in legal practice—comes from curiosity, effort, and the willingness to learn from mistakes.

Action Items:

1. Reframe fear as curiosity: Instead of "I have to figure this out," try "I get to learn this." A learner's mindset reduces pressure and increases adaptability.

2. Challenge internal resistance: If you find yourself avoiding tasks out of fear or perfectionism, ask, "What's getting in my way?" Identify the blocker and take a small, concrete step forward.

3. Try something new every week: Whether it's introducing yourself to someone, attending an event, or reading something unfamiliar, leaning into small changes builds adaptability and confidence.

Chapter 40

Do Female Lawyers Have to Play by Different Rules?

Natalie Loeb & David B. Sarnoff

Dear Coaches:

> **I'm a sixth-year female associate. Some of my male colleagues have a habit of taking credit for my work or ideas, and are sometimes brash enough to do it in front of me in meetings (you may know the type—you contribute an idea, and someone else rephrases it to make it sound like it was theirs).**
>
> **The last time this happened, I asserted that the idea was mine, and after the meeting my boss (a male partner) told me that I shouldn't speak up when someone else takes credit for my work or ideas because it makes me look bad. I want to make partner, and not being fairly credited for my ideas, work, and contributions could impede my goals. I disagree with my boss, but do you think I should follow his advice? How do I handle the situation?**
>
> ***—Silenced by a Partner***

Natalie: Your question made me bristle a bit. I have shared this experience, and I too have wondered how to handle it. Thank you for your courage in submitting it. There are a few ways for me to answer this question. Because of who I am, I have specific lived experiences. One of those lived experiences is building a professional career as a woman. Over time, as I look back over thirty years, there have been some key experiences that have taught and shaped me. I am going to share them with you and then leave you with a few questions to think about as you choose how to handle the situation you describe in your question.

I remember the time I was co-presenting with a male at a legal conference: My co-presenter would assertively attempt to grab the clicker to our PowerPoint presentation from my hand in order to take the lead in the presentation during what we previously agreed to be my section of the presentation. I held tight to the clicker, I stood my ground, and I continued with the presentation with a confident tone and appropriate volume to continue engaging the audience. I received many accolades afterwards for my presentation. And the presenter did apologize afterwards and told me he's not good at "partnering" on presentations. It was the last time we presented together.

I remember the time a CEO I was coaching told me my tone and voice sounded "childish" and like a "little girl." It took me off guard. I had to step back in the moment to manage the emotional impact of his statement and instead ask a question in a lower, slower tone with more direct eye contact in order to move our discussion forward productively. This wasn't easy, but a good choice at the time. After leading that meeting, I self-coached myself and asked what went well and what could I do differently next time. And I did in fact learn a valuable lesson from that experience: Pay attention to my own self-regulation when speaking about topics that ignite my personal passion, to help the recipient of my information focus on *what* I'm saying rather than *how* I'm saying it. This is a good lesson for all, but especially for women who may be more easily dismissed in the workplace.

Now let's think about *your* experience, which, from your question, appears to stand out to you because it was with a male colleague as opposed to female colleagues. As a female senior associate, I can see how the encounter makes you wonder . . . is it because I am a female? How may it impact my career? I can't answer that for you; however, here are some questions to ask to self-coach yourself in hopes of gaining some clarity on what you can do:

1. How do I want to present myself and be seen in these situations? What actions will get me there? Who's support or guidance can I seek out as I make these decisions?

2. Are there male or female mentors in the firm that can step in to help me untangle this type of situation or provide advice on what they have seen work before?

3. What role, if any, do I play in these situations? How do I respond? Is how I am responding helping the situation or hindering the situation?

4. Is there any part of the feedback that is useful? Is there anything I can take away that will make me a better lawyer? What actions can I take?

I realize these are tough questions. You may answer them and feel powerless. *Or* you may answer them and feel more power. If the road leads to "powerless," you have additional questions to ask yourself about the culture of the firm and the support of your growth there. If the road leads to feeling more power over the situation, proceed.

Be prepared for both missteps and successes. And be prepared to learn from both. Missteps will require grit and resilience. Success will require humility and confidence. Either way, as you can see, you will learn from this journey.

If your observation, and perhaps those of others, is that behaviors like "taking credit for others' ideas" and "shutting down" smart associates when they want to make productive contributions to discussions are consistent behaviors, start to look around and sense the workplace culture of your practice group or firm. You then have another decision to make. Do you want to exercise your leadership and seek support and guidance to create a new intentional culture that models giving credit where credit is due and welcoming the thoughts of smart associates? Or do you want to seek out another firm where the culture already aligns more closely with your values and actions.

Either way, I have learned that these types of reflective questions require time and good analytical thinking (which I'm sure you have); so allow yourself the time to think everything through.

I hope this helps as you consider your actions the next time you find yourself in this type of situation.

David: Thank you for sharing your story. Like Natalie, I had a visceral reaction to reading your question. Also, I want to commend you for your courage in asserting yourself when claiming ownership over your work product that someone else tried to claim. I find your boss's response to be highly concerning for multiple reasons. In my opinion, his response was unethical and unprofessional. Furthermore, his statement that claiming rightful ownership "made you look bad," without commenting on the behavior of the person who wrongfully appropriated your work, is a warning sign for me.

As Natalie said, if bias towards women or considering it acceptable to claim someone else's work is endemic in the firm culture, you may want to evaluate whether this is the right firm for you. If colleagues and supervisors are willing to cross the line when it comes to other people's ideas and work, where else will they cross the line when it comes to inappropriate behavior or ethics? For many people in the workplace, conflict arises when our personal values are being challenged or tested. From what I am hearing from you, this seems to be an example of one of those times. As an additional lookout, in my many years connected to the legal profession, I have noticed that the same people who take credit for other people's work and ideas are the ones, in repeated cases, who blame others for their mistakes and bad decisions.

I agree with Natalie that you should engage in self-exploration and ask yourself questions that may take you out of your comfort zone but will hopefully lead to you discovering what values you will not negotiate, your worth, and your tolerance for bad behavior. While you indicated that your goal is to make partner at this firm, I believe that you should also consider exploring the lateral market to see if there are opportunities at firms or in-house legal departments that more closely align with your values. When I was in executive search for many years, I would counsel clients that they are not obligated to do anything except to educate themselves about other potential opportunities. Whether or not you move forward with an opportunity is completely up to you. If your preference is to dig in and go for partner at your current firm, you can also investigate the lateral market after you are hopefully elevated to partner.

As a practical matter, as you develop successful ideas and work product, you may want to create a record of those ideas and work product, and "cc" a trusted colleague on emails. By creating a record, you have documentation to support your claims if your ownership is ever called into question. Also, you have the backup in performance reviews to advocate for your performance and contributions. You also may want to discuss your experience with other female associates and see if any have had a similar experience to yours and, if so, bring it to the attention of a trusted female partner, HR, or leadership. If the problem persists and you are not getting support internally, you may want to consult women's legal network groups or bar association committees for guidance and advocacy. As an aspiring leader at the firm, you also may want to consider looking out for junior associates who may be susceptible to the inequity that you are experiencing. You can play an important role for new associates and be an informal mentor or ally to help break the cycle of this behavior.

Best of luck. And remember: follow your values.

Key Takeaways and Action Items

Key Takeaway One

Speaking Up for Yourself Is a Form of Leadership, Not a Liability

Asserting ownership over your ideas and contributions is a courageous and necessary act, especially in environments where others may try to minimize your role. While it may not always be received well, staying silent can be more costly in the long run.

Action Items:

1. Continue to assert yourself professionally by claiming your contributions during meetings. Use confident, composed language (e.g., "To build on the idea I raised earlier . . .").
2. Document your contributions in writing when possible (e.g., in follow-up emails or internal notes), and "cc" trusted colleagues when appropriate.
3. Reframe self-advocacy as a leadership behavior and practice it with calm conviction—not aggression—to avoid playing into biased perceptions while staying true to your voice.

Key Takeaway Two

Culture Matters—And Values Conflicts Are Warning Signs

The partner's comment that speaking up "makes you look bad" signals a culture where power is rewarded over fairness. Long-term success requires alignment between your values and your workplace environment.

Action Items:

1. Self-coach through reflective questions: What are your non-negotiable values? Can you thrive here long-term? Is there room to advocate for change?

2. Explore your options: Quietly assess the lateral market or in-house roles that may align more with your values—even if you ultimately stay.

3. Identify allies: Seek mentorship from trusted female or equity-minded leaders inside or outside the firm who can offer support and help shift culture.

Key Takeaway Three

You Are Not Alone—Build Networks and Be the Ally You Wish You Had

Many women and underrepresented professionals have shared similar experiences. Building and leveraging networks can offer support, advocacy, and collective strength.

Action Items:

1. Connect with other women in the firm to compare experiences and, if appropriate, raise patterns to HR or firm leadership.

2. Join external groups like women's bar associations or legal networks for advice, mentorship, and empowerment.

3. Mentor others: Use your position to support junior associates who may be facing the same inequities—modeling the leadership and advocacy you're working to embody.

Chapter 41

"Why Do I Have To? Nobody Did It for Me"—Addressing Generational Diversity in Law Firms

Natalie Loeb & David B. Sarnoff

Dear Coaches:

> **I am a senior partner in a large law firm. I emailed my associate a question, and they texted me back an answer. If I send an email, I expect an email. If I send a text, I expect a text. I did not communicate my expectations to the associate. Why should I have to?**
>
> ***—Trying to Bridge the Generational Divide***

David: For the first time in history, there are five generations in the workplace: the Traditionalists or Silent Generation (1928–1945), Baby Boomers (1946–1964), Gen X (1965–1980), Millennials (1981–1996), and Gen Z (1997–2012). While there are numerous topics to address regarding generational diversity, I want to focus on law firms, particularly the perceived gap between Baby Boomer and Gen X partners and their Millennial and Gen Z associates. These challenges often stem from a lack of shared life experiences, differing career goals, work commitments, inconsistent communication, lack of feedback, and preference for technology.

There is a significant opportunity to bridge these divides through mutual understanding and effective communication. By recognizing and valuing each generation's unique perspectives, law firms can foster a more inclusive and collaborative environment, ultimately enhancing overall performance and employee satisfaction.

In my conversations with several law firm partners and associates, I've found that while there are more similarities than differences, stereotypes based on extreme behaviors of all generations tend to get most of the media attention and form a shortcut perception based on bias. This bias manifests in the workplace in several forms. Though studying generations is not an exact science, data indicates preferences among generations for how they view work, communicate, use technology, and build relationships. Chris De Santis, author of *Why I Find You Irritating: Navigating Generational Friction at Work*, points out that parenting and education significantly impact how generations show up at work.[1]

Baby Boomers, who play a significant role in leading law firms, grew up with parents who experienced the Great Depression and World War II. They were often told to listen and not speak, leading to a workplace structured in a hierarchical, command-and-control manner. Gen X, known as the "latchkey kids" with two working parents, were encouraged to ask questions to confirm understanding but typically did not challenge authority. Millennials and Gen Z were raised in more collaborative and interactive classrooms, where they were not only asked to question but also to challenge processes and structures. Some experienced flipped classrooms, where teachers video-recorded lessons for students to watch outside class, dedicating class time to discussion and problem solving. This is a stark contrast to the educational experiences of Baby Boomers.

How does this generational diversity show up in law firms? Here are some examples:

A Gen X partner shared that they used to believe associates lacked work ethic, initiative, and seriousness. After spending significant time meeting and listening to associates, the partner realized their bias. They found that associates actually want to understand the importance

1. Chris De Santis, Why I Find You Irritating: Navigating Generational Friction at Work (2022).

and meaning of their work and how it fits into the bigger picture of legal strategy and client service. Associates don't want to just be given tasks in the abstract; they want to know how their work connects to the broader goals and why it is meaningful. This partner noted that while it takes time to communicate expectations and understand associates' goals, it ultimately creates a more effective and productive workplace. It is also important to invest the time to give developmental feedback on assignments and professional development. Redlining is not feedback and associates typically accept changes without an understanding of the "why."

This partner, who focused on working long hours and developing business early in their career, observed that Millennials and Gen Z associates prioritize their personal time and advocate for their wellness differently than older generations. This partner had respect for this self-advocacy which would have been unthinkable when the partner was an associate.

A mid-level associate who joined their firm during the COVID-19 pandemic struggled to develop practical skills and learn the practice of law. This associate would hear partners discuss how collaborative it was working in person, being in a law library, or working on due diligence trips. Then over this past year, the firm started requiring associates to be in the office more frequently. The associate said that as they spent more time working in the office during the day, they understood what the partners were talking about. The associate experienced a significant increase in spontaneous learning, being able to go into a partner's office and ask a question, sit in on a client phone call, or observe a deposition and found it invaluable to their professional development.

A Baby Boomer partner noticed that associates in general do not always participate in firm social events or outings with clients after hours. This partner shared that they once returned from vacation to attend a client event, only to find associates unavailable or unwilling to attend the same event. A Millennial associate explained that they don't see the need to socialize with colleagues after work, as they have other priorities. They asked, "Why can't we cultivate these relationships during the workday instead of expecting to do it on nights and weekends?"

Another consistent piece of feedback from partners was that fewer associates seem interested in developing business for their firms. While the population of rainmakers has always been small, there is concern about a shrinking pipeline of associates willing to build client relationships and generate business. In most cases, generating business can be a second full-time job to practicing law. Associates I have spoken with tend to say they are not averse to learning how to generate business but were never shown how to or given an understanding as junior associates that this would be an expectation. Partners believe that associates would benefit greatly from a better understanding of the business and economics of law firms.

Addressing generational diversity in law firms involves recognizing and bridging differences in communication styles, work values, and relationship-building approaches. By fostering mutual understanding and effective communication, law firms can create a more inclusive and collaborative environment, enhancing overall performance and satisfaction.

Natalie: David provided an excellent summary about the different values, needs, and expectations of the generations in today's workplace. Let's add another layer to what seems to complicate and/or increase some of the tensions in today's intergenerational workplaces. Like David said, different generations have had different life experiences. While acknowledging that we can't expect each person in the same generation to have the same set of values, expectations, and needs, there is enough research to prove that we can expect some similarities. Let's look at feedback. We have seen over the years that each generation has their own philosophy in regard to feedback.[2] It's not uncommon for those in the Traditionalist/Silent generation to dismiss feedback. In fact, if feedback is given, it is usually only because something is wrong. The expectation for this generation is that work will be completed as it should be and feedback is only necessary if something needs to be corrected or done over. So "no news is good news."

When the Baby Boomers entered the workplace, the annual performance evaluation was developed and formalized. Due to this process, leadership learned to rely on the annual review process as the only mechanism for feedback. As a result, ongoing feedback didn't seem necessary and instead all feedback would be delivered and expected to be received at the annual performance review. Unfortunately, this

---

2. See chapter 29, Is Praise As Important As a Paycheck?, for additional discussion of generational differences in feedback philosophies.

system cultivated a culture where employees were often surprised or even angered when they received critical or constructive feedback at the annual review. The response often was "why didn't anyone tell me earlier?"

From that process, the next generation of Gen Xers decided they didn't want to be caught off guard, so would start to ask their managers "How am I doing?" This often made leaders who weren't used to giving feedback uncomfortable. Without the confidence to give feedback in a constructive manner, managers often avoided the topic or gave vague untimely awkward feedback instead. Ultimately, this led to increased frustration for both the feedback giver and the feedback receiver. As a result, the next generation of employees, the Millennials, decided they needed more efficient feedback. And it was found that offering FAST (Frequent, Accurate, Specific, and Timely) feedback to Millennials helped to meet their professional needs. What this method of feedback ignored was the way it was delivered. And this is why Generation Z has tweaked and developed an additional way for feedback to be delivered; meeting both their performance and emotional needs. This method includes delivering feedback in a timely, constructive, collaborative, empathetic, and balanced manner.

Whew! A lot to take in. As David described above, not only do we need to think about who we are, and our own experiences formulating our feedback delivery methods, we also need to consider whom we are communicating with and which generation they may be in. From there, we then need to consider the best way to deliver the feedback to maximize productivity, morale, teamwork, and well-being to be effective.

Over the years, the field of organizational psychology has taught us a lot about how to maximize performance, build trust, and create healthier workplaces. As our legal workplaces continue to evolve, we continue to learn. When we know better, we do better. As we all strive to create workplaces where we bring out the best in each other, to deliver exceptional work to clients, we must accept that even if nobody did it for you, we will be more effective leaders if we do what is best for others, treating them in an equitable manner. In short, move beyond the golden rule of treating others as you would like to be treated, and instead, treat others as they prefer to be treated. And then message me on LinkedIn and let me know how it went.

Key Takeaways and Action Items

Key Takeaway One

Assumptions About Communication Norms Create Friction

Each generation has different communication preferences shaped by the technology and social norms they grew up with. Expecting others to "just know" your expectations without articulating them leads to misalignment and unnecessary frustration.

Action Items:

1. **Clearly communicate your preferences:** If you expect email replies to emails, state it. Use statements like, "For documentation, I prefer responses via email—thanks!"
2. Ask about others' preferences too. Building mutual understanding increases collaboration and reduces misinterpretations.
3. Be flexible when possible, adapt your own style occasionally to meet others where they are, especially across generational lines.

Key Takeaway Two

Feedback Expectations Vary Greatly by Generation

From "no news is good news" to "collaborative and empathetic feedback," each generation has distinct expectations around how and when feedback should be delivered. A one-size-fits-all approach to performance conversations is ineffective in today's multigenerational workplace.

Action Items:

1. **Learn the feedback styles associated with each generation:** Use FAST feedback (Frequent, Accurate, Specific, Timely) with Millennials, and balanced, empathetic feedback with Gen Z.

2. **Tailor your delivery:** Consider who you're speaking to and adapt accordingly to ensure your message is received with clarity and care.

3. **Check in periodically:** Ask, "Is this kind of feedback helpful to you?" to improve future communication and demonstrate responsiveness.

Key Takeaway Three

Equity Requires Intentional Leadership, Not "What Worked for Me" Thinking

Relying on outdated workplace norms or personal experience as the standard risks alienating younger generations. Effective leaders adjust their approach to bring out the best in others, not just replicate their own path.

Action Items:

1. **Move from the Golden Rule to the Platinum Rule:** Don't just treat others how *you* want to be treated, treat them how *they* want to be treated.

2. **Challenge generational biases:** Ask yourself whether frustration stems from legitimate performance issues or from different work styles or values.

3. **Invest in learning across generations:** Host generational workshops or panels at your firm to foster understanding, reduce stereotypes, and build inclusive leadership practices.

Chapter 42

From Bates Stamp to Blockchain: How Immigrant and First-Gen Attorneys Bridge the Generational Divide in the Legal Profession

Anjli Garg & David B. Sarnoff

Introduction

The legal profession today hosts an unprecedented convergence of five generational cohorts: Traditionalists, Baby Boomers, Generation X, Millennials, and Generation Z. Each brings unique perspectives, values, and expectations that shape their approach to career paths, work-life balance, skill development, communication, feedback, and leadership. When these perspectives are harmonized, they create a dynamic and high-performing environment. However, in many firms, these differences result in generational divides, siloed interactions, and communication gaps that hinder mutual respect, knowledge transfer, and learning. We believe that immigrant and first-generation attorneys ("First-Gen Attorneys") are an untapped resource for bridging these differences and fostering cross-generational collaboration.

This chapter explores how First-Gen Attorneys have the potential to unify generations if properly supported and empowered to do so, because they often reflect the values and perspectives of multiple generations. If law firms can successfully harness this group's bridging potential, together, they can foster stronger collaboration, innovation, and engagement across all generations—creating an inclusive culture that not only enhances attorney engagement and retention but also drives firm profitability and long-term success.

Tapping into the Strengths of First-Gen Attorneys

First-Gen Attorneys' adaptability, resilience, grit, and cross-cultural awareness are often the keys to their success as lawyers and their ability to connect with colleagues across age groups. Additionally, as discussed in more detail below, First-Gen Attorneys respect and share the traditional values of senior colleagues while embracing the dynamic, inclusive culture sought by younger generations. This seeming duality makes them uniquely positioned to translate and bridge generational divides, contributing to a more cohesive and collaborative workplace.

First-Gen Attorneys' Cross-Generational Traits

First-Gen Attorneys, regardless of their generational cohort, embody traits from multiple generations. For example, First-Gen Attorneys are similar to:

- **Traditionalists**, in the sense that they are raised to value loyalty, hierarchy, and respect authority;
- **Baby Boomers**, in the sense that they are deeply committed to hard work, achievement, and perseverance;
- **Gen Xers**, in the sense that they are independent, resourceful, and adept at navigating professional landscapes without formal mentorship;
- **Millennials**, in the sense that they are adaptive, inclusive, and value workplace flexibility due to their experience of fitting into spaces not originally designed for them; and
- **Gen Zers**, in the sense that they are open to innovation.

However, unlike many Gen Z professionals, First-Gen Attorneys often hesitate to advocate for themselves, workplace resources, and fairness, due to a combination of factors:

- **Assimilation pressure:** The pressure to assimilate and mask cultural differences to succeed in environments that aren't reflective of them or their experiences;
- **Systemic barriers:** The significant barriers to success, including implicit bias, limited mentorship opportunities, exclusion from informal networks, and the need to prove their competence at higher levels than their peers; and
- **Cultural humility:** Their own learned cultural humility, which often makes them shy away from self-promotion.

This paradox—possessing cross-generational strengths while struggling with self-advocacy and systemic barriers—makes the potential of First-Gen Attorneys both invaluable and underutilized.

Firms that invest in collaborating with their First-Gen Attorneys aren't just fostering inclusivity, they're improving productivity, retention, and client satisfaction. By unlocking this group's ability to bridge generational gaps, firms can reduce attrition costs, improve knowledge transfer, and cultivate a more engaged workforce—ultimately boosting profitability and long-term growth.

Empowering First-Gen Attorneys to Bridge Generational Divides

Engaging First-Gen Attorneys in cross-generational collaboration requires creating an environment where they feel empowered to step into leadership roles. Without this support, they may hesitate to take on the informal role of generational bridge-builders, depriving firms of their unique ability to unify teams and enhance collaboration. Firms can achieve this through:

- **Structured programs:** Provide structured mentorship and feedback opportunities that recognize their strengths and create pathways for them to emerge as leaders.

- **Open communication:** Foster an environment where advocacy is encouraged and rewarded so that these (and all) attorneys feel safe in asking for support and advancement opportunities.
- **Recognition and reward:** Acknowledge and support the efforts these attorneys provide in bridging cultural and generational gaps—a benefit that ultimately enhances firm cohesion and productivity for all attorneys.

Generational diversity, when managed effectively, strengthens law firms by fostering innovation, collaboration, and client engagement. Research consistently shows that diverse teams outperform homogeneous ones in problem-solving, decision-making, and productivity. The benefits of a multigenerational team include:

- **Diverse perspectives**, which foster creative problem-solving and strategic insights.
- **Stronger client relationships**, as attorneys reflect a broader range of generational and cultural backgrounds.
- **Cross-generational mentorship**, enabling knowledge-sharing in both directions.
- **Enhanced innovation**, as younger attorneys introduce fresh approaches and technological fluency.

First-Gen Attorneys amplify these benefits by offering unique perspectives that often synthesize the values of different generations as well as lived experiences. For instance, their adaptability and understanding of cross-cultural dynamics enable them to propose solutions that appeal to multiple generational cohorts, enhancing team cohesion and decision-making. Their lived experiences also position them as champions of inclusivity and empathy, as they naturally recognize the importance of valuing diverse voices and experiences.

Motivating All Attorneys to Invest in Bridging Generational Divides

In order to successfully bridge generational divides, all attorneys within the firm must embrace this common mission. This involves inspiring and motivating established and junior attorneys to step outside of their comfort zones to truly understand, appreciate, and learn from each other.

Motivating the Established Guard

- **Legacy and influence:** By mentoring associates, the established guard ensures that the firm's future reflects their values. This is especially important as we expect a tidal wave of Baby Boomer retirements in the next few years. The window for knowledge and experience sharing is closing fast. How well this opportunity is leveraged will directly impact the effectiveness of the next generation of leaders.
- **Client expectations:** Multigenerational teams align with diverse client needs.
- **Personal fulfillment:** Many senior lawyers find renewed purpose through meaningful collaborations with junior colleagues.

First-Gen Attorneys can play a pivotal role in inspiring senior colleagues to embrace these motivations. Their success stories, achieved despite systemic barriers and often without structured mentorship, highlight the gap that formal mentorship could fill. By sharing their unique experiences, they encourage the old guard to see mentorship not just as a responsibility but as an opportunity to leave a lasting impact.

Motivating the New Guard

- **Career growth:** Senior attorneys' insights are essential for the new guard's professional development.
- **Shaping culture:** Engaging across generations allows for greater influence in firm direction.
- **Belonging:** Fostering relationships across generations strengthens workplace inclusion.

First-Gen Attorneys can model how younger professionals can approach senior colleagues with curiosity and respect while advocating for change. Their embodiment of cross-generational values demonstrates that bridging generational divides is not about compromising values but about integrating diverse perspectives to create a stronger, more unified culture based on mutual understanding.

In a nutshell, First-Gen Attorneys can play a pivotal role in helping the established guard and the new guard to reach common ground, because they embody both the established and new guard values and motivations.

The Role of Law Firm Leadership

Law firm leadership plays a pivotal role in modeling inclusive behavior and creating an environment where generational diversity thrives. There is a saying in professional development that "leaders model the behavior they expect of others." If leaders are not out front advocating for specific change and leading by example, particularly in bridging generations, success becomes far less likely. Effective leaders:

- Model curiosity and respect in cross-generational interactions.
- Implement mentorship programs that foster mutual learning.
- Encourage open communication, aligning expectations across age groups.
- Ensure firm policies reflect flexibility and innovation while preserving institutional knowledge.
- Recognize and reward the contributions of attorneys who bridge generational and cultural divides.

Generational diversity, while complex, presents a unique opportunity for law firms to cultivate a richer, more collaborative culture. The firms that recognize and nurture First-Gen Attorneys' potential won't just create a more inclusive culture, they will build more resilient, high-performing teams that drive sustainable success. With intentional leadership, open-mindedness, and proactive strategies, generational differences become not a challenge but a competitive advantage.

A Fictionalized Case Study for Your Consideration

Maria D'Souza, a first-generation immigrant and junior associate at a prestigious corporate law firm, quickly learned that excelling in legal analysis and client work was only part of the equation for success. Despite graduating at the top of her class from a top-tier law school, she struggled to navigate the firm's unspoken social norms. Unlike her colleagues with family connections in the legal industry, Maria had to figure out firm politics on her own.

She found herself excluded from informal networking circles, where key client opportunities and mentorships were often brokered. When she sought feedback on her performance, she received vague advice about needing to "fit into the firm's culture" without clear guidance on what that meant. As the daughter of immigrants, she carried the weight of her family's high expectations, seeing her legal career as the fulfillment of their sacrifices, while also being an outsider lacking role models who could help her understand and navigate the nuances of law firm dynamics.

In addition, Maria faced implicit bias. Senior partners frequently assigned her to diversity initiatives rather than high-stakes cases, assuming she was a better fit and would be more fulfilled by representation efforts than complex corporate transactions. Clients occasionally mistook her for a junior staffer rather than the lead attorney on their cases.

Determined to change her trajectory, Maria sought mentorship from attorneys with similar backgrounds outside of her firm who had navigated comparable challenges. With their guidance, she learned to advocate for herself, strategically align with influential sponsors, and push back against limiting assumptions. She also collaborated with firm leadership to implement structured mentorship programs for First-Gen Attorneys, helping bridge the gap between talent and opportunity. Her ability to navigate these challenges ultimately strengthened her leadership skills and positioned her as a mentor for others facing similar struggles.

Questions for Reflection

We included this fictionalized case study and the below questions as a practical, engaging way to illustrate key takeaways in a real-world context. It is our expectation that this case study will help readers see how concepts applied in nuanced, complex situations, reinforce understanding and retention. We also believe that a well-crafted case study transforms abstract ideas into actionable insights, making this chapter's message more impactful.

1. What specific challenges did Maria face as a First-Gen Attorney in her law firm?
2. How did implicit bias affect Maria's career opportunities and interactions?
3. How might her experience have differed if she had come from a family with legal connections?
4. What strategies did Maria use to overcome her challenges?
5. How might Maria—and her firm—have benefited if structured mentorship programs had existed earlier?

Key Takeaways and Action Items

Key Takeaway One

First-Gen Attorneys Are Natural Bridge-Builders Across Generations

First-Gen Attorneys uniquely blend traditional values (loyalty, work ethic, respect for authority) with the adaptability and inclusivity of younger generations, making them powerful connectors in multigenerational firms.

Action Items:

1. **Identify and Engage First-Gen Attorneys:** Conduct voluntary self-identification or listening sessions to understand their experiences, challenges, and ideas for improving cross-generational collaboration.
2. **Leverage Their Perspective:** Involve First-Gen Attorneys in firm committees, task forces, and DEI initiatives where their insights can help harmonize generational expectations.
3. **Highlight Success Stories:** Showcase examples like Maria's journey to demonstrate how First-Gen Attorneys can strengthen culture and encourage others to model their bridging role.

Key Takeaway Two

Support and Empowerment Unlock First-Gen Attorneys' Potential

Without structured support, many First-Gen Attorneys hesitate to advocate for themselves, limiting their impact and depriving firms of their bridging capacity.

Action Items:

1. **Create Structured Mentorship and Sponsorship Programs:** Pair First-Gen Attorneys with senior mentors and sponsors to open doors to high-value work and informal networks.

2. **Foster Psychological Safety:** Encourage open dialogue, normalize asking for feedback, and celebrate those who advocate for resources and fairness.

3. **Recognize and Reward Bridge-Building Efforts:** Publicly acknowledge contributions that foster cross-generational collaboration and tie these behaviors to performance reviews.

Key Takeaway Three

Law Firm Leadership Must Model Inclusive, Generationally Savvy Behavior

Leadership sets the tone for whether generational differences become a strength or a source of division.

Action Items:

1. **Model Curiosity and Respect:** Leaders should actively engage with attorneys from all generations, asking questions and demonstrating interest in different work styles and motivations.

2. **Align Policies with Generational Needs:** Update firm practices (e.g., flexibility, professional development pathways, communication norms) to balance institutional knowledge with innovation.

3. **Invest in Training:** Offer workshops on generational awareness and emotional intelligence to help all attorneys appreciate diverse perspectives and collaborate effectively.

Chapter 43

Is There Life After Law? Career Transitions for Attorneys

Natalie Loeb & David B. Sarnoff

Dear Coaches:

> **A few fellow partners at my firm have been talking about next steps in their careers—some are considering big changes. It's made me feel unsettled and wonder if I should be thinking about a change too. But I'm not sure what that would even look like—change to what? And how? All I know is practicing law. How do I start figuring this out?**
>
> ***—Dreaming Beyond the Billables***

David: You're not alone in feeling unsettled when colleagues start discussing transitions. These conversations often spark self-reflection, especially among lawyers who have spent decades committed to their profession, serving client needs and in many cases contributing to the sustainability of the firm. For many, the thought of "what's next" may appear when a trigger nudges it forward: a health scare, burnout, the arrival of grandchildren, the retirement of a close colleague, or simply the creeping sense of being tired of practicing. Sometimes the nudge is subtle, other times it's substantial, but either way, it's worth paying attention to.

The most intimidating part is not knowing what may be next. After years of structuring your identity around being an attorney and maybe a law firm partner, imagining something different feels like stepping into uncharted territory. That's why the first step isn't to make dramatic and instant change but rather to ask better questions and explore. What do you want more of in your life? Time with family? Travel? Work that feels more purposeful? And what do you want less of? Long hours, client pressure, constant business development? And what do you want to remain the same? Intellectual challenge, collegiality, solving problems? Even sketching those answers starts to narrow the possibilities.

It's important to note that this question isn't limited to partners. Many associates leave the law too, often for very similar reasons. Some find that the pace, hours, and pressure simply aren't sustainable for the long term. Others realize they're not inspired by the work itself or that they want to use their skills in different ways. I know this firsthand: I started in a firm as a paralegal, worked my way up to mid-level associate, and after nine years I was burned out. Stepping away wasn't easy. I had invested years of study, tuition, and effort to build an identity around being a lawyer. But transitioning opened the door to career changes that aligned more closely with my strengths and passions. Associates and partners alike wrestle with these decisions; the common thread is having the courage to recognize when it's time for change and not to force yourself through actions that drain you of energy and well-being.

Practical readiness matters too. Financially, can you step back without jeopardizing your security? Emotionally, are you prepared to let go of the role and title that have defined you for so long? Lifestyle is another consideration. Do you picture yourself working part-time, traveling more, or pouring energy into community or nonprofit work? These questions don't all need immediate answers, but they ground the dream in reality.

As for what "change" might look like, there's a wide spectrum. Many senior partners find fulfillment on corporate or nonprofit boards, where their strategic and governance skills are highly valued. Others move into consulting, advising organizations on compliance, risk, or leadership. Teaching and mentoring can be deeply rewarding, whether in law schools, CLE programs, or through professional associations. Some lawyers discover purpose in volunteering or leading nonprofits. And for those who are financially comfortable, travel, writing, or creative pursuits finally get the space they've long deserved.

For junior and mid-level attorneys, your legal education and experience have prepared you for a variety of professions that rely on critical thinking, collaboration, and problem-solving. The skills you've honed, for example, analyzing complex information, communicating persuasively, and managing competing priorities, are highly transferable across industries. Some of the careers that former junior and mid-level lawyers often transition into include, but are not limited to, compliance and risk management, where understanding regulations and mitigating exposure is paramount; in-house counsel roles, offering closer integration with business strategy; consulting, where problem-solving and client service are key; legal recruiting, talent development, or law firm management, supporting the growth of other professionals; or entrepreneurship and corporate operations, proving that a legal foundation opens the door to a wide array of meaningful and fulfilling careers.

If you're unsure, experiment in small steps. Try joining a board while still practicing. Guest lecture at a law school. Volunteer on a nonprofit committee. Attend subject matter conferences and network in industries or topics that interest you. These low-risk explorations help you discover what energizes you and what doesn't. Talking to colleagues who've already transitioned is also invaluable. Ask what surprised them, what was harder than expected, and what advice they'd give to someone just starting to consider it.

Perhaps the hardest part for many lawyers is redefining success. For decades, success has been measured in billable hours, client wins, and origination credits. In the next chapter of your career, it may be measured in time with family, intellectual engagement without constant pressure, or the satisfaction of giving back. That isn't a loss, it's an evolution.

Natalie: I challenge your comment "all I know is law." I am not doubting you are a highly talented and knowledgeable lawyer. I am suggesting that there is more to who you are. At a time like this, introspection is the deep work one needs to do to help make some of the intentional decisions suggested by David earlier.

Like many executive coaches, I have a coach. Like you, I sometimes think about a "next chapter" or transition. A few things have triggered it for me; one being a frightening health scare and the other being the delightful birth of our first grandchild. At the same time, I love the work I do, and it gives me purpose while meeting interesting people. The biggest reward is seeing others take ownership of their behaviors and actions, leading to the successful outcomes they desire.

Successful outcomes they desire. There you go. David reminds us that next chapters/transitions are particularly unsettling when you may not know what will be next. It is harder to leave something behind without clarity on what you are moving towards in the future.

The self-reflection David mentioned will help you to begin to gain clarity. When my clients think about next chapters, I often share a document with them that my coach shared with me. It is called the "Why? document." This document is meant to challenge, inspire, and guide the reader to dig deep into one of life's biggest questions: *Why?*

Why? A single-word question that provides all of the answers you need to create the freedom, happiness, and success that you desire in your next chapter. *Why?* A question that too many lawyers never explore; and if they do, they don't explore it deep enough.

German philosopher Friedrich Nietzsche once said, "He who has a why can endure any how."

Beginning with the *how* may seem logical, but the answers to your *how* questions are rarely clear when you begin. Your *how* doesn't inspire the energy and passion to create your most powerful vision, the grit necessary to maneuver through the challenges, and the foresight to pave the path to your next chapter. It's the *why* that brings these strengths and qualities to the surface and fuels your strength and courage for your next steps.

Close your eyes and envision your *why*. How do you feel? Does your heart beat a little faster? Do you feel impassioned? Do you experience joy in your heart or butterflies in your gut? Most significantly, does it bring tears to your eyes? Yes, tears. I'm not talking about watery eyes, I'm talking about deep, meaningful tears. That is how you know when you've finally found your real *why*.

Begin with the following questions and after each one ask *why? Why is this true? Why is it important to me? Why do I feel so strongly about this?* When you believe you have the answer, ask again—*Why?*

Use your feelings as the gauge; they will tell you when you finally arrive at the real answer.

- What is the most important thing in the world to me?
- When I lose all track of time, I am usually (doing what)?
- I get most excited and passionate when I talk about (what)?
- What world issue matters most to me?
- What are my personal values?

To find what you really want to move towards, the single most important piece of information to wrap your heart and mind around is to find your *Why?*

Key Takeaways and Action Items

Key Takeaway One

Transition Begins with Self-Reflection, Not Action

Before making any major career moves, attorneys should pause to explore what they truly want more of, less of, and the same in their professional and personal lives. Clarity precedes change.

Action Items:

1. **Conduct a Personal Audit:** List what energizes and drains you at work; look for themes about purpose, balance, and fulfillment.
2. **Ask Yourself Powerful Questions:** Identify what success means to you now—beyond billable hours and titles.
3. **Experiment Safely:** Test ideas by joining a board, volunteering, or guest-lecturing before committing to a new path.

Key Takeaway Two

Redefine Success and Identity Beyond the Role of "Attorney"

After years of defining themselves by their legal careers, many lawyers struggle to imagine life beyond law. True transition requires letting go of old measures of success and rediscovering personal identity.

Action Items:

1. **Explore Transferable Skills:** Write down your strongest legal skills (analysis, communication, advocacy) and map how they apply to other fields.
2. **Connect with Peers Who've Transitioned:** Conduct informational interviews to understand real-world paths and challenges.
3. **Visualize the Next Chapter:** Create a vision statement for your ideal professional life—consider purpose, pace, and lifestyle alignment.

Key Takeaway Three

Purpose ("Why") Fuels Sustainable Change

Lasting career transitions are grounded in understanding *why* you want change, not just *how* to make it happen. Purpose provides motivation, resilience, and direction.

Action Items:

1. **Complete a "Why" Exercise:** Ask yourself, "Why is this important to me?" five times in succession for each goal until you reach the emotional core.
2. **Align Choices with Values:** Identify your top five personal values and use them as a decision-making compass for next steps.
3. **Engage a Coach or Mentor:** Partner with a professional who can help you clarify your purpose and hold you accountable for aligned action.

Case Study

Balancing the Scales in Labor & Employment

Background

Fletcher & Ames LLP has one of the top labor and employment practices in the country, handling everything from discrimination class actions to sensitive internal investigations. The practice is busy and growing, with increasing demands from clients for guidance on ESG, DEI, and mental health initiatives.

Despite its stellar reputation, the L&E group has seen higher-than-usual associate attrition and mixed reviews in the firm's engagement survey. Feedback revealed that some associates feel stretched too thin, unclear about performance expectations, and left out of key client-facing opportunities.

Key Participants

- **Karen Li (Partner and Practice Chair):** Strategic thinker and well-respected by clients. She has been tasked with improving retention and creating a more inclusive, sustainable work culture.
- **Devon Brooks (Partner):** Excellent litigator with a reputation for high standards. Known for the phrase "sink or swim," he tends to give little feedback until something goes wrong.
- **Sonia Patel (Counsel):** Recently promoted and excited to shape the group's culture. She advocates for formal mentorship and more transparency in work allocation.

- **Luis Romero (Mid-Level Associate):** Skilled and ambitious but struggling with burnout after covering multiple depositions while short-staffed. He has quietly started exploring in-house opportunities.
- **Emma Johnson (Junior Associate):** Highly capable but feels overlooked because she is remote two days a week. She is hesitant to request more client-facing work for fear of seeming "needy."
- **Maya Chen (Practice Group Administrator):** Oversees staffing and coordinates CLE and training programs. She notices stress levels rising but worries about raising concerns with busy partners.

Scenario

During a busy quarter:

- Devon assigned Luis a large, urgent brief with no context about deadlines other than "ASAP." When Luis submitted it, Devon rewrote significant portions and told him in front of others, "This isn't usable."
- Emma logged into a virtual team meeting and remained quiet. Afterward, she told Sonia she doesn't know whether she's doing well or falling behind because she rarely receives feedback.
- Karen learned in a partner meeting that two other mid-level associates had recently resigned, citing stress and lack of mentorship as key reasons.
- Sonia suggested piloting a well-being check-in program and creating a rotating work-allocation system to ensure client opportunities are distributed fairly. Devon resisted, saying, "Nobody did that for us—we figured it out ourselves."
- Maya drafted a report highlighting workload imbalances and offered ideas to redistribute tasks, but hesitated to share it with Karen, concerned it would be seen as complaining.

Karen now faces a critical moment: the firm's leadership expects her to present a plan to address attrition, improve associate experience, and show the group is living its stated commitment to inclusion and well-being.

Learning Themes and Integration of Chapter Insights

1. **Equitable Feedback and Growth**
    - Clear, fair, and constructive feedback is essential to help all associates grow and stay engaged.
    - *See* chapter 34, Is a Lack of Equitable Feedback Hindering Your Path to an Inclusive Workplace?
2. **Mental Health and Well-being**
    - Chronic stress leads to burnout and attrition if unaddressed.
    - *See* chapter 37, Why Partners Shouldn't Ignore Associates' Mounting Stress, and chapter 35, Advocating for Your Attorneys' Mental Health.
3. **Belonging and Accessibility**
    - Inclusion requires intentionality so that remote, introverted, or diverse attorneys feel equally valued.
    - *See* chapter 36, Prioritize Belonging and Accessibility in Your Next Position.
4. **Generational Mindset Shifts**
    - Dismissing modern support systems perpetuates inequity and hinders culture change.
    - *See* chapter 41, Why Do I Have To? Nobody Did It for Me—Addressing Generational Diversity in Law Firms.
5. **Gender Equity & Bias Awareness**
    - Subtle biases must be acknowledged and mitigated in staffing and evaluation processes.
    - *See* chapter 40, Do Female Lawyers Have to Play by Different Rules?

Positive Leadership Behaviors in the Case Study

- Sonia advocated for systemic solutions like mentorship and fair work allocation, showing leadership initiative.
- Maya collected data on workload imbalances and proposed solutions, demonstrating courage and ownership.
- Karen engaged with leadership about attrition rather than ignoring the problem, signaling a willingness to act.

Developmental Behaviors to Address

- Devon's public criticism of Luis undermined morale and trust. Feedback should be private, specific, and developmental.
- Associates like Emma lack clarity on expectations, risking disengagement and attrition.
- Resistance to cultural change ("we figured it out ourselves") perpetuates inequities and fails to meet current talent expectations.
- Failure to normalize well-being check-ins leaves stress unspoken and unaddressed.

Facilitator's Guide

Balancing the Scales in Labor & Employment

Key Learning Themes

- **Wellclusion = Well-being + Inclusion:** A healthy, inclusive culture balances performance expectations with psychological safety and equitable growth opportunities.
- **Equitable Feedback Is Critical:** Timely, fair, and constructive feedback helps associates learn and signals investment in their development.
- **Culture Change Requires Leadership:** Shifting away from "sink or swim" mentalities requires intentional modeling and reinforcement by partners.
- **Belonging Drives Retention:** When associates feel seen, supported, and fairly staffed, they are more likely to stay and thrive.

Positive Leadership Behaviors to Reinforce

- Sonia's proactive proposals for mentorship and staffing fairness.
- Karen's willingness to engage leadership on attrition concerns.
- Maya's data-driven approach to workload distribution.

Developmental Behaviors to Address

- Devon's lack of constructive, private feedback.
- The group's missed opportunity to normalize discussions about stress and well-being.
- Inadequate communication with remote associates about performance and opportunities.
- Resistance to change framed as nostalgia ("nobody did it for us") instead of a chance to build a better system.

Reflection Questions for Readers

On Feedback and Development

- How do you deliver feedback in a way that supports learning rather than discouragement?
- Do all associates in your group receive the same quality and frequency of feedback?

On Well-being and Belonging

- How do you check in on associate workload and stress in a meaningful, non-performative way?
- What steps can you take to ensure remote or quieter team members feel fully included?

On Generational and Cultural Mindset

- Where might you be holding onto "we had it harder" thinking?
- How could reframing this mindset improve your ability to lead and retain talent?

Application

- **Feedback Must Be Timely and Fair:** Associates cannot succeed if expectations are unclear or feedback is delayed.
- **Stress Is a Leadership Issue:** Partner involvement in well-being initiatives is not optional—it's essential for retention.

- **Inclusion Is Action, Not Intention:** Actively create opportunities for participation, visibility, and career growth for all attorneys.
- **Change Requires Champions:** Culture shifts stick when leaders model new behaviors and hold others accountable.

Suggested Reader Exercise

After reading this case study, write down:

1. **One way you can improve feedback equity** in your practice group (e.g., set a recurring check-in to review work product privately with each associate).
2. **One step you can take to address associate well-being** (e.g., introduce quarterly workload conversations, encourage mental health resource use).
3. **One generational or cultural mindset** you are willing to shift (e.g., replacing "sink or swim" with "develop and grow").

www.ingramcontent.com/pod-product-compliance
Lightning Source LLC
LaVergne TN
LVHW052219200926
848481LV00001B/153